New and Exr

Approac

Writing Lives

NEW AND EXPERIMENTAL APPROACHES TO WRITING LIVES

EDITED BY JO PARNELL

First published 2019 by
RED GLOBE PRESS

Red Globe Press in the UK is an imprint of Springer Nature Limited, registered in England, company number 785998, of 4 Crinan Street, London, N1 9XW.

Red Globe Press® is a registered trademark in the United States, the United Kingdom, Europe and other countries.

ISBN 978–1–352–00721–3 hardback
ISBN 978–1–352–00718–3 paperback

This book is printed on paper suitable for recycling and made from fully managed and sustained forest sources. Logging, pulping and manufacturing processes are expected to conform to the environmental regulations of the country of origin.

A catalogue record for this book is available from the British Library.

A catalog record for this book is available from the Library of Congress.

TABLE OF CONTENTS

FOREWORD

Caroline Mcmillen

As a scientist, it was with some trepidation that I accepted the opportunity to write a foreword to a book on new and experimental approaches to writing lives. In the stratified and segmented world of research, it would be generally understood that there are more differences than similarities between the scholarly lives of scientists and writers. It would seem evident to the research community that how an idea is formed, explored, and captured through narrative in the fields of science and life-writing would be so different that only the experience of living an academic life could provide a point of contact. This book is a bold experiment which challenges those preconceptions.

This collection of essays tests the original idea that bringing together scholars with new, different, and experimental approaches to life-writing will challenge the basis on which we understand our own lives and those of others. Setting out to explore the lives of objects and things, the use of map-making and cartography in life-writing, and the unpacking of the role of biography, literary docu-memoir, and obituary as forms of life-writing is an innovative approach which leads us to rethink how we understand the narrative of a life and the context of family, communities, and culture. The focus on how the line, the voice, the form of media, and the story act as vehicles for capturing a life either at a point in time or through memory allows us to understand how innovation in forms of writing informs our understanding of what comprises the elements of a life beyond chronology.

In the world of scholarship, whether in the field of science or life-writing, original ideas explored through experimental approaches by scholars of substance will invariably change our thinking. New insights are possible, however, only when a collection of essays has been sourced and edited with the forethought and precision required to deliver a collective body of work that can challenge orthodoxy. This collection of essays represents a clear example of such an approach; it is an important work and one which will have a sustained impact on the development of the field of life-writing.

ACKNOWLEDGEMENTS

I wish to thank my close family and friends for their understanding and for putting up with the 'do not enter' sign on my study door while this book was coming to fruition. My deepest thanks also go to all the contributors who appear in this book and made it happen. Their keenness for the project was exhilarating and inspiring. I wish to also thank my colleagues. I owe a debt of gratitude to the University of Newcastle, Australia, and the School of Humanities and Social Sciences for welcoming me into their community and making it possible to present my work both at the university in symposiums and on a national and international scale at major conferences, something that I had never even dared to dream about. In the course of my studies, I have been extremely fortunate and privileged and honoured to have had fine teachers and exemplary supervisors who willingly passed on their knowledge and modelled excellent research skills. These people showed me the way and helped me to grow. I am particularly indebted to Vice-Chancellor Professor Caroline McMillen for her friendship, support, and guidance over the years that she has been at the university and for her continued support for my projects, for being enthusiastic about my research studies, and for doing me the honour of writing the Foreword for this book. I also owe a debt of gratitude to Professor Catharine Coleborne for her continued support for my projects, for being enthusiastic about my research studies, and for doing me the honour of welcoming me into the community.

I am especially indebted to Emeritus Professor Hugh Craig FAHA, formerly my supervisor for all my higher research studies and now my dear mentor, for modelling excellent research skills and fine teaching, for all his care in helping me to evolve as a scholar and a writer, and for making the continuing journey so enjoyable. I am also indebted to him for writing the Introduction to this book, for editing the editor, and for being a wise guide and good friend. In addition, I must also thank Emeritus Professor Hugh Craig for inadvertently introducing me to Associate Research Professor Julie Anne Taddeo of the University of Maryland in the United States. At Hugh Craig's urging, while I was still only a research higher degree candidate in the MPhil and a year before I was enrolled in the PhD programme at the University, I forwarded Julie one of my essays on Catharine Cookson. As a result, Julie invited me to write a chapter for her Ashgate book, a world-first academic work on Cookson as a serious writer, and I gained an excellent long-time friend, via email, who follows my progress and urged me to continue with my plans to write this book. I have known Julie Taddeo for many years, via email; then, purely by happy coincidence, we met face to face only a few years ago, in London.

Whenever an idea for a book comes to mind, I run it past Hugh, and we discuss it; hence, this book grew out of a perceived need to highlight some of the new and/or experimental approaches to writing lives that are beginning to emerge or have newly emerged or evolved, as deserving of full recognition in the hallowed halls of the auto/biography (A/B) text corridor. The urge to 'do' something constructive and write a book on this topic, a book that others might find helpful in their own work, eventually reached the stage where I approached the Macmillan International Higher Education division and met their acquisitions editor, Rachel Bridgewater, and later, Emily Lovelock, and the publisher Jenna Steventon. I would like to say a special thank you to these people for their guidance through the publishing process and for always answering my questions so promptly. I owe a large debt of gratitude to Rachel, Emily, and Jenna for their continuous support and encouragement in bringing the project to fruition.

On a more personal basis, I wish to thank Dr John Goswell and his wife, Felicity Goswell, for all their care and support and, in particular, Dr John for his wise advice on handling my life and health during the time I was putting this book together and, incidentally, a time when the world seemed to descend on our family and I became frantically busy. This brings me finally to my beloved husband, Bob, who had been battling cancer all during this time; I thank him for his wonderful attitude to life, for his understanding of my need to work; for his tolerance, his caring, and his love; and for taking the risk of popping into my study at various times, saying, 'You need to take a few minutes' break now; come and walk with me in our garden.'

EDITOR'S PREFACE

Jo Parnell

Why do we need a book on new and experimental approaches to writing lives, and why do we need such a book right now? This edited collection of critical essays is the first of its kind to offer a serious study of an area that is commonly acknowledged by most writers as worthy of scholarship, but it is nevertheless an area that has never actually been properly and openly addressed in the syllabus. *New and Experimental Approaches to Writing Lives* is a comprehensive study of some ways of writing lives that demonstrate an entirely new or experimental form, an unusual hybridisation, an innovative multi-hybridisation, or an approach to a form that is relatively new in that it may possibly have already appeared to some small degree at some time and that can be, or has been, adapted or evolved to create text that is fresh and new and different.

In answer to my email of early 2017, informing Craig Howes of IABA (International Auto/Biography Association, World) fame and Professor, Center for Biographical Research, University of Hawaii at Mānoa, of my intent to write this book on new and experimental approaches to writing lives, he said that, for him, the 'big thing here is that digital humanities, automediality, autographics … etc., etc., all are such prominent and widely-practiced life 'writing' genres that addressing' these forms 'must be an essential part of our teaching' (Private email, 8 Jan. 2017). In a later email, Howes refined these 'musings':

> The many emerging futures of life writing are increasingly visual and virtual. … [A]ll have swiftly become such widely-employed life 'writing' media that addressing not only their texts, but their practices, must become a major concern for those who teach and write about representing lives. A collection that addresses how to approach such texts, and just as valuably, that provides direction on how to teach their production, and offers course assignments and learning outcomes, can only be a welcome and timely addition to our resources for studying lives. (Private email, 18 Dec. 2018)

Here, I will add that in this age of the Internet, 'digital humanities, auto-mediality, lives online,' and forms such as graphic memoir—so-called by Sidonie Smith and Julia Watson (168–69) and which Gillian Whitlock calls autographics (Whitlock, 'Autographics' 965–79)—and other visual-verbal-virtual texts that once were actually considered as lying outside the conventional A/B text corridor are, to this day, areas that still await being fully embraced and given their rightful place as areas that are properly and openly addressed in the syllabus scholarship. All are now such prominent and widely practised life 'writing' genres that addressing new and experimental approaches to writing lives not just as texts (digital, print, and interchangeable) but as practices must 'be an essential part of our' lives as teachers and producers of such works if life-writing as a genre is not to falter and possibly stagnate.

Recently I was asked where I see the future of life-writing going from here. How does one answer that briefly? As Howes exclaimed when I took the liberty of running it past him, that question demands a further book or book series, 'or a major key-note think-piece that would probably … delay lunch or dinner' (Private email, 10 Dec. 2018). Consequently, I am now contemplating a further book on the subject. There has always been that grey area of writing lives (our own and those of others) differently from the accepted norm of the conventional A/B text corridor. Elsewhere, in my 2016 report on the Inaugural IABA Asia-Pacific Chapter Conference, which was held at the Flinders University City Campus, Adelaide, South Australia, in 2015, I noted that the question 'Where to from here?' was the subject of the conference Plenary Roundtable Session, 'Unsettle.' As the panellists' talks indicated, more recently, there are 'others,' 'writings' we all recognise and can connect to, such as discussion board and forum entries; blogs and multimedia literary productions; and asylum seeker or refugee zines. Somehow, even though some of these 'writings' or depictions may seem to have no apparent borders or easily perceived system, we instinctively know they are life-writing. Moreover, in their own way, they are in fact forms that are self-referential, often reflexive by implication, and, to some degree or another, revealing of the writer or creator or collector. The problem is, though, how do we categorise them, what label do we use, how do we tag and explain them in order to understand exactly where and how they can fit into the accepted life-writing genre? In my report on the conference, I also noted that

> [t]he general consensus at this roundtable session was that by their introduction and acceptance as new, named, forms

and categories within the genre, these new and unusual ways
of writing lives could serve to pave the way for broadening
and enhancing the life writing genre to take it into the future,
and so prevent a possible stagnation of the genre. (Parnell 31)

So there have always been, and still are, experimental writings of one sort or another floating around the outer fringes of life-writing. Life-writing is such that the genre seems to attract those elements. With the advent of the Internet, these more experimental traditions have been thrown into sharp relief. More and more people are writing about themselves and the things we see and hear in the course of every day and putting these depictions out on show via the Net, in a readily available space where everybody can see and access them. With experimental creative practices being accepted and commonly acknowledged as a part, indeed a fact, of ordinary life, along with even newer developments in the advances in Internet technology, and with world politics and ideologies undergoing sweeping changes, people's ideas and ways of looking at things are also changing. Increasingly, these experimental creative practices are resulting in the production of new experimental literary texts and cutting-edge methodologies in writing lives, creating a whole new platform for practitioners to seek and invent even newer and fresher ways of writing lives.

Of course, nothing in writing is *absolutely new*; everything and every approach has a precedent of some sort. For instance, unusual self-referential, self-reflective writing is not strictly new; it did not just suddenly touch down. All the various forms and modes and fashions of writing lives have behind them a rich and diverse history that stretches all the way back to St Augustine's *The Confessions of St. Augustine* (written about 397 CE and published in approximately 400 CE) and beyond, to other, less reflective or non-reflective self-referential forms still further back. Being an erudite scholar, St Augustine would have been aware of the first-hand accounts written as third person narratives by Julius Caesar: the *Commentarii de Bello Gallico* (Commentaries on the Gallic War) (c 49–48 BCE), in which Caesar describes the battles that took place in the nine years he was fighting the Gallic Wars, and *Commentarii de bello Civili* (Commentary on the Civil War) (c 40 BCE), an account by Caesar of events that took place between 49 and 48 BCE in the civil war against Gnaeus Pompeius and the Senate. What Julius Caesar called his 'Commentarii,' we now call early memoir.

Even though St Augustine's *Confessions* is commonly referred to as the first autobiography ever written, it is neither memoir nor autobiography.

But it does provide an unbroken record of his pattern of thought, and it did, and continues to, influence recognised life-writing genres such as memoir and autobiography. For one thing, it introduced new techniques, methods, perspectives, and ways at looking at writing lives differently. In his 'confessions,' St Augustine seemingly did not have a system. As well, his texts did not appear to have borders. Rather he indulged in texts built on observations and descriptions of human motives and emotions. His self-reflective, self-referential texts demonstrate a highly complex interaction of in-depth analyses of will and thought, together with an exploration of the inner nature of the human self. Yet St Augustine's *Confessions* did have a specific form which had implied precedents in the traditions, manner, and fashions of both the wider Christian literature of the times and the church writings of the community to which he belonged, as well as in the context of the Church and the happenings within that world at the time. Furthermore, St Augustine's *Confessions* had its prototypes in the other works and many of the letters he wrote. The thirteen books that made up St Augustine's famous work also had its designated term *confessions*, terminology that he coined specifically to explain and define his writings. St Augustine's innovative works established one of the main traditions in European self-referential writing, thus setting a precedent that allowed future generations of writers to expand borders by seeking new modes and methods, as well as a host of terms specifically coined to differentiate and describe particular 'new' ways of writing lives.

Then, sometime between 1599 and 1602, thousands of years after St Augustine wrote his *Confessions*, Shakespeare pointed out in *Hamlet* that the telling of one's own life must always differ from how someone else might tell it or tell their own story: when Shakespeare's Hamlet begs Horatio 'tell my story' (*Hamlet* 5.3), it sounds so simple and straightforward. What can be so difficult about telling your own story or telling that of someone else? But the complexities and difficulties inherent in telling someone else's story, or in telling your own story, are unending, and writers keep inventing new ways of doing this. In a way, this business of writing lives is like a moving train in that it never stands still. So this is why this scholarly collection makes so much sense right now, not only in labelling, describing, and analysing such texts and the detailed explanation of the production of such texts but also in offering critical feedback and specific assignments and examples combined with critical approaches.

It seems to make sense that this book, *New and Experimental Approaches to Writing Lives*, should be a collection of essays written by scholars who are research and teaching academics, and practitioners of writing lives in their own fields. Our contributors (from Hong Kong, the United States, North America, the United Kingdom, and Australia), in combination, provide a multidisciplinary approach to lives in literary and poetic forms (digital, print, and interchangeable). This book is a collection of scholarly essays that are thematically driven. Individually, the essays are fair examples of some of the 'new' and/or experimental forms that are now emerging and making their appearance as deserving of a place in scholarship.

Given the title and the content, it also makes sense that the book should follow an unusual form rather than one which is fairly conventional and more usual or, in this case, rather ordinary. Rather than taking a conservative approach to structuring, this work has been structured to imply new growth springing out of the 'old.' This work echoes the progression of the cycle of life—a natural, continuous cycle which has no beginning and no end. The book begins with essays on 'obituaries' and the forgotten, which carry the implication of a death preceded by a life preceded by a birth and similarly the implication of what has gone before. The 'old' appears to be 'dead' but only until it has been reframed in such a way that one is able to look beyond and back into the past to find the preceding generations and to where whole families and notable people are visible, out on show, and new life is found in, springs out of, or is rediscovered from that which at first impression *seems* to be 'dead'—or lost, inanimate, forgotten, past, or even overlooked. Each of the essays is an exploration of the new life, or literary forms, springing out of the 'old,' accepted approaches to writing lives. Thus, these essays take the reader through a steady progression of various new and unusual, and experimental forms of life-writing, through to 'youth' and then finally to young children as writers; and this progression carries the implications of 'new' beginnings and hence a fresh celebration of new and experimental approaches to writing lives.

 Works Cited

Augustine, of Hippo, Saint, 354–430. *The Confessions of St. Augustine,* translated by Rex Warner. New American Library, 1963.

Caesar, Julius. *The Gallic War: Commentaries on the Gallic War with an Eighth Commentary by Aulis Hirtius,* translated by Caroline Hammond, 1st ed. U Oxford P, 2008.

Damon, Cynthia, editor. *C. Ivli Caesaris Commentariorvm: Libri III De Bello Civili*. Rev. ed. U Oxford P, 2015.

Parnell, Jo. 'Report on the Inaugural Asia-Pacific Conference November 2105.' *European Journal Life of Writing,* vol. V, 2016, pp. 26–33, R26–Rs33. DOI: doi.org/10.5463/ejlw.5.204

Shakespeare, William (1599–1602). *The Tragedy of Hamlet, Prince of Denmark*, in *The New Oxford Shakespeare: The Complete Works Modern Critical Edition*, edited by Gary Taylor and Terri Bourus, pp. 1993–2001. U Oxford P, 2016.

Smith, Sidonie, and Julia Watson. *Reading Autobiographies: A Guide for Interpreting Life Narratives*, 2nd ed., edited by Louise Castner. U Minnesota P, 2010.

Whitlock, Gillian. "Autographics: The seeing 'I' of the comics." *Modern Fiction Studies,* vol. 52, no. 4, Winter 2006, pp. 965–75.

INTRODUCTION

Hugh Craig

Successful life writing animates the lives of its subjects so that readers can enter into others' experiences and vicariously live lives parallel to their own. These stories, like their siblings, invented fictional stories, predate writing and go back to the dawn of language itself.

There is always a balance between established and new ways to present life writing. Familiar modes of narrative take the burden off audiences, who can rely on trusted conventions and an existing shared understanding with writers, but there is also a role for innovation. New approaches catch our attention. New ways of understanding experience and new kinds of experience require new modes of expression.

This book brings together a variety of innovative approaches to life writing, all dedicated to renewing and refreshing this thriving area of creative work. The chapters offer theoretical backgrounds, worked examples, and practical exercises, giving students and novices the impetus to embark on a first story and giving practised writers ways to develop new strengths and hone their technique.

Dr Amanda Norman's chapter on obituaries is an unexpected but fitting place to start for the collection. It seems that obituaries are increasing in popularity, perhaps, Norman argues, because in troubled times, it is heartening to read how others have survived and sometimes thrived. Obituaries are life writing marked by the terminus of life, when death abruptly gives a retrospective form to the shapeless succession of moments that make up everyday experience.

Alfred Nobel was motivated to create prizes celebrating human achievement because he read his own obituary, which had appeared in error. It focused on the terrible consequences of his dynamite-manufacturing business. This is Norman's introduction to the idea of the therapeutic self-written obituary. Viewing one's own life from an imagined standpoint of its end, says Norman, may be a valuable way to galvanise how to live.

Obituaries have a public, official dimension. In summing up a life, they reflect and influence core values. What is important to record about a life? What is the balance between outward achievement, inward being, and relations with family and friends, between 'task-oriented' and 'person-oriented' elements? And who should have an obituary—the already well known, heroes and villains, or those who had a quiet, persistent impact on others? Furthermore, women are under-represented in obituaries. What does that say about how their contributions are valued?

Professor Donna Lee Brien's chapter on object biography takes us into the world of Thing Theory. A thing is an object that has shed its usual function and thus confronts us as a resistant and obstinately material entity rather than one which fits snugly into a human purpose. Brien argues that objects are able to live and grow, with a series of uses and states through time which are worthy of a biography. Objects are connected to each other in 'rich webs,' says Brien, further increasing their utility for life writing. Human lives are lived in relation to objects and things. Objects and things, whether precious or everyday, whether found in a natural state or fashioned by human beings, anchor memories and make ongoing physical existence possible. The object biography genre has produced a biography of cod and a biography of one set of the tiny Japanese carved figures called netsuke.

The idea of object biography defamiliarises biography itself, adding a hint of the uncanny, which Freud defined as moments when the boundary between the living and the inanimate is breached. It also highlights the time dimension of life writing. Attributing a capacity to change through time to objects, which we normally think of as fixed and unchanging in form, draws attention to the relations between mere persistence through time (this table was here yesterday) and organic life (a person feels differently from moment to moment).

What makes an apparently ordinary life worth writing about, so that readers with no connection by way of family or acquaintance will take an interest? In Chapter 3, Emeritus Professor David Walker ponders this question and offers two established writers as guides—the German novelist W. G. Sebald and the British writer Alan Bennett. Sebald combines a mysterious lack of explicitness, close observation and reflection in his haunting narratives. Bennett is an acute recorder of everyday middle-class English life, seeing meaning, humour, and pathos in otherwise painfully mundane detail.

Walker is a professional historian turned family memoirist and his background helps him see how to write 'lives outside of history.' What are we to make of the giant onion grown by his grandfather, which is put on display in a shop in a small town in South Australia, in a year which brought the Russian Revolution and the Battle of the Somme? Walker's answer is that the onion speaks of ordinary but important lives lived in a culture of self-sufficiency and within the bonds of community.

Walker describes how in his recent work he has escaped from a dependency on documentary sources. In bringing episodes from the past to light, too much information can be a burden, and blanks in the record can be an inspiring challenge to creative reconstruction (this side of 'outright invention,' Walker cautions). In the same way, Walker says, his failing eyesight, ruling out the reading of documents, led him to explore his own memory and to his 'seeing things more clearly.' The stimulus of images from old photographs, even where context is lost, and the realisation in age that family traits are inescapable are further aids to writing a family history narrative. These stories complement grander historical narratives, pitting commonplace but intensely lived experience against political and military exploits and events.

Dr Jo Parnell also explores the interrelations of factual and imaginative truth. Her concept of the literary docu-memoir has as its starting point Tony Parker's extended interviews with real-life subjects, but she draws the line at Parker's melded identities and stories. Her approach is to make an agreement with her subjects from the beginning that they are to be presented as themselves in the completed work. Indeed, as she notes, her subjects have a need for recognition, after a long experience of being overlooked and having their testimony doubted, and she aims to create for them 'a literary space in which to claim a sense of identity.'

Colour and texture is given by the documentary effect of incidental factual materials and photographs. Literary docu-memoir also creates a three-dimensional experience for the reader, by rendering in detail the context of the interviews and the experience of the interviewer. The interviewer puts on a 'fictional cloak' as writer, striving, paradoxically, to create truth by acknowledging the context of imagination and feeling for both subject and interviewer.

Parnell takes from Parker the belief that ordinary people in their interaction with a sympathetic interviewer can touch on 'deeper realities,' philosophical and poetical insights which might otherwise not have emerged over the course of their normal reflective and interpersonal life. This fits with her idea of the truth of a personal 'myth' which crystallises a life story.

The first volume of the autobiographical writings of the Norwegian writer Karl Ove Knausgaard appeared in 2009 and attracted intense interest. They portrayed the unremarkable events of Knausgaard's life in excruciatingly minute detail, but readers in Norway and then in the rest of the world found them entirely compelling. Workplaces in Norway introduced Knausgaard-free days to give workers some relief from the obsession with his work. The series won numerous literary prizes in Norway and abroad. Meanwhile, some members of Knausgaard's family were vocal in their rejection of the way they are portrayed in the series.

In Chapter 5, Dr Michael Sala focuses on the first volume of the sequence, *Min Kamp 1*, translated into English as *A Death in the Family: My Struggle: Book 1*. Sala explores the nature of the literary act performed by the book, its novelty, and its dark and paradoxical aspects.

In the second part of Knausgaard's book, the narrator-protagonist is cleaning his father's house, making it ready for the latter's funeral; seemingly aiming to redeem the family's reputation in their circle from his father's long-drawn-out, public, and squalid act of self-destruction; and presumably aiming to do the same with the wider public of his readers. Yet as Sala points out, the recital of this work has the opposite effect and leaves an indelible impression on the reader of the filthy state of the house before cleaning and of the degradation of his father's breakdown.

Sala shows how Knausgaard combines two different approaches to autobiography. One stems from Rousseau's *Confessions* (written in two parts—books I to IV 1765–67 and books VII to XII 1769–70—and originally published in 1782) and turns on the writer's admission to the world, in print, of a shameful act or desire, a confession which guarantees the authenticity of his narrative. The other is well represented in Vladimir Nabokov's autobiographical work *Speak, Memory* (1951). As Sala puts it, Nabokov here deploys a range of literary techniques 'that pit the traumatic event against the literary mechanisms of its presentation' and so frames confessions in 'a sense of play and arrangement' rather than offering unmediated revelation. Knausgaard's confessions are artful as well as frank, as Sala demonstrates. In making his 'commodification' of self, the Norwegian writer is making something public and at the same time submitting to a 'private desire to confront himself'—an unstable, potent mixture of motives.

Life writing generally starts with a chronological focus. Associate Professor Sonya Huber offers an interesting alternative, writing based on place rather than time—what she calls '[m]ap-based essays.' She describes a project to explore the invisible boundary between Bridgeport and Fairfield in Connecticut. Bridgeport is a decaying industrial city. Fairfield is a wealthy enclave. The boundary she says is a 'scar' full of intensely lived conflict and injustice. Her project includes repeated walks along part of this boundary, some of which is hard to access, traversing abandoned spaces and forgotten back corners. She celebrates the role of the flâneur, wandering with 'no specific task,' as a child might.

Huber sees her self-imposed restriction to one defined territory as an instance of the 'constraint' which the 1960s French Oulipo group championed as a source of creativity. After some years of work, she has a densely populated map which holds all kinds of material in a geographic container, as well as the narratives of individual visits. '[W]hat happened here' is just as important as 'what happened when,' as it is in the Native American creation stories that Huber cites.

The walk or the visit as the basis for writing goes back to epic quest narratives, as Huber shows, combining the 'suspense' of approaching a destination with the 'episodic drama' of events along the way. Walking, she says, is an activation of the city system put in place by planners and developers, just as a speech act is an instantiation of a language. Walkers can 'remake place' in the face of a world which is made 'placeless' by the modern imperative to traverse the globe at the highest speed possible. A new place can be a 'trigger' to bring to consciousness the parts of the self which are tied to the home environment but not otherwise available.

Huber describes a way writers can collect creative material through visits to places identified and given meaning through a map. Dr Vanessa Berry presents a second 'cartographic approach to life writing.' This time the maps follow experience rather than directing it. They offer a way of visualising past experiences, especially those with a deeply personal resonance. They are less literal representations of a physical terrain and more guides to a landscape of feelings.

Berry includes as an illustration the 17th-century French map called *Le Pays de Tendre*, which shows the way to love. This may follow the River of Inclination or alternative routes through villages named 'Billets Doux' (love letters), 'Petits Soins' (little trinkets), and 'Tendresse.' *Le Pays de Tendre* shows the power of representing the imaginative and emotional through a mapped landscape, along the lines of Bunyan's work *Pilgrim's Progress* (cited in Huber's chapter), in which the pilgrim Christian negotiates the Slough of Despond, Vanity Fair, and so on. These are maps and fictional territories which map 'the invisible,' a 'story map' as opposed to a 'grid map.'

A second map reproduced in the article shows Berry's own 'significant sites' and memory places from when she was eight years old, in the mid 1980s. Drawings and hand-written captions depict a Sydney landscape with the places that had a grip on her childish imagination and feelings. School is marked with a skull and crossbones. A poppy stands for the suburb of Croydon, where the writer's father grew up in a house with poppies in the front garden, known only to Berry through stories.

The digital realm brings new expressive possibilities for the writer. It also challenges the basis for life writing by introducing a new sense of the self. Dr Emma Newport's chapter focuses on the GIF—the short, looping online video which captures a meme, a minimal cultural unit which can be almost instantaneously and almost universally shared across the cybersphere. Newport connects these tiny, independent entities to the principle of brevity in life writing going back to Samuel Johnson's 'little lives' of writers. She sees the GIF and the collections of GIFs, such as those on Giphy.com and in Dennis Cooper's GIF novel *Zac's Haunted House*, as aids to the writer in moving beyond the commonest form of writing on the Web, which involves what she calls 'emotive first-person' commentary in blogs and posts, towards something more fragmentary, mobile, and inherently digital.

Newport shows that the GIF, which takes a moment of experience and finds in it something that is shared and that resonates for a whole culture, can suggest alternatives to the idea of the self as stable and fixed. The GIF is always in motion and always prone to take on new meanings when detached from its original context. It is irreverent, and its predominant mode is bathos. No grand or self-important gesture can survive looping round in a more or less instant repetition, and no one meaning to any event can survive this detached, relentless, circular trajectory. The '21st-century self' that it can help us see is an ephemeral, relational thing which is always 'veering' away towards something new.

Life writing and lyric poetry seem to have little to do with each other. Life writing creates a sequence; lyric poetry dwells on a moment. Life writing is built around a person in history, but lyric poetry may be impersonal and choric. Nevertheless, new writing about lives may take the form of lyric poems, which is the subject of Professor Page Richards's chapter. Rita Dove's *Thomas and Beulah* (1986) showed the way, and two books of biography in poems by Marilyn Nelson (2001) and Ruth Padel (2009) respectively have followed. Lives can be created out of lyric moments rather than as prosaic sequences. Kim Cheng Boey's *Gull between Heaven and Earth* (2017) is another specialised example, a biography of the 8th-century Chinese poet Du Fu which creates biographic and subjective contexts around surviving individual poems.[1]

The promise of lyric poetry for life writing is of lives depicted as 'beads on a necklace' rather than as a progressive narrative. There is, then, the possibility of dismantling established fixed sequence, which can serve the cause of '[p]ostcolonial reconstructions,' 'temporal self-resistance' and the dethroning of the familiar, dominant individual focus of biography. Richards argues that lyric poetry, in its pre-Romantic forms at least, was 'symbolic, anonymous, and … universal.' It is something like the opposite of history, being associated with the irrational—for example, Shakespeare groups the poet with the 'lunatic' and the 'lover'—and with the subjective first person rather than the objective third person.

Richards dwells on the force of lyric prosody in creating circularity and backwards movement through rhyme and lineation, what she calls 'backwards sonic pull.' The lyric invokes 'the ineffable' and so breaks any sense of completeness and internal coherence. In some forms, there is no speaker, only a sense of the language itself or a language community speaking. Richards emphasises the need for the new in life writing, for ways to tell 'our stories afresh' (quoting Geoffrey Davis), replacing forms which are 'visibly outworn' (quoting Charles Johnson). The 'intersections of biography with lyric poetry' offer one enticing path to this renovation of life writing.

Innovation in life writing is often discussed as an axis between the factual and the fictional. How much can the imaginative and emotional resources of fiction enrich biography and autobiography? What are the limits beyond which creative non-fiction loses the privileges of its connection with the real and joins the realm of the invented and fantastical? There is a second axis to consider as well, however, that of form. This is most obvious in the case of the biographical poems discussed by Dr Jessica L. Wilkinson in Chapter 10. Poetry also returns us to the role of the fictional in biography and subverts the usual mantra of a virtuous adherence to documented fact.

Wilkinson's chapter discusses four examples of 'poetic biographies' and their successes in bringing fiction-like and emotional perspectives to rendering the lives of historical figures. Poetry 'acknowledges … the limitations of language,' in the words of Cole Swenson, quoted by Wilkinson, and thus can serve a more reflective practice of biography. Edward Sanders's biographical poem *Chekhov* (1995) is discussed in the chapter in terms of its 'swerve' from the ruling conventions of biography. Wilkinson also points out that the freedoms associated with verse allows Sanders to foreground his own contribution, through his signature hyphenations (e.g., 'doom-drum' and 'shoot-ups') and elisions (such as 'quick'ning'). Wilkinson cites Sanders's own commentary about poetic biography being new territory for poetry—'a voyage into the description of *historical reality*'—and a shake-up of biography. Sanders's experiments in 'playing' with factual details make one wonder how we are to judge the truthfulness of this sort of biography. Is it simply on the grounds of intuitive persuasiveness? In that case, how can we avoid simply falling into accepting what one generation or one group prefers to believe about a historical figure? Ruth Padel's *Darwin: A Life* (2009; also discussed by Richards) is Wilkinson's next example. Padel shows what Wilkinson argues is an unnecessary deference to biography. Padel does not call her work a biography, because it is not based on a comprehensive work of scholarship, and she adds marginal annotations with conventionally bio-graphical references, qualifying the authority of her freer interpretation of Darwin's life career in the poem. Wilkinson stresses the success and power of the experiments with form in the poem, which she suggests echoes the 'collision of fact and hypothesis' which is the hallmark of Darwin's scientific work.

Wilkinson also treats a second poetic biography of Darwin, Emily Ballou's *The Darwin Poems* (2009). This work, Wilkinson suggests, moves further from conventional biography than Padel's venture in the same genre. She invents 'subjective perspectives' based on selected and adapted voices from the Darwin archive. Wilkinson argues that this takes her closer to what Cole Swenson calls the domain of 'imagina-tion' rather than of 'idea.' In one case, Ballou blends two Darwin note-books, one of scientific observation and one of notes on his family, with a third, of her own 'jottings,' to create a poem. Wilkinson's last example is Dennis Cooley's poetic biography of the Manitoban outlaw Bloody Jack Krafchenko. Cooley focuses on fleeting glimpses of his subject and takes no interest in nailing down facts about him. Biography in this case is 'experiment and play.' Wilkinson's writing tasks ask the student writer to take on the first-person perspective on the subject and to introduce themselves into the frame with reflections on the process of writing.

The penultimate chapter in the collection is a rousing call to action for more ambitious and more stirring life writing. Dr Willa McDonald aims at younger writers in particular, those who may conceive of the memoir as simply the immediate recycling of memories (she brings up one imag-inary title in this connection: 'Krazy Me at Kuta Beach'). The message is applicable to any writer, however. McDonald asks aspiring writers to target specifically and separately the intellect, the emotions, the body, and the spirit. She challenges the authority of the memory for the writer. She reminds us that memories are not fixed but rather actively constructed in the moment. Memories are motivated. They are produced to maintain the integrity of our sense of self and our sense of a personal history. If memory is fallible and never disinterested, then what are the memoirist's obligations to truthfulness? McDonald here cites Philippe Lejeune's 'autobiographical pact.' Writer, reader, and publisher commit to an agreement that the writer is representing their world. As McDonald says, this is far from simple, however, and the work of W. G. Sebald, Bruce Chatwin, and Helen Garner reminds us of how perilous and exciting the borderland between fact and fiction is. The exercise of the intellect, through taking account of wider social and political developments and through documentary research—'details that make the work glow'—is one of the four pillars of good writing. In the exploratory personal essay pioneered by Michel de Montaigne, the questioning intellect is paramount. Emotion can come through the well-crafted persona, through dialogue, and through not telling but showing, via action and other means. Restraint is one of the keys to achieving emotional affect.

Connecting 'with being a fleshly, bodily presence in the world' is another key to vivid writing. Body language and bodily reactions (e.g., blushing, crying, and yawning) have a truthfulness and an immediacy in human communication which the writer can take advantage of. Life writing connects with meaning at the level of the spirit. The best life writing is distilled wisdom that takes readers to depths and to heights. It can be an unflinching enquiry about the life we lead and about the way selves inhabit the world, which will, in the words of Annie Dillard, 'press upon our minds the deepest mysteries, so we may feel again their majesty and power.'

Non-fiction stories adapted for children are the focus of Professor Kate Douglas's chapter, Chapter 12. She discusses two books: One is by the comedian Ahn Do, telling the story of his life in Vietnam during the Vietnam War, his journey on a refugee boat to Australia, and his life as a new immigrant. The other is by Malala Yousafzai, describing the attempt on her life and its consequences and her experiences as an activist agitating for education for girls in Pakistan. Both books are collaborations with illustrators, and Douglas suggests that this is one way they might stimulate thoughts about new and unusual ways of writing lives. The writer shares the material of the life story with other creative forces, to reach new audiences and to explore new dimensions within and implications for it.

A second way is through adaptation to a specific audience—in this case, children. The two aspects come together in the question of how to deal with the representation of violence and suffering. Even more than writers, illustrators grapple with the problem of how graphic to be in showing traumatic events given the age of their readers.

Yousafzai was shot in the head by members of the Taliban in their attempt to end her campaign for equal education for girls. In her book for children, this is not depicted except in the simple statement that 'dangerous men tried to silence me.' Douglas notes that this is immediately followed by a triumphant declaration: 'But they failed.' The illustrations neither represent this event nor its aftermath in Yousafzai's facial injuries. In this way, Yousafzai escapes the trap of being defined by this event and gives optimism a powerful impetus.

Adults writing for children, as Douglas shows, can take advantage of a powerful double point of view. In Do's *The Little Refugee*, for instance, the language of the narrative is childish, suggesting an engaging innocence; at the same time, the adult awareness of the mature narrator provides a context of information that the child could not have known at the time. Do as a young child knows only the warmth of his family and the richness of their life in a Vietnamese village, but the adult Do adds an awareness that death and suffering were all around.

Yousafzai's writing is itself the most important avenue of her activism. '[L]ife stories are a powerful genre,' as Douglas says, and this can be transposed to writing for children. Reading autobiographical writing may play an important role for children, alongside the reading of the more usual fictional works. Life stories can help show young readers that they can be 'capable problem-solvers who identify issues and take action to solve them' in the words of Prisca Martens and her co-authors, quoted by Douglas.

Yousafzai's book for children is called *Malala's Magic Pencil*. As a child, she longed for a magic pencil to solve the problems she saw around her. As an adult, she can see that her life story reveals a different kind of magic at work in the powerful effects of speaking out through her blog and her books. Do's book likewise has a strong, positive arc. Do goes from a confrontation with pirates on a refugee boat to recognition in his new country when he is elected class captain, then implicitly through his later success in his career as a comedian. Whether or not readers of the present volume consider adapting their work for children, these two books prompt ideas about a double awareness in narration and about the power of the moral that comes with a life story. They also remind us of the way fanciful and childish imaginings can sometimes be realised in different but equally satisfying forms in the everyday adult world.

The twelve essays, with their targeted exercises for writers and their lists of further reading, have a collective impact and provide individual insights. No reader will be able to escape the feeling that life writing is a supremely difficult endeavour. How on earth can the writer of today, starting on a new biography and memoir, add something to the stock of wise, innovative, and entertaining life writing that already exists? On the other hand, there is hope through the new perspectives on existence and experience that open up with each twist of the cultural spiral, demanding their own spokesperson. New generations need their voices to be heard. Moreover, the power of form can be put beside the might of content. The chapters are a tribute to the role of craft and technique in taking writers through barriers to new achievements, so that they can move from 'Krazy Me at Kuta Beach' to memoir or biography that is both embodied and spiritual and both felt and intelligent.

 Works Cited

1. Boey, Kim Cheng. *Gull Between Heaven and Earth*. Epigram Books, 2017.

FOUND LIVES: REFRAMING THE LOST, THE INANIMATE, AND THE HIDDEN

1 OBITUARIES: BEHIND THE FINAL TRIBUTE

Amanda Norman

An obituary is a public announcement of the recent death of an individual, together with information about the upcoming funeral. According to Glennys Howarth and Oliver Leaman the obituary can 'be described as a published notice of the details of a person's death together with a biography cataloguing' the deceased's past life (334). In Manel Herat's view also, "The meaning the word [obituary] has nowadays is 'a record or an announcement of a death or deaths, especially in a newspaper; usually comprising a brief biographical sketch of the deceased' (*OED*)" (118). The obituary notice is not usually written by a person prior to their own death but rather by others on what they remember or want known about their newly deceased. For Jennifer King, 'Obituaries are the first draft of a person's [entire] history and act as a snapshot of society at a particular point in time' ('Backstory' 2017). Mushira Eid presents a wider picture when she points out that obituarists often reflect aspects of their culture, their gender, and themselves in their writing: obituary notices 'conform to a certain format and reflect aspects of the social context within which they are written—its values and perhaps its attitudes towards death, its people and perhaps how they view themselves and, by implication, their perception of gender' (14). Importantly, Douglas Vipond sees that although they are "often overlooked, obituaries are an important form of 'epideictic' or ceremonial discourse, 'composed in order to celebrate or reaffirm the community values' Crowley 1990, 157)" (Vipond 102).

Obituary writing, even though an experimental approach to and unusual form of life-writing, has some characteristic elements. Apart from the notice of death and the funeral arrangements, it can—but does not always—include factors such as a sketch of the life achievements or accomplishments of the deceased, a mention of a characteristic or physical feature of that person, and a mention of surviving family (Narayan; Conventions of obituary writing; The Remembrance Process). Known for their brevity, the lengths of obituaries may nevertheless vary considerably. They can be anything from a few lines to a paragraph to even a page or more: 'a short straight-to-the point announcement' or 'an epic account of a person's life,' and they can be 'sad, sweet, inspiring, and even funny' in their delivery (Terranova).

In this chapter, I draw on examples of obituaries that provide an alternative way of exploring life-writing. I also focus on how obituaries can chronicle personal and professional identities. In this, I draw on obituaries that have been written about individuals in mainstream society who are not so much recognised as private persons but rather for their uniqueness to their profession. I include a discussion on how obituaries can be sourced, collated, and analysed for scholarly research: 'despite the implied potential of obituaries as residential provinces for exploring social phenomena, they have often been neglected as research sites' (Bonsu 202; Herat 118).

Brief historical overview

The earliest forms of obituary can be traced back to (at least) ancient Rome, to the Acta Diurna, a papyrus newspaper which included 'prominent death announcements' (Terranova). In Britain, 'the obituary art in its first incarnation' in print was 'practiced by the newsbook compilers of 17th-century England, notably during the Restoration' (Starck, 'Posthumous' 267). This practice, which was limited to the obituaries of the 'notables,' the wealthy, the famous, and the aristocracy, was continued in the following centuries, in newspapers such as the iconic British newspaper, *The Times*, which first published in the 18th century. In the introductory pages to *The Times Great Victorian Lives* (2007), Ian Brunskill reveals that 'In its early days, [*The Times*] approach to obituary coverage had been haphazard' (viii). Moreover, 'Notable deaths had been recorded from the French Revolution onwards, but there was no great consistency of quality or tone' (vii). During 1841–42, under the new leadership of editor John Thadeus Delane, though, the newspaper's journalists sought new and creative ways of attracting wider readership, including to their obituary section, especially with obituaries of those who had been deemed notable in life (vii–viii). Even so, in Britain—and in the United States—in the early 1800s and even into the early to mid 1900s, obituaries of less-notable deceased people often contained little more than the deceased's name, date of birth, cause of death, place of residence, and surviving family, if that (Brunskill *The Times,* vi–viii; Meyerink).

In the United States, even though newspapers had been in regular circulation since 1704, 'the traditional biographical obituary … primarily developed after the U.S. Civil War' (Meyerink). To begin with, these were usually fairly basic: 'As the interest in local news grew, newspapers added more and more information and a wider range of people to their traditional death notices'; although 'there will not be an obituary on every person who died in the latter half of the 1880s, you will find them for a very large number of adults, especially those who had been a resident in a community for a number of years' (Meyerink). In time, in both the United States and Britain, and in many other countries as well, the obituary came to include brief biographies, poems, prayers, and even pictures of the deceased (Meyerink).

Numerous writers (e.g., Árnason et al. 2003; Fowler and Biesla 2007; Meyerink 2017; and Starck 2006a, 2006b, 2007, 2008, 2009). have noted a significant rise in interest of obituaries during the late 20th century in many countries. Britain, along with many other nations, has for many years published obituaries of famous people and ordinary people, although since the 1980s, these have attracted a significant growing readership and have become a popular read in the public arena (*The Economist,* 'The art of the obituary.'). Subsequently, obituary writers from varying backgrounds beyond newspapers have responded to this growth by developing a style of life-writing that is anecdotal, discursive, and elegantly concise (*The Economist,* 'The art of the obituary'). These days, the obituary columns in national newspapers have become a source of entertainment, fascination, and intrigue of celebrated lives, and they are growing in popularity (*The Economist*; Narayan ; Brunskill, *Great Lives: A Century in Obituaries*).

Josephine Livingstone, in her article 'The Art of the *New York Times* Obituary,' reveals that in the present age 'most obituaries' that appear in *The New York Times* usually 'run to 800 words … although they can go down to 500 or up to thousands in the case of, say, a dead pope' (14 Apr. 2017). Moreover, "When celebrities are 'ailing' (their word), the obituarists start drafting" before that celebrity has actually died (Livingstone). The obituaries editor for *The New York Times*, Bill McDonald, in 'Talk to the Newsroom' (25 Sept. 2006), notes that in the modern-day United States, in the major cities and the largest print newspapers—different from what happens in local newspapers—only the obituaries of celebrities and other recognisably significant newly deceased people (e.g., politicians, popes, royalty) are considered newsworthy, and because they are news items, no payment is required. Conversely, as Lux Narayan points out, in the United States, in big city newspapers such as *The New York Times*, prominent people in society, who nevertheless are not celebrities or otherwise recognised as significant to the masses, usually have longer (paid) obituaries which contain information about their achievements in life and status in society (Narayan). McDonald agrees: Families of all deceased people who are not celebrities or otherwise recognisably significant must pay to place their obituaries in the paper: 'the paid [obituary] notices are classified ads … . placed in the paper or on the Web by the classified advertising department, which operates independently of the news department' (McDonald, *The New York Times* 'Talk to the Newsroom' 25 Sept. 2006). Such notices can have as much space as they wish because they generate revenue; 'We, on the news side, who only spend revenue, are generally promised … half a page,' sometimes 'less, sometimes more, depending on how many ads are sold' (McDonald, *The New York Times* 'Talk to the Newsroom').

Behind the print

Obituaries can be considered in terms of what they reveal about aspects of an individual's life story, garnered from recorded facts and the collective memory of the deceased's close family and friends (Fowler, *The Obituary as Collective Memory*). Bridget Fowler and Esperança Bielsa in their 2007 article on their joint study of 883 samples of noted obituaries consider the question, in Western societies, of 'who is selected for certain key national newspapers … with particular reference to their social origins, educational backgrounds and nationality' (203–4). They find that 'collective memory is intertwined with remembering the dead'; 'systematic forgetting affects certain ethnic groups, nationalities and classes disproportionately'; 'the impact of elite higher educational establishments' is evident across the Western world (203); and the noted obituaries are 'overwhelmingly of men' (221). 'Yet certain signs of movement within the obituary world can also be detected: women start to appear in their own right, the Third World begins to be represented and wider arrays of occupations have become the source of obituary portraits' (203).

In contemporary obituaries in the Western world, the social privilege of people is not restricted to the memory of the 'dominant class'—the 'power bloc, ie those social groups aligned together by similar background and experience, notably of public schools' and wealth and 'class'—alone (Fowler and Biesla 220–22). Even though the noted entries still contain the 'dominant' groups, entries are 'skewed towards the higher professions,' celebrities, 'politically elite,' and suchlike (222), and within that core they are skewed towards the predominant nationality and after that the ethnicity—in the United States, for instance, the Black population and the Jewish population, for example—most favoured by a particular paper (Fowler and Biesla 220–21). Regardless of these factors, "the frequent *family* transmission of privilege is still overshadowed by the 'mountain climb' image of the individual's biographical trajectory dominant in these [noted] obituaries" (Fowler and Biesla 222). These days, obituary editors in national newspapers aspire to include all those who have helped to shape or inspire the modern world beyond the arena of villains and heroes (*Economist*; Meyerink).

Eid, in her study of obituaries, looked at 'sexism in language' and gender in obituaries across cultures (16), specifically newspaper obituaries in which both genders are 'represented' (14). Eid aimed to measure 'gender (in)equity and change in the obituaries' (16). Within this study, she found that people create patterns of 'linguistic behaviour so as to resemble' the group(s) which they wish to be either identified with or distinguished from (16–17). To give the best possible spread for her study, Eid chose three different languages and their corresponding cultures: Arabic (Egypt), Persian (Iran), and English (US) (15). Eid saw that linguistically, of the three, Arabic is Semitic and hence stands alone and that the other two, being Indo-European, are 'more closely related' (15–16). Culturally, Egypt and Persia are predominantly Islamic and hence stand together, and the last given is predominantly Judeo-Christian: 'These choices,' she believed, 'are diverse enough to allow for sufficient difference and similarities to emerge' (16). Eid's study confirmed her initial discomfiture on gender inequality: generally, though 'in some parts of the world more so than in others, women have been denied equal access to the public domain,' and men took precedence over women even in death (14–15). Further, through obituaries, gender inequality expressed itself in both linguistic and non-linguistic ways, no matter how educated the woman and no matter her professional status (14, 16–18). This was true regardless of cultural, orientation and size differences between the obituaries and changes (including time) to obituaries, such as length of text and information given (76).

Approaches such as selecting a period of years and then collating obituaries during ten-year intervals can provide a period long enough to determine whether change has taken place. The Christa Rodler et al. research study on gender and society highlighted how gender stereotypes were portrayed in work-related roles. The aim of the study was to investigate changes 'in gender stereotypes by an unobtrusive method' (827): 'Descriptive words in the obituaries of female and male leaders'—people who had held leadership positions in life—'were analyzed with regard to task-orientation and person-orientation' (840). The sample obituaries chosen were from those published in four German-language newspapers between 1974 and 1998 and covered both genders equally (827). Rodler et al. give their reasons: 'With regard to gender, this approach focuses … not on how men and women actually differ but how people *think* that they differ (Deaux 110)' (Rodler et al. 827). Rodler et al. explain that 'In assigning attributes to male and female leadership performance, observers are biased by subjective social realities and by stereotypes' (828). Further, whether leaders are, or are merely regarded as, successful 'depends heavily on followers' implicit theories of leadership' and 'there is strong evidence for the existence of a leadership prototype'—one invariably 'cloaked in masculine terms' (Rodler et al. 828). That is, in general, leadership success is not only based on the competencies of leaders but also affected by subordinates' behaviours, assumptions, and perspectives of leadership attributions, by factors that are subjective, and by those largely based on biological sex (Rodler et al. 827–28).

The Rodler et al. study results showed that female 'gender images' differed markedly from male ones every year—with the exception of 1992 and 1998, when the gender stereotypes showed some similarity (Rodler et al. 827). Overall, the study showed that 'there is a balance between task- and person-orientation' (840). Importantly, Rodler et al. found that running parallel with this obvious evidence of social change, traditional views seem to have changed over the term of the study; the obituaries indicated that there was an increase in the numbers of women 'in intermediate leadership positions,' which in turn indicated 'a decline of gender barriers to opportunity,' and this 'observable convergence of gender images' could give rise to the hope that 'gender stereotypes of leaders' will change over time (841). Nevertheless, what was also clearly shown by the obituary content is that while 'female images' may seem to have changed somewhat over the years studied, male stereotypes have remained the same (839).

Studies such as the three just given provide examples of how differing facets of lives can be explored through obituaries alongside the context of the time. In approaching obituaries as a distinct form of discourse, Rae A. Moses and Giana D. Marelli find that obituaries are 'window[s] that provide' a 'view into a culture and … are one of the elements out of which literate cultures are built' (123). In addition to these types of contemporary obituaries, a two-volume work of short biographies, *Brief Lives* (1626–97), written by 17th-century historian and gossip John Aubrey, forms a historical perspective of how lives can be recorded and analysed (Buchanan-Brown; Scurr; Webb). This gives emphasis to how individuals not only contribute to instigating change but also shape the fabrics of society in which they are immersed, thus supporting the rationale of obituaries of both the famous and known and the relatively unknown being worthy of academic study: Jarboe , says Reem Bassiouney, 'argues that obituaries are a good source of documentation of facts about both ordinary and famous people' (Bassiouney 66). "Knutson adds that obituaries are 'formal pieces, designed to eulogize important community and national figures'" (qtd. in Bassiouney 66).

Learning in obituary

In a 2017 conference, data analyst Lux Narayan presented 'The Conventions of obituary writing,' an international talk about what he considered valuable in the reading of obituaries. Over a period of twenty months, Narayan analysed two thousand *New York Times* entries of (paid) obituaries of mostly famous people and found that after taking away the first and last few words of an obituary—the person's name, funeral details, and the bereaved—all that remained was a full biography in brevity and a descriptor of that deceased person's achievements over a lifetime. Narayan then fed these descriptors into a computer programme that throws out the superfluous words—'and', 'the,' and so on—leaving only the most significant words. From these, he deduced that obituaries could help predict future trends, and that maximised achievement is most likely to occur in mid life and reflectivity (Narayan). Although the sample that Narayan analysed was demographically small, and all were *New York Times* entries, his talk emphasised the developing popularisation and shared international forums in presenting and studying obituaries, otherwise considered a limiting short space narrative of the deceased (Narayan).

Obituaries are considered to be a family's, a community's, and a society's final public tribute to an individual when they die (see Herat 117–24, 135). Herat warns that 'Obituaries, it should be noted, go beyond the limits of a mere announcement of a demise; they are also a means of affirming the cultural background, religion, social status, and immigration patterns of the deceased and their family' (118). Samuel K. Bonsu takes this a step further when he notes that Lawuyi 'identified obituaries as socially legitimised advertisements of deceased and bereaved persons, often built on the aspirational rather than the true identities of the people in the text' (202). That is, 'An obituary's ability to bridge the gap between actual and inspirational identities relies on the fact that texts are often written by people other than the deceased' and are hence 'imbued with the personal and social identities of both the bereaved family and the deceased' (Bonsu 202). This allows the writer to 'project themselves into the text' in a 'fashion consistent with the bereaved's perspectives, but not necessarily in line with' that 'espoused' by the deceased person in life (202).

Life, not death

Nigel Starck says in his article 'Revelation, Intrusion, and Questions of Taste: the Ethical Change for Obituary Writers' that 'It is widely accepted that the emphasis on obituary composition should be on capturing life rather than death' (373). He notes that newspapers' obituary columns, especially those outside of the paid advertisement sections, 'deliver their posthumous review with a formidable authority' and 'have the capacity to offend and wound' those who are related or connected to deceased and remember that person 'with a familiarity not necessarily available' to 'the readership at large' (372). 'At the same time,' says Starck, 'there is a duty to present formidable authority' to 'satisfy the historical record' (372). Consequently, for writers and editors and for publishers, this presents an ethical dilemma about 'what measure of intimate information should be revealed' and, in particular, about the cause of death, especially if self-inflicted regardless of whether it was intentional suicide or otherwise (372). Starck adds that 'Then there is the matter of qualification for the page itself' (372). In the world's current sociopolitical clime and with advent of terrorism, whereas 'newsworthy' obituaries were formerly concerned with 'society's more prominent citizens whose histories could be safely compiled from,' say, the files, 'obituary practice has been extended in recent times to offer an egalitarian coverage' (372). As a result, 'Obituary desks have had to intrude on grief and seek information from the newly (and violently) bereaved' (372).

In his book *Life After Death the Art of the Obituary* Starck notes the *Sydney Morning Herald*'s former editor-in-chief, David Bowman, once saying that in the present times, 'in an era when we must all pretend to be young,' obituaries 'have caught on'; that 'In the English-speaking world' at least, 'a newspaper of quality hardly seems complete these days without a regular obituary page'; and that 'Perhaps, in an age of bewildering change, it buoys one up to discover how others survived their times. The best obituaries, after all, capture life; they are not about death' (Starck, *Life After Death* ix). Commenting on Bowman's findings, Starck reiterates his words in the earlier article 'Sex after death': 'The best obituaries, after all, capture life; they are not about death' ('Sex' 338; 'Revelation, intrusion' 373). Starck further notes that in the present day, obituaries 'have shrugged off the subfusc language of old, introducing in its stead a fusion of irreverent assertion and candid assessment,' resulting from the 'obituary transformation, a phenomenon of the 1980s,' and that Hugh Montgomery-Massingberd, 'widely acknowledged as the driving force in this movement's British manifestation … was influenced by an earthy exclamation within the stage adaptation of John Aubrey's *Brief Lives*' (Starck, 'Sex' 338–39).

Jason B. Phillips (2007) reports on his recent study that in it he examined obituaries from the *New York Times*, from 1899 to 1999, 'at three points to illuminate changing conceptions of death' (325). Phillips found that the obituaries indicated that 'descriptions of biophysical aspects of the dying process are marginalized over time and that there is a more frequent use of language that emphasizes death-resistant themes in the most recent obituaries'; he concludes that this finding 'exemplifies the observation of increasing claims to authority over mortality by individuals in recent decades' (Phillips 325). This would seem to indicate that with the ever-increasing advancement in medical technology, people have hope of greater longevity.

Noted and newsworthy, not national celebrity

Reading the obituaries of those who are well known within their professions and community, but less known nationally, allows one the opportunity to gain a deeper sense of what an obituary can reveal and an idea of how it can be approached as a form of writing for others. Ted Wragg, professor at Exeter University, UK, was one such character. Combined, Wragg's many obituaries portrayed him through his social identity while endeavouring to retain a persona to which the reader could relate.

In *The Times* obituary of Friday 11 November 2005, written by Will H. Woodward, Ted Wragg is lauded as the 'Educator who confronted the complexities of teaching with wisdom and humour over three decades' (Woodward, *The Times* 11 Nov. 2005). Woodward wrote for more than one newspaper. *The Guardian* described Wragg in their obituary of Friday 11 November 2005, written by Woodward: 'Ted Wragg: Education guru whose ideas were embraced by teachers and energised our schools' (Woodward, *The Guardian* 11 Nov. 2005). The obituary that appeared in *The Guardian* focused on career aspects and Wragg's criticisms of the political climate of the time. It did not gloss the character but made Wragg appear as a real individual caught in the politics of education and as one who did not hide his views. *The Independent* obituary of Friday 11 November 2005, written by Richard Garner and titled 'Professor Ted Wragg: Campaigning educationist and tease of government in merciless newspaper columns' recorded Wragg's criticism of exams and focused on a popular television programme to which he contributed and on his work as 'a columnist for several national newspapers in his time' (Garner). *The Times* were more conventional in their approach, beginning their obituary with Wragg's contribution to education, his authorship, and his own professional background as a professor at a university. *The Telegraph*, in their editorial obituary of 10 November 2005, 'Professor Ted Wragg,' documented Wragg's relationship with Chris Woodhead, the former chief inspector of schools in 1998, and gave some background of their disputes, which followed on to his disputes with the Prince of Wales (*The Telegraph*).

These various obituaries, as verified by journal articles written by appreciative students, others, and various academics—such as Sara Delamont in her article 'Ted Wragg: An appreciation,' to name but one—who either knew him or knew of him, had been able to encapsulate Ted Wagg's controversies, his passions, the chronicles of his life, and his contributions to education, all in one brief experimental form of writing.

Ethics and creativity

In speaking of his 2007 study of a hundred obituaries of deceased academics, which were published in 'quality national newspapers,' Malcolm Tight states that in life-writing, new genres and hence methods are necessary to complement more familiar approaches (127). However, in approaching some other's obituary with flair and creativity, there is the potential issue of the obituary becoming an entertainment piece rather than a befitting obituary. As G. Thomas Couser clearly spells out in 'The obituary of a face,' writing an obituary for someone else necessitates that the writer take a more tentative and respectful attitude.

In 'The obituary of a face' Couser notes that Lucy Grealy's obituary that appeared in *The New York Times* allowed the implication that she had died by suicide because of her unhappiness about her facial disfigurement (1). Couser points out that *The New York Times* obituary was at odds with Grealy's previously published autobiography chronicling her lifelong struggles not only to triumph over adversity by accepting her face as it was but also to assist others to accept her evident physical disability (1). Obituaries, as Couser notes, aim to encapsulate how an individual looked to the world, not how the world looked to them (1–2). In Grealy's obituary, though, the writer insinuated that Grealy's facial disfigurement played a more sinister role, culminating in her death (1). 'If one accepts [Joel] Feinberg's argument' that 'it is possible to harm' the dead's 'surviving interests,' says Couser, 'then Lucy Grealy's obituary can be seen as a particularly ironic example of death writing inflicting posthumous harm on its subject' (1). 'On this matter,' writes Couser, 'the obituary's author, Christopher Lehmann-Haupt, was at once circumspect and irresponsible. While declining to specify a cause of death, the obituary presented its circumstances in a sequence that implied one' (2).

In a self-written obituary, the writer does not have the ethical restrictions of which Couser speaks and can be as indulgent and creative as they see fit. Isabelle Rubin LaBelle proposes, in her 1987 work with disturbed adolescents, the writing of a projected self-written obituary as a way of galvanising how one wants to live their life, and she posits that the activity has therapeutic properties that enhance personal growth (538). For LaBelle, this activity itself becomes a poignant part of the writing in how one thinks about life (538–39). LaBelle also considers the broader application: she finds that writing the self-written obituary to be 'a therapeutic technique,' one which is 'widely applicable as a projective as well as practice tool' and which can be used with 'people of all ages.' For example, 'Older clients frequently [discovered] that writing their obituaries revealed to them aspects of themselves they had never known' and brought them to review how they had lived their life (539).

Obituary writing is a purposeful form, in its entirety, of life-writing with accuracy and authenticity. Alfred Nobel (1888), the inventor of dynamite, was stunned to read in his local newspaper that he had died. The paper had mistakenly written about him instead of his newly deceased brother. The obituary read the merchant of death is dead'. It went further to say that he was an individual who became rich by killing more people than had ever been done by a single other before. Although the obituary revealed the authentic facts about Nobel, it was the legacy left that was of greatest concern to him. Subsequently Nobel took immediate action and changed his legacy. After reading the mistaken obituary, he founded the Nobel Prize international awards. He is now remembered for the Nobel Peace Prize rather than for dynamite, his original invention. Thus, becoming aware of his finite existence intensified Nobel's delight of his time left and resulted in his seeking richer and more authentic ways to live his life (Shaw).

Conclusion

As Eid, Rodler et al., Fowler and Biesla, Tight, and others discussed in this chapter show, comparative studies of obituaries from any given time and covering any cultural, linguistic, gender, or social context are important forms of research. As the research studies discussed here seem to indicate, obituaries contain 'implied potential … as residential provinces for exploring social phenomena' (Bonsu 202; Herat 118); further, they are also important forms "of 'epideictic' or ceremonial discourse, 'composed in order to celebrate or reaffirm the community values'" (Crowley 157, qtd. in Vipond 102).

Looked at from a different perspective—that is, as a piece of biographical writing in brevity—an obituary written by one person for another reflects aspects of the deceased person's identity and the social perception of the one who is writing the tribute for public reading (Herat; Fowler; Howarth and Leaman; King; Narayan). As Couser shows in his article 'The obituary of a face,' though, writing about another necessitates respect and a duty of care to the deceased and the bereaved (1–15). Conversely, as LaBelle shows, in self-written obituaries, the writer can be as indulgent and self-appreciating as they see fit (538–39). With projected self-written obituaries, even though the writer cannot generally determine the cause of actual death, the projected way that death may occur can be included, elaborated on by the writer (LaBelle 538–39). In being creative about death, obituaries can reveal how people perceive life.

Thus, obituaries can be considered in terms of what emerges from and they expose about an individual's life story and the meanings within their life, their society, and the world in which that individual lived (Fowler and Biesla); rather than simply being a commentator of death the obituary 'is generally much more concerned with life than with death' (Starck, 'Death Can' 923). In effect, the obituary treats the individual as universal singular, and in the literary move recognises that each individual life is itself a singular accomplishment which demands recognition: A life, like the stories that can be told about it, never ends (Denzin 78–80). Ultimately, the obituary is about crafting a narrative that links together events, experiences, and perceptions, with an opportunity to create an identity (Jackson, 'The Dying Art of Obituary Writing'). It is from this perspective that obituary writing is significant as a forever new and experimental approach to writing lives (Bytheway and Johnson).

 ACTIVITY

Practice exercises for writing an obituary

1. **Styles of writing**

   Choose the life of a controversial person or someone who has died in controversial circumstances from over fifty years ago.

   Select two to three obituaries of this person, from different sources.

   Read the obituaries and consider the following:

   What is the overall tone of each obituary?

   Are the writers sympathetic in their approach?

   Are they descriptive?

   Are they limited in context?

   How are the identities of the individuals depicted in each obituary?

   Do the obituaries reflect the society of the time?

   Now select a well-known individual, known through their work, public persona or contribution to society. Source and read six obituaries from different media. Describe their tone and style and the comparative impact they have on you.

   How do you find these writers' narrative techniques?

   Did any themes emerge?

   Did you get a sense of who the individual was?

   Were the obituaries written with the individual or the reader in mind?

Consider the following:

Tone

Content

Emotional words included

Identity of the individual—and how they were described

2. Writing for others

Ask yourself, do I know this individual, or is the individual someone outside of public knowledge?

What information is needed?

What would you include?

How would you describe the remembered individual?

Where would you share the completed obituary?

Search online and source any sites you deem of value in contributing to the world of obituary writing.

3. Writing a projected self-written obituary

Writing one's own obituary is a form of developing an individual creative style of autobiographical writing.

Map your life story using the following themes to organise your thinking according to the following:

Recollection

Connections

Projections

By approaching an obituary using these broad themes, one can gain a better understanding of both the connection and the distance between a current life state and projected aspirations within a finite space.

Once you have completed these steps, use the following areas to develop your obituary further. Your objective is to ask yourself, what do I want individuals to remember about me? Keep in mind the following concerns:

A list of accomplishments

Anecdotes and happenings in life

A timeline

Ask others for their input, to make your writing more objective.

Study a photograph of yourself, one that represents a time and place you feel is significant to your life, and write a self-projected obituary.

After a day or so, look at your self-projected obituary, study the approach you have used in writing, and write a second self-projected obituary taking a different approach. Experiment by repeating this exercise over a short but reasonable period of time. You might also experiment with form and the layout of your self-projected obituaries.

 ## Recommended Reading

Boler, Sandy. "Marit Allen: 'Vogue' fashion editor and costume designer on 'White Mischief' and 'Brokeback Mountain'." *The Independent*, Saturday 1 Dec. 2007. www.independent.co.uk/news/obituaries/marit-allen-vogue-fashion-editor-on.

Brunskill, Ian, and Andrew Sanders. *Great Victorian Lives: An Era in Obituaries.* HarperCollins Publishers, 2007.

Couser, G. Thomas. 'The obituary of a face: Lucy Grealy. Death writing and posthumous harm.' *Auto/Biography,* vol. 12, no. 1, 2004, pp. 1–15. doi.10.1191/0967550704ab001oa.

Eid, Mushira. *The World of Obituaries: Gender across Cultures and over Time.* Wayne State UP, 2002.

Fowler, Bridget. *The Obituary as Collective Memory.* Routledge, 2007.

Fowler, Bridget, and Esperança Bielsa. 'The lives we choose to remember: A quantitative analysis of newspaper obituaries.' *The Sociological Review,* vol. 55, no. 2, May 2007, pp. 203–26. dx.org/101111/j1467-954X.2007.00702.x doi.10.111/j.1467-954x.2007.00702.x

Massingberd, Hugh, editor. *The Very Best of the Daily Telegraph Books of Obituaries.* Pan Books, 2001.

———. *The Daily Telegraph Third Book of Obituaries: Entertainers.* Pan Macmillan, 1997.

Montgomery-Massingberd, Hugh. and David Watkin. *The London Ritz: A Social and Architectural History,* photographs by Keith Collie. Aurum Press, 1980.

Montgomery-Massingberd, Hugh, editor. *Daily Telegraph Book of Obituaries: Celebration of Eccentric Lives.* Vol. 1. Paperback ed. Pan, 1996.

 ## Works Cited

Árnason, Arnar, et al. 'Letters to the dead: Obituaries and identity, memory and forgetting in Iceland.' *Mortality,* vol. 8, no. 3, Aug. 2003, pp. 268–84. DOI:10.1080/1357627031000159981 2. Accessed 15 May 2017.

Buchanan-Brown, Jim, editor. *John Aubrey: Brief Lives,* selected and edited with introduction, glossary and notes by Jim Buchanan-Brown, foreword by Michael Hunter, Paperback ed. Penguin Classics, 2000.

Bassiouney, Reem, editor. *Al-Arabiyya. Journal of the American Association of Teachers of Arabic,* vol. 44 and 45. U Georgetown P, 2012.

Bonsu, Samuel K. 'The Presentation of dead selves in everyday life: Obituaries and impression management.' *Symbolic Interaction,* vol. 30, no. 2, Spring 2007, pp. 199–219. doi.org/10.1525/si.2007.30.2.199 *JSTOR.* www.jstor.org/stable/10.1525/si.2007.30.2.199. Accessed 15 May 2017.

Brunskill, Ian. *Great Lives: A Century in Obituaries.* Times Books, 2005. HarperCollins, 2005.

———. *The Times Great Victorian Lives.* Times Books, 2007.

Bytheway, Bill, and Julia Johnson. 'Valuing lives? Obituaries and the life course.' *Mortality,* vol. 1, no. 2, Routledge, 1996, pp. 219–34.

Conventions of obituary writing—Amazon ASW WJEC CBAC LTD 2017 resource.download.wjec.co.uk.s3.amazonaws.com/vtc/2016-17/16-17_3-23/pdf/obituary/. Accessed 10 Oct. 2017.

Couser, G. Thomas. 'The obituary of a face: Lucy Grealy. Death writing and posthumous harm.' *Auto/Biography,* vol. 12, no. 1, 2004, pp. 1–15. doi.10.1191/0967550704ab001oa. Accessed 15 May 2017.

Crowley, Sharon. *The Methodical Memory: Invention in Current-Traditional Rhetoric.* U Southern Illinois P, 1990.

Delamont, Sara. 'Ted Wragg: An appreciation.' *Teaching and Teacher Education,* vol. 22, no. 4, May 2006, pp. 523–24. doi.org/10.1016/j.tate.2006/01.001. Accessed 15 May 2017.

Denzin, Norman K. *Interpretive Biography.* Qualitative Research Methods, Vol. 17, series editor, John Van Maanen et al. Sage Publications, 1989.

The Economist. 'The art of the obituary.' Obituaries, 24 Dec. 1994. www.economist.com/1994/12/24/the_art_of_the_obituary. Accessed 16 May 2017.

Eid, Mushira. *The World of Obituaries: Gender across Cultures and over Time.* U Wayne State P, 2002.

Fowler, Bridget. *The Obituary as Collective Memory.* Routledge, 2007.

Fowler, Bridget, and Esperança Bielsa. 'The lives we choose to remember: A quantitative analysis of newspaper obituaries.' *The Sociological Review,* vol. 55, no. 2, May 2007, pp. 203–26. dx.org/101111/j1467-954X.2007.00702.x doi.10.111/j.1467-954x.2007.00702.x. Accessed 17 May 2017.

Garner, Richard. 'Professor Ted Wragg.' *The Independent,* Friday 11 Nov. 2005. medium.com/thrive-global/how-the-merchnt-of-death-turned-patron-of-peace-and-what-that-means-to-you. Accessed 17 May 2017.

Herat, Manel. 'Avoiding the reaper: Notions of death in Sri Lankan obituaries.' *International Journal of Language Studies,* vol. 8, no. 3, July 2014, pp. 117–44. www.hira.hope.ac.uk/../herat83%20%281%29.%20 obituraries%20publication%20pdf.pdf. Accessed 17 May 2017.

Howarth, Glennys, and Oliver Leaman, editors. *The Encyclopedia of Death and Dying.* Routledge, 2001.

Jackson, H. 'The dying art of obituary writing.' *Press Gazette.* 2007. www.pressgazette.co.uk/the-dying-art-of-obituary-writing/. www.pressgazette.co.uk/story.asp?storyCode=38457&sectioncode=1. Accessed 18 May 2017.

King, Jennifer. 'Backstory: The art of obituary writing—it's about life, not death' ABC Backstory. Posted 16 Nov. 2107, updated 13 Dec. 2017. www.abc.net.au/news/about/backstory/digital/2017-11.obituary-writing/915446. Accessed 15 Dec. 2017.

LaBelle, Isabelle Rubin. 'Obituaries by Adolescents: A therapeutic technique.' *Social Work,* vol. 32, no. 6, 1 Jan. 1987, pp. 538–39. dx.doi.org/10.1093/sw/32.6.538. Accessed 15 Dec. 2017.

Livingstone, Josephine. 'The Art of the *New York Times* Obituary.' 14 Apr. 2017. newrepublic.com.article/142044/art-new-york-times-obituary. Accessed 15 June 2017.

McDonald, Bill. 'Talk to the Newsroom: Obituaries, Editor Bill McDonald.' *The New York Times.* 25 Sept. 2006. www.nytimes.com/2006/09/25/business/media/25asktheeditors.html. Accessed 15 June 2017.

Meyerink, Kory L. 'Obituaries: More Than Meets the Eye, Read All About It.' Genealogy.com posted 2017. www.genealogy.com/articles/research/76_kory.html. Accessed 17 Dec. 2017.

Moses, Rae A., and Giana D. Marelli. 'Obituaries and discursive construction of dying and living.' *Texas Linguistic Forum,* vol. 47, 2004, pp. 123–30. www.salsa.ling.utexas.edu/proceedings/2003/moses&marelli.pdf. Accessed 22 June 2017.

Narayan, Lux. 'What I learned from 2,000 obituaries.' TEDNYC Jan. 2017. YouTube, posted March 2017. www.ted.com/speakers/lux_narayan_ what_i_learned_from_2_000_obituaries ru-clip.com/video/JlbwchclCBo/ what -i-learned-from-2-000-obituaries-lux-narayan.html. Accessed 22 June 2017.

Phillips, Jason B. 'The changing presentation of death in the obituary. 1899–1999.—NCBI.' *Omega-Journal of Death and Dying,* vol. 55, no. 4, December 1, 2007, pp. 325–46. doi.10.2190/OM.55.4.g www.ncbi.nlm. nih.gov/pubmed/18027647. Accessed 22 June 2017.

The Remembrance Process. 'How To Write An Obituary—A-Step-by-Step Guide 2017.' www.RemembranceProcess.com. Accessed 15 Dec. 2017.

Rodler, Christa, et al. 'Gender stereotypes of leaders: An analysis of the contents of Obituaries from 1974 to 1998.' *Sex Roles: A Journal of Research,* springernature.com online journal, vol. 45, no. 11–12, Dec. 2001, pp. 827–43. doi.org/10.1023/A:1015644520770 link, springer. com/journal/11199. Accessed 22 June 2017.

Scurr, Ruth. 'John Aubrey and our golden age of life writing,' *The Guardian*, Australian ed., 28 Feb. 2015. www.the guardian.com/profile/ruth-scurr. www.the guardian.com/books/biography. Accessed 14 July 2017.

Shaw, Jodie. 'How the 'Merchant of Death' Turned Patron of Peace.' Thrive Global, 12 Jan. 2017. thriveglobal.com/stories/how-the-merchant-of-death-turned-patron-of-peace/. Accessed 14 July 2017.

Starck, Nigel. Posthumous parallel and parallax: The obituary revival on three continents. *Journalism Studies,* vol. 6, no. 3, 2006a, pp. 267–83. doi.org/10.1080/14616700500131828. Accessed 14 Jul. 2017.

———. *Life After Death: the art of the obituary*, edited by Sybil Nolan U Melbourne P, 2006b.

———. 'Revelation, intrusion, and questions of taste: the ethical change for obituary editors,' *Journalism Practice,* vol. 1, no. 3, 19 Sept. 2007, pp.373–82. doi.org/10.1080/17512780701505069. Accessed 14 July 2017.

———. 'Death can make A difference: A comparative study of 'quality quartet' obituary practice.' *Journalism Studies,* vol. 9, no. 6, 11 Nov. 2008, pp. 911–24. doi.org/10.1080/14616700802227886. Accessed 14 Jul. 2017.

———. 'Sex after death: The obituary as an erratic record of proclivity.' *Mortality*, vol. 14, no. 4, 30 Mar. 2009, pp. 338–34. doi. org/10.1080/13576270903223671. Accessed 14 July 2017.

The Telegraph. 'Professor Ted Wragg.' Thursday 10 Nov. 2005. www. telegraph.co.uk/news/obituaries/1502670/Professor-Ted-Wragg.html. Accessed 14 July 2017.

Terranova, Jacob. 'The History of the Obituary.' The history of the obituary—Frazier Consultants. Blog post. February 9, 2017 www.frazerconsutants. com/2017/02/the_hitory_of_the_obituary. Accessed 14 July 2017.

Tight, Malcolm. 'Dead academics: What we can learn about academic work and life from obituaries?' *London Review of Education,* vol. 6, no. 2. July 2008. pp. 125–35. doi:10.1080/1474846082185045. Accessed 14 July 2017.

Vipond, Douglas. *Writing and Psychology: Understanding Writing and Its Teaching from the Perspective of Compositional Studies*. Praeger, 1993.

Webb, Simon, editor. *Aubrey's Brief Lives Omnibus Edition,* introduction and notes and edited by Simon Webb. Langley Press, 2017.

Woodward, Will H. 'Obituary: Ted Wragg.' *The Guardian*, Friday 11 Nov. 2005. www.theguardian.com/news/2005/nov/11/guardianobituaries. pressandpublishing. Accessed 15 Jul. 2017.

_____. 'Professor Ted Wragg: Educator who confronted the complexities of teaching with wisdom and humour over three decades.' *The Times*, 11 Nov. 2005. www.thetimes.co.uk/edition/news/ professor-ted-wragg-jznxcv0r5. Accessed 15 July 2017.

2 OBJECT BIOGRAPHY: WRITING THE LIVES OF OBJECTS, ARTEFACTS, AND THINGS

Donna Lee Brien

It is commonplace to suggest that individuals and societies are saturated, even drowning, in the objects that are the products of the contemporary commodity culture and that our memories and identities depend on this material culture (Horton and Kraftl). Yet these things have not been widely understood as worthy of being the objects of inspiration for life writers. As Thing theorist Bill Brown has asked, 'What habits have prevented us—prevented you—from thinking about objects, let alone things? Or more precisely, perhaps: what habits have prevented you from sharing your thoughts?' (7). An innovative type of life writing, not only does object biography offer a form for such writing practice, but once mastered, it can also be used in other subgenres of writing about lives, as well as in a wide range of fiction and non-fiction narratives.

This chapter provides a guide to object biography, which takes non-human things, objects, and artefacts—which I will hereafter largely use the word 'object' to describe—as the subject of biographical life stories. These subjects can include features of the natural world, physical sites and locations, buildings and monuments, objects of consumer and popular culture, art works, media products, pieces of fashion and jewellery, businesses and other enterprises, and types and brands of foods and beverages, as well as animals and other non-human beings. Considerating the various and shifting ways an object may have come into being and then been used and understood through time is crucial because, as these things pass through the world, they—like individuals—live through unique life cycles, during which they accumulate life histories.

These histories, the object biography proposes, can be expressed as life narratives. In profiling the object biography as an inventive way of writing lives and providing a guide to its form and its features, this chapter will discuss a number of object biographies, as well as authors who have successfully used object biographies in their work to demonstrate the applicability of the form.

Object biography

The concept of conducting and writing biographical studies of objects was raised three decades ago by cultural anthropologist Igor Kopytoff, whose influential work in this area suggested that to more fully understand the objects that are such a significant part of the human world and its history, they need to be thought about and scrutinised from more than just one point in what can be understood as their 'lives.' That is, it is useful and revealing to look at objects in terms that extend beyond the original purpose for which they were made or constructed or the current way they are being used. Instead, the various and shifting ways an object may have been used and understood are not only important but revealing. In this, objects are understood to not be static and unchanging, but rather, as Vesa-Pekka Herva posits, they can be thought of as able 'to live and grow not unlike organisms' (215). Once conceived in such terms, an object's life cycle—in terms of conception, birth, growth, life, death, disposal, and decay—can fit neatly into a chronological, biographical narrative, although—as in all biographical writing—this is not a requisite. Jody Joy, for instance, raises the idea that object biographies can be non-linear (i.e., non-chronological) (544)—as is the case in biographical and writing more generally (Brien 'Welcome').

The purpose of an object biography, as Robert Smith and Gemma Watson explain, is to uncover, explore, and narrate an object's journey 'from manufacture to disposal, tracing its changing uses and meanings' (5). Rosemary A. Joyce and Susan D. Gillespie's edited collection, *Things in Motion: Object Histories, Biographies, and Itineraries*, adds the idea of charting spatial 'itineraries' as part of an object biography, in the process that traces the journeys that an object makes from the place of its development and manufacture to where it is used and maintained and on to where it comes to rest or decay. This involves mapping the routes via which such objects move and circulate, together with the means by which they are moved. This involves noting the whereabouts of objects due to their moving due to economic, ritual, or personal exchanges and recognising how they might be reproduced and circulated in various media. A number of archaeological studies suggest that the exchange of portable objects plays an important and transformative role in how objects are perceived, valued, and understood (Peers), but less- and non-moveable objects, such as monuments, statues, and buildings, and even cities, also gather layers of use and reuse, and interpretation and reinterpretation, around themselves through time.

Ellen Swift discusses the modification, recycling and reuse which can be part of an object's life cycle—in particular those 'moments of object transformation,' which can result in an 'extended lifespan' and which are thus necessary to incorporate into what she calls 'the later stages of object biography' (167 – 68), in this particular example looking at the fate of a number of Romano-British bracelets. This study is also illuminating in its illustration of what Swift calls the 'divergent life histories' (202) of individual examples of the same type of object. After its period of man-ufacture, distribution, and initial use, a bracelet could, for example, be deposited in a temple or grave; it could be lost or discarded; or it could be melted or cut down and/or reshaped into a smaller bracelet, ring, or other object, such as a hook. Moreover, these—or other—processes could again be revisited on these refashioned objects, while once lost or discarded bracelets could be found and themselves altered.

Herva posits that objects can have what can be described as an invis-ible 'afterlife' (although not terming it as such). In a study of the objects deliberately hidden in ancient Minoan buildings, Herva explains that 'breakage and deposition do not necessarily bring to an end the use-life of an artefact'; instead, this may just 'mark another phase in object biography ... [since these objects] may well continue to be functional ... even though they are no longer visible and nothing is done with them' (223). Jody Joy uses the concept of reincarnation to describe the new life enjoyed by objects 'whose lives extend beyond different systems of understanding' (541), referring to objects which outlast specific civilisa-tions and to the meanings those people gave them and the uses to which they put them.

In practice, such enquiry involves the revealing process of investi-gating both the various ways objects have been used through their his-tories and how they have been understood and valued (or not) through time (Joy). Significantly, such object life stories contain evidence of rich webs of connection. There are links, bonds, and networks of correlations between objects and the societies and cultures through which they have passed, as well as to the events and people with which they have been associated. Chris Gosden and Yvonne Marshall suggest that it is this connective underpinning of an object's biography that gives that object and its functions significance and meaning in the present. Most object biographies indeed begin from an understanding that there is a relationship, an 'inextricable link between things and people,' and this can be explored 'by focusing on the meanings constructed around objects' (Langdon 580).

As Gosden and Marshall explain, the core premise of object biography—that 'objects do not just provide a stage setting for human action but are integral to it' (169)—recognises not only that objects gain meaning and significance through their use by—and relationships with—people but also that these objects actively affect the world which they inhabit and the individuals with whom they come into contact. Herva describes this in terms of the 'sociality between humans and non-human entities' (215), and Susan Langdon provides an extended example of this sociality in action in her investigation of how material culture influenced the construction of individual identity in the post-Bronze age in Greece. Joy adds the concept of 'drama' to the object's life cycle, suggesting that this sociality can be both troubled and performed, while Fabienne Moine suggests that the social lives of objects can also be political in their intent.

Art history, archaeology, and other non-fiction object biography

The field of art history has embraced the writing of object biographies, although the resulting narratives have not always been identified as such. English art dealer Jeremy Maas is an authority on Victorian painting who penned early examples with his illustrated life histories of two major works, William Frith's *The Prince of Wales's Wedding* and Holman Hunt's *The Light of the World*, the latter narrative of which includes the triumphant tour of one of the three versions of this painting of Australasia. Grant Wood's painting *American Gothic* has attracted two such book-length published life histories, both of which discuss the painting's creation, initial reception, and subsequent interpretation, as well as information on the lives and afterlives of the house and people represented in this iconic work (Biel; Hoving). Carola Hicks's series of biographies of art objects similarly trace the life stories of well-known major works. Her *The Bayeux Tapestry: The Life Story of a Masterpiece* traces back to the days of the tapestry's manufacture and then forward to a surprising range of subsequent uses and interpretations, and it includes the only near survival of the needlework during a number of times of war and other turmoil. In *The King's Glass: A Story of Tudor Power and Secret Art*, Hicks explains not only why the design of the windows of Cambridge's King's College Chapel was altered during the decades of their manufacture due to the political machinations of the day but also the various uses that individuals have made of the narratives they contain in the intervening centuries. Her posthumously published *Girl in a Green Gown: The History and Mystery of the Arnolfini Portrait* relates the intriguing story surrounding the creation and subsequent circulation, ownership, and understanding of Jan van Eyck's enigmatic masterpiece. In these absorbing investigations, alongside her obvious knowledge of art history, Hicks brings to bear her considerable skill as a biographer, which she had demonstrated in her much-praised biography of the life of the 18th-century Lady Diana Spencer. Interestingly, Maas had also written a compelling full-length biography, of leading 19th-century art publisher and dealer Ernest Gambart.

Despite the primacy of object biography in writing about archaeological finds, Joy notes that such full life histories of individual objects are only rarely written in that discipline. Joy cites Janet D. Spector's book-length study featuring a single awl from Wahpeton Dakota Village in North Dakota as a rare example of such an archaeologically based object biographical study. Reviewer Gretchen Green calls this 'a breath of fresh air for the field of archeology,' noting how Spector writes about the awl as 'adventurous and refreshing' (277–78). Recently, Nanouschka Burström has posited that archaeological object biography 'needs to be revitalized' by being written by better writers who might '[pay] attention to the different [narrative] strategies and myriad possibilities for writing object lives' that are possible (65), and Joy asserts that creativity is key to writing such biographies.

Mark Kurlansky's bestselling *Cod: The Biography of a Fish that Changed the World* can be seen as giving rise to what may be identified as a subgenre of popular contemporary object biographical publication. In this book, Kurlansky traces the history of the cod fish, charting its rise as a popular food source to its current declining numbers. The use of the label 'biography' for a detailed life study on a type of foodstuff was timely in terms of sales and marketing, instituted at a moment when reader interest in both biography and food writing was marked (Brien 'Rewriting'). While Kurlansky used the more common term of 'history' to describe his later object biographical studies of salt and New York oysters in *Salt: A World History* and *The Big Oyster: History on the Half Shell*, his *Cod* gave rise to a significant number of named biographies of food and food products (Brien 'Rewriting'). Other object biographical texts attracting a popular readership include biographies of places, such as of Sydney (Birmingham), Australia (Rolls), London (Ackroyd), and Detroit (Martelle); other popular object biographical texts include restaurant biographies and gastrobiographies (e.g., Brien 'Porky times'; A. Brown).

Memoir and biography

A number of creative non-fiction writers have used object biography in their work. British ceramicist Edmund de Waal was acclaimed for this approach in his award-winning family memoir *The Hare with Amber Eyes* (2010). This book narrates the story of five generations of his family by investigating the story of their collection of miniature Japanese wood and ivory carvings. De Waal's own description of his narrative clearly places these objects in a position of central importance in his storytelling, referring to the narrative as both 'the biography of a collection and the biography of my family' ('Writing'). A famed ceramicist, de Waal also writes about how these objects inspired a central theme in this writing: 'how objects embody memory—or more particularly, whether objects can hold memories' ('Writing').

Memoirist Bambi Ward describes how she used object biography to investigate a series of pieces of a porcelain dinner service which she inherited. In this, Ward illustrates how writing an object biography for these pieces of crockery, which accompanied members of her Holocaust-survivor family from Europe to Australia, enabled her to develop a more nuanced understanding not just of these objects themselves but also of the surprisingly important role they played in her family's life. A significant realisation was that this meaning extended far beyond the 'appearance and characteristics' of the objects themselves, which, Ward states, were not to her personal taste (10). Writing about these pieces' lives, tracing them back to the factory where they were made, and then discovering the subsequent part they played in her family's life choices enabled Ward—as a memoirist—to gain not only an understanding of these objects and her family but also a deeper realisation about some aspects of herself. In this case, Ward also brings a perceptive consideration of aspects of taste and aesthetics into her writing.

Objects can also provide a source of data and/or content in what could be classed as speculative biographies—biographies that openly include conjecture (Brien 'The Facts'). Marele Day's *Mrs Cook: The Real and Imagined Life of the Captain's Wife* is a highly imaginative portrayal of the wife of the great navigator, a woman who lived to ninety-four but whose entire life usually rates only a few lines in even the most detailed biographies of her husband. The first mention—usually noted between Cook's return to England from Newfoundland in November 1762 and his appointment, the next April, to return to survey the coast of that island—is that, on 21 December 1762 James Cook married Elizabeth Batts. Often added to this is the information that Elizabeth was thirteen years younger than her husband, and although they were married for fourteen years, they spent little more than four years in physical proximity to each other due to Cook's extensive voyaging. Other relevant information includes that Elizabeth gave birth to the couple's six children, but three died as infants, and those who survived early childhood all predeceased their mother. When Cook was killed in Hawaii in 1779, it was twenty months before his wife knew of his death, and when she died in 1835, she had been widowed for fifty-four years and never remarried. No letters between the couple have survived, and there is no mention of Cook's wife, family, or children's deaths in any of his journals or other written reports. Apart from the 1835 obituary that she cites at the end of her novel, Day found little written about Elizabeth that she could use.

Yet, when Elizabeth died, her London home was filled with memorabilia from her husband's exotic travels, and many of these objects are now held in various museum collections. Day made highly sensitive and imaginative use of these artefacts, which include Elizabeth's childhood alphabet tiles, a porcelain teapot, a tapa cloth vest that she began to embroider for her husband when he left on his last voyage, and the carved 'ditty box' in which the crew preserved a lock of Cook's hair after his death. An accomplished novelist, Day's descriptions of these objects and their relationship to Elizabeth become central and revealing parts of *Mrs Cook*. In this, Day's main focus is always on Elizabeth and how she copes with her husband's absences and the tragic deaths which too often punctuate her domestic life, while her husband's considerably more familiar (and celebrated) achievements become the backstory to this biography. Despite this, ironically, Day's is one of the few biographical narratives in which Cook himself appears vividly human; as Mark Tredinnick has described, 'after all these years living as a myth ... [Day's narrative] put flesh back on those scattered bones' (73).

Conclusion

These object biographies illustrate Kopytoff's foundational assertion that such biographically based inquiry can reveal not only fascinating information about the objects under consideration but also provide original contextual information about the times in which these objects were seen, used, viewed, or otherwise 'active,' as well as about the people who came in contact with them. The influence of these narratives also extends to the readers of such biography, with Kopytoff further suggesting that during the process of reading such texts, the consumers of object biography examine their 'cultural ... aesthetic, historical, and even political' responses to these narratives (67). Additionally, writers can profitably use object biography as a component of their narratives. The following writing exercises will be helpful to writers who may wish to adopt, or adapt, the form of object biography in their own work.

 ACTIVITY

Writing exercises for practice in writing object biography

These exercises step writers through the processes of beginning, researching, and writing object biographies. They are activities suitable for writers to use individually or as a component of group activities. These exercises contain information on how to begin writing object biography by describing objects in detail, tracing an object's locations and relocations, and exploring an object's production, ownership, use, and functions through its lifespan. They can be completed by writing on sheets of paper or in a journal or by typing into a computer document.

Exercise 1: Beginning writing object biography: describing objects

The first step in writing an object biography is to compose a rich description of the object, one that will draw in readers. This exercise requires one piece of fruit or a vegetable (whole or cut apart) or one individually wrapped chocolate or other sweet that is familiar to you. You will also need writing materials. Other kinds of foods can also be used, as long as they can be tasted, but please choose something that is well known to you rather than something more exotic or unfamiliar. The objective of this exercise is to practise writing interestingly about even the most of quotidian objects, by using the five senses.

To begin, set up five pieces of paper or computer files with the name of the object and the following five senses—sight, sound, smell, taste, and touch. Then place your fruit, vegetable, or sweet in front of you and contemplate it for at least a full minute, concentrating on assessing the foodstuff by using just one of the five senses at a time. Begin with how it looks. You can pick it up to scrutinise it from every angle, but concentrate on how it looks rather than how it feels. Then, write a description of this item by using just one of the five senses. Spend at least three minutes, and up to five minutes, drafting this description. The only direction is to try to avoid clichés or other tired descriptions.

Repeat this exercise four times, each time focusing on another sense, again spending at least a minute observing the object before starting writing for three to five minutes. This exercise should be completed in the following order—sight, sound, smell, taste, and touch. That is, describing how the object looks, sounds, smells, tastes and feels. Again, do your best to avoid obvious clichés as you work.

Next, use these five pieces of description as notes to write a description of the object in no more than 250 words. Here, the focus is on composing a vivid, powerful, and resonant description of the object, being especially aware of avoiding trite and formulaic descriptions. Once you have done this, reflect on which of the senses you found the most useful during this exercise, especially in your writing a fresh description of something which is common in your everyday environment.

To evaluate this writing, locate a good and a poor example— in terms of whether it is vivid and interesting or banal and boring—of writing about fruit, vegetables, or sweets. Examples of both fiction and non-fiction writing are suitable for this context, and anthologies and culinary magazines will provide a rich source of materials for you. Having contemplated these samples and identified what is vivid or obvious in these texts, edit your piece as required to further improve it.

You can then repeat this exercise with other fruit, vegetables, sweets, or the object you are writing about. This exercise is especially useful in focusing on writing about an object by using descriptions other than how it appears visually, as these modes of perception often receive less attention in descriptive writing than sight.

Exercise 2: Objects in space: tracing an object's locations and relocations

Just like humans, many objects move through space during their lives, and these movements can be charted and then written about as key components of the object biography.

For this exercise, choose a physical object you have, that you have owned, or that you have otherwise known about for some time. Create a timeline divided into years or decades, whichever is most suitable for this object. For example, a dress that you have owned for a decade will need a different timeline than an heirloom you inherited that has been in your family for generations.

Note along this timeline the different places your object has been. Go back to the object's creation or manufacture and—if you can—even further back, to its design. As an example, your dress might well have been manufactured in a different location than where it was designed.

Once you have what is essentially a list of locations, start to add a series of dot points of information about one of these places in terms of the date it relates to. This will necessitate some research, which can be initially conducted online. Try to collect some images of the location. Continue researching until you have enough information to draft a 250-word description of that place as it was in the time you are describing it.

This can then be repeated for the other locations. You can also create a map of these locations, which will also provide some further information on how these places relate to each other.

Exercise 3: Exploring an object's production, ownership, use, and functions through its lifespan

For this exercise, you are going to continue to use the object you wrote about in Exercise 2 and the timeline you have already constructed. In writing object biography, researching and logging the history of an object's production, ownership, use, and functions are essential. This research can be conducted as any other historical research is conducted, using archival and online resources. This research then needs to be organised onto a timeline and then written into a narrative.

To begin, list any details you know about the object in terms of its production, ownership, use, and/or functions. Then add these to your timeline, using exact dates (or approximate dates if you cannot determine exact ones). As in the Exercise 2, then choose one of these aspects of the object's life history and note down, using dot points, any information you know or can find out about it. Remember to include any damage, repairs, or reuse. This will again necessitate some research, which can be initially conducted online. Again, try to collect any relevant images. Continue researching until you have enough information to draft a 250-word description of one aspect of your object's production, ownership, use, or functions through its lifespan.

 Recommended Reading

Alberti, Samuel J. M. M. 'Objects and the Museum.' *Isis*, vol. 9, no. 4, 2005, pp. 559–71.

Brien, Donna Lee. 'The Rise and Fall of *Masterchef Magazine*: An Object Biography.' *Text, Journal of Writing and Writing Courses,* Special Issue 25, 2014. www.textjournal.com.au/speciss/issue25/content.htm.

Brown, Al. *Depot: Biography of a Restaurant (With Recipes)*. Random House, New Zealand, 2014.

Crew, Gary. *Strange Objects: A Novel*. Heinemann, 1990.

Crielaard, Jan Paul. 'The cultural biography of material goods in Homer's epics.' *Gaia: Revue Interdisciplinaire sur la Grèce Archaïque,* vol. 7, 2003, pp. 49–62.

Kuipers, Alice. *Life on the Refrigerator Door: Notes Between a Mother and Daughter, A Novel.* HarperCollins, 2007.

Levine, Karen. *Hana's Suitcase: A True Story.* Allen & Unwin, 2003.

Lord, M. G. *Forever Barbie: The Unauthorized Biography of a Real Doll.* William Morrow, 1994.

MacGregor, Neil. *A History of the World in 100 Objects from the British Museum.* Allen Lane/Penguin, 2010.

Mansfield, Stephen. *The Search for God and Guinness: A Biography of the Beer that Changed the World.* Thomas Nelson, 2009.

Saunders, N. J. 'Biographies of Brilliance: Pearls, Transformations of Matter and being, c. AD 1492.' *World Archaeology,* vol. 31, no. 2, 1999, pp. 243–57.

Sewell, Anna. *Black Beauty.* Jarrold & Sons, 1877.

Thomas, Nicholas. *Entangled Objects: Exchange, Material Culture, and Colonialism in the Pacific.* U Harvard P, 1991.

 ## Works Cited

Ackroyd, Peter. *London: The Biography.* Chatto and Windus, 2000.

Biel, Steven. *American Gothic: A Life of America's Most Famous Painting.* W. W. Norton, 2005.

Birmingham, John. *Leviathan: The Unauthorised Biography of Sydney.* Random House, 1999.

Brien, Donna Lee. 'Rewriting a national cultural food icon: a gastrobiography of Vegemite.' *Text, Journal of Writing and Writing Courses,* Special issue 9, 2010a. www. textjournal.co.au/speciss/issue9/Brien.pdf. Accessed 20 Nov. 2017.

———. '"Porky times': A Brief Gastrobiography of New York's The Spotted Pig." *M/C Journal,* vol. 13, no. 5, 2010b, pp. 1–10. journal.mediaculture. org. au/index.php/mcjournal/article/view/290. Accessed 20 Nov. 2017.

———. '"Welcome creative subversions': Experiment and innovation in recent biographical writing." *Text, Journal of Writers and Writing Courses,* vol. 18, no. 1, 2014. www.textjournal.com.au/april14/brien.htm. Accessed 20 Nov. 2017.

———. '"The facts formed a line of buoys in the sea of my own imagination': History, fiction and speculative biography." *Text, Journal of Writing and Writing Courses,* Special issue 28, 2015. www.textjournal.com.au/speciss/issue28/Brien.pdf. Accessed 20 Nov. 2017.

NEW AND EXPERIMENTAL APPROACHES TO WRITING LIVES

Brown, Al. *Depot: Biography of a Restaurant (With Recipes)*. Random House, New Zealand, 2014.

Brown, Bill. 'Thing Theory.' *Critical Inquiry*, vol. 28, no. 1, 2001, pp. 1–22.

Burström, Nanouschka M. 'Things in the Eye of the Beholder: A Humanistic Perspective on Archaeological Object Biographies.' *Norwegian Archaeological Review*, vol. 47, no. 1, 2014, pp. 65–82.

Day, Marele. *Mrs Cook: The Real and Imagined Life of the Captain's Wife*. Sydney: Allen and Unwin, 2002.

Gosden, Chris, and Yvonne Marshall. 'The cultural biography of objects.' *World Archaeology*, vol. 31, no. 2, 1999, pp. 169–78.

Green, Gretchen. 'What This Awl Means: Feminist Archaeology at a Wahpeton Dakota Village [review].' *The Annals of Iowa*, vol. 53, no. 3, 1994, pp. 277–78.

Herva, Vesa-Pekka. 'The life of buildings: Minoan building deposits in an ecological perspective.' *Oxford Journal of Archaeology*, vol. 24, 2005, pp. 215–27.

Hicks, Carola. *Improper Pursuits: The Scandalous Life of an Earlier Lady Diana Spencer*. St Martins Press, 2001.

———. *The Bayeux Tapestry: The Life Story of a Masterpiece*. Chatto & Windus, 2006.

———. *The King's Glass: A Story of Tudor Power and Secret Art*. Chatto & Windus, 2007.

———. *Girl In A Green Gown: The History and Mystery of the Arnolfini Portrait*. Chatto & Windus, 2011.

Horton, John, and Peter Kraftl. 'Clearing Out a Cupboard: Memory, Materiality and Transitions,' in *Geography and Memory: Explorations in Identity, Place and Becoming*, edited by Owain Jones et al., pp. 25–44. Palgrave Macmillan, 2012.

Hoving, Thomas. *American Gothic: The Biography of Grant Wood's American Masterpiece*. Chamberlain Bros, 2005.

Joy, Jody. 'Reinvigorating object biography: reproducing the drama of object lives.' *World Archaeology*, vol. 41, no. 4, 2009, pp. 540–56.

Joyce, Rosemary A., and Susan D. Gillespie. *Things in Motion: Object Histories, Biographies, and Itineraries*. SAR Press, 2015.

Kopytoff, Igor. 'The cultural biography of things,' in *The Social Life of Things*, edited by Arjun Appadurai. pp. 64–91. U Cambridge P, 1986.

Kurlansky, Mark. *Cod: The Biography of a Fish that Changed the World*. New York: Walker and Co., 1997.

———. *Salt: A World History*. New York: Walker and Co., 2002.

———. *The Big Oyster: History on the Half Shell*. New York: Ballantine Books, 2006.

Langdon, Susan. *Art and Identity in Dark Age Greece, 1100–700 BCE*. U Cambridge P, 2008.

Maas, Jeremy. *Gambart: Prince of the Victorian Art World*. Barrie & Jenkin, 1975.

———. *The Prince of Wales's Wedding: The Story of a Picture*. Cameron & Tayleur, 1977.

———. *Holman Hunt and the Light of the World*. Scolar Press, 1984.

Martelle, Scott. *Detroit: A Biography*. Chicago Review Press, 2012.

Moine, Fabienne. 'The Politics of Objects: Eliza Cook's Biographies of Things.' *Cahiers Victoriens et Édouardiens,* vol. 83, 2016. cve.revues.org/2620. Accessed 20 Nov. 2017.

Peers, Laura. '"Many tender ties": The shifting contexts and meanings of the S Black Bag." *World Archaeology,* vol. 31, no. 2, 1999, pp. 288–302.

Rolls, Eric. *Australia: A Biography*. U Queensland P, 2000.

Smith, Robert. and Gemma Watson., editors. *Writing the Lives of People and Things, AD 500–1700*. Ashgate, 2016.

Spector, Janet D. *What This Awl Means: Feminist Archaeology at a Watipeton Dakota Village*. Minnesota Historical Society Press, 2013.

Swift, Ellen. 'Object Biography, Re-Use and Recycling in the Late to Post-Roman Transition Period and Beyond: Rings made from Romano-British Bracelets.' *Britannia,* vol. 43, 2012, pp. 167–215.

Tredinnick, Mark. 'Books: Discovery Channels.' *Bulletin with Newsweek,* vol. 10, Sept. 2002, p. 73.

de Waal, Edmund. *The Hare with Amber Eyes*. Chatto & Windus, 2010a.

———. 'Writing a very personal book.' *Edmund de Waal*. 2010b. www.edmunddewaal.com/writing/the-hare-with-amber-eyes/about. Accessed 20 Nov. 2017.

Ward, Bambi. 2014 'A taste of Herend Hungarian porcelain: Aesthetics, object biography and writing memoir.' *Text, Journal of Writing and Writing Courses,* Special issue 26, 2014. www.textjournal.com.au/speciss/issue26/Ward.pdf. Accessed 20 Nov. 2017.

3 BURRA'S GIANT ONION AND THE BATTLE OF THE SOMME

David Walker

'There is no such thing as an ordinary life' (Twain, *Mark Twain's Note-books* 49). All lives are extraordinary. All lives have their secrets and speak to the times and circumstances in which people live. Yet it remains true that most people do not leave substantial documents that trace their life journey let alone their interior world. When researching for my book *Not Dark Yet, a personal history* (2011), a family history narrative with a difference, I found there were large gaps in the family records. As I discovered, though, few lives go *entirely* undocumented: all who enlist in the armed services have detailed war service files, and all who marry, give birth, and die (hard categories to escape) generate records. I was surprised at the range of sources available, and I found that the gaps in the family records had their own kind of challenge and interest. I became intrigued by how best to reveal or reach undocumented lives by taking an experimental approach when writing lives. This experience led me to consider some of the processes involved in producing a *personal* work combining elements both of memoir and of family history. In this chapter, using *Not Dark Yet* as a practical demonstration, I examine the ways in which a writer can capture 'ordinary' lives and the importance of doing so.

Revealing personalities

I have come to think of my family as formed by two personality types. My mother was quirky, unpredictable, and sometimes blunt to the point of rudeness. She came into the world with a long and not at all musi-cal name: Glasson Maude Wallace Bourne. The Bournes were a rascally lot, with an appetite for mischief and breaking the rules. The second personality type entered the frame in the early 1930s. Glasson was greeted by a well-dressed young man as she got off the tram to attend Adelaide's Challa Gardens Teachers' College. She noticed with approval his handmade shoes, neat tie, and gentlemanly hat. This was Gilbert John Walker, first son of churchgoing Methodists from Burra, in the dry north of South Australia. Gilbert's father, Oswald, owned a shop selling boots, shoes, and drapery. Gilbert's parents were unassuming people, comfortably off rather than rich. Gil and Glasson married in Adelaide in 1936 and spent their adult lives entwined in the great bureaucracy of the South Australian Education Department. They were on file.

I was the third child, a postwar bright idea. The American writer and essayist Flannery O'Connor said, 'Anybody who has survived his childhood has enough information about life to last him the rest of his days' (84). I became a cultural historian with an interest in how Australian writers had sought to build a national culture in the first half of the 20th century. At university, one of 'my' figures (one of those I explored in my doctoral thesis), was the Melbourne-based writer and critic Vance Palmer. Palmer had heaped scorn on the 'suburban draper,' whose stupefying narrow-mindedness supposedly stood in the way of all things creative, progressive, and visionary. I was troubled by his attitude. My family were not really suburban, a saving grace, but they were certainly drapers. They also sold boots, which was slightly better because they were more manly, but there was no escaping that this was a shamefully middle-class background.

I did not need Palmer to tell me that my family was not particularly interesting. For many years, it never occurred to me that they might have a history worth telling. What was there to tell? At first sight, it seemed there were not too many notable achievements worth mentioning. At the height of our fame as a family, my grandfather Oswald Walker had been mayor of Burra. His name still appears on the charming rotunda at the town's photogenic centre. In old photographs, placed just behind the rotunda in the town square, one can clearly see a large sign bearing the words 'Walker and Sons.' But how can these people become objects of interest? There seemed to be no escaping the fact that the Walkers led quiet, uneventful lives. They left few records. There were no letters or diaries. There were however, some photographs. Oswald was a keen amateur photographer. It is rare to find a family photograph from predigital times with a date or an indication of who had been captured on camera. With Oswald's photos, some could be identified, but many could not.

It is intriguing how across time the photograph moves from being a literal document that needs little explanation to something far more enigmatic and strange. We no longer clearly understand the context, the social codes, and the people looking back at us. Nevertheless, photographs can open up a fascinating speculative field of hints, clues, and possibilities. Much of the appeal of photographs, though, lies precisely in the narrative gaps: as Marianne Hirsch says, 'The conventionality of the family photo provides a space of identification for any viewer participating in the conventions of familial representation; thus the photo can bridge a gap between viewers who are personally connected and those who are not' (251). Although Hirsch is specifically referring to photos preserved in the Jewish Museums, her words could equally apply to almost any photo to which the viewer is drawn. Such photos create a bond between 'the image and the referent'; they contribute to the individual or collective memory or both, depending on the photo and the context, as well as the purposes for which it is intended (Hirsch 51).

Interrogating the visual and the narrative gaps between the pictures strongly contributes to one's sense of identity, belonging, and history (Hirsch 134). Seen in this light, photographs open up a fascinating speculative field of hints, clues, and possibilities. For example, Jo Spence's Freudian theories, readings, and essay interpretations of her personal and family photos 'fill in the gaps of [her] autobiography' (Hirsch 131–32). Spence's 'essays focus not on life story but on photographic projects and theoretical/practical issues' with which she had been concerned: "'the autobiographical is expanded to include the 'political' and the 'photographic' on either side of the 'personal'" (Hirsch 131–320). Spence's 'first-person narrative and the self-portraits that underwrite it cast the autobiographical subject in a great range of roles and identities, both within and outside the family' (Hirsch 132).

The fascination of the ordinary and haunting photography

While it may seem pretentious to say so, I was influenced by the novelist and literary critic Winfried Georg Sebald and his astonishing mix of memoir, speculation, and historical reflection that placed what appeared to be ordinary lives at the centre of the devastating conflicts of the 20th century. In his handful of books, notably *The Emigrants* (1992–93), *The Rings of Saturn* (1995), and *Austerlitz* (2001), Sebald's themes on memory and loss of memory, both personal and collective, and on the decay of societies and traditions, civilisations, and objects take us to the heart of memoir, history, and the human condition. Frequently likened to

Virginia Woolf, Gunter Grass, and Marcel Proust, Sebald is regarded as one of the most important writers of the times (Ward).

Among recent writers, none have raised more questions for me than Sebold. A German expatriate living in England, Sebold came late to writing and left it far too early. He died in a car accident, leaving behind some enigmatic, powerful, and hard-to-categorise works, a mix of memoir, recollected meetings and historical digression. Each of his books is scattered with a number of uncaptioned photographs. These photographs are strange, mysterious documents. While invariably blurred, indistinct, and seemingly nondescript, they haunt the text, pointing to what we can never know about the real figures and real lives allegedly captured by the camera. The Holocaust is never far from the background. It looms over Sebold's text, ever-present but rarely named directly. How Sebold achieves his haunting effects is hard to determine; his stories are remarkable for their obliqueness. Sebold can hardly be reduced to a manual, yet his novels offer profound lessons in the power of the indirect and in how apparently small details build into deep and consequential modern fables. Reading Sebold made me think differently about my own family and not least the silent unfolding of a history that took a quiet young man from Burra to the war. I found it was one thing to write as a historian about WWII, quite another to write about the personal experience of my uncles who served in that war.

In a different way, I was struck by the strange musings of the British writer and satirist Alan Bennett. The fascination of the ordinary had not altogether escaped me. I had enjoyed the writings and monologues of Bennett. Bennett has a relentless and critical eye for the humdrum business of the daily life of his middle-class upbringing in Leeds. In the book *Untold Stories* (2005), Bennett's parents (with their horror of attention-seeking and their ordinariness), his family, and what it means to be British are all well captured by his comedy. These were lives so remarkably uneventful and dull that they seemingly defied writing and memoir altogether. Yet Bennett's forensic analysis of speech, dress, and manners, the tiny rituals of daily life, both open up a middle-class world and demonstrate new ways of writing about the ordinary and the everyday. One such example is his engrossing account of his father, a man almost entirely defined by the small domestic world around him. Through the persistent accumulation of small details—the way his father wore his cardigan, his careful speech, and the absolute regularity of meals and daily rituals—Bennett creates a haunting portrait of a thwarted life. Bennett's striking portrayal of his father taught me that in telling a life, no detail is too small or too trivial. The cardigan had a story to tell about its owner.

Behind this, Bennett explores profound questions, particularly that of authenticity. Bennett did not so much put himself into *Untold Stories*; rather *Untold Stories* offers insights into Bennett himself. In *Untold Stories*, Bennett says, 'For a long time, years even, it seemed to me I had nothing to put into what I wrote; and nor had I. I did not yet appreciate that you do not put yourself into what you write; you find yourself there' (545). From Bennett, I also learnt that it is more important to observe than to judge, although that can be a hard lesson to apply to one's own parents and family.

Finding value in undocumented lives

While few historians would regard objectivity as entirely possible, formal traditions remain strong; it remains a rule of the craft that taking a rigorous approach to evidence and a balancing of competing views are vital to the writing of good history. There is a growing awareness that the historian's experiences, ethnicity, gender, class, and identity can have a profound influence on questions they think are worth examining and on how history is written and what we understand history to be. In writing *Not Dark Yet*, I drew on but also stepped away from my formal training in the historian's craft. I stepped away from the traditional role of the historian seeking objectivity to find another, more 'personal' voice.

Yet because of my historical training, I wanted not just to capture a family tale or a record but to take a wider view, setting ordinary lives within the broader context of the Australian story. By locating the 'personal' within the broader framework of a historical period, the narrow specificity of much autobiographical writing can be enriched with cultural and political detail that informs those intangible forces that help shape lives. By narrating the personal histories of a family, many cross-currents, eddies, and whirlpools can illuminate revealing and overlooked complexities in the river of a national history and important themes in a national culture.

Like many people, on first considering their forebears, I thought I saw people with unassuming and—even more worrying to a historian—undocumented lives. Yet as I researched the family background for *Not Dark Yet*, it became increasingly clear; it just took a dogged persistence and some lateral thinking to search unusual records. I also found that there was no need to panic about gaps left in the family record. They can present their own kind of challenge and interest and can provide room in a narrative for historical imagination, speculation, and a touch of the novelist's art. I also found that different conventions and approaches were needed as I tried to record my family history and to set it in a wider, more general context. While I wanted to locate the 'personal' within the broader framework of Australian history, the reverse was also true. I now wanted the 'personal' to inform and illuminate this history. After tracking down what records I could, there remained one difficult task. Before even starting writing, I needed to convince myself that my 'personal history' was worth writing—not just worth writing but could be written at all.

Dealing with too much information

Historians can get hung up on records. Too often they think: no records, no story. With no documents, or few, lives can be hard to learn about, but at the same time, too many documents can be overwhelming. For instance, I had thought that one of the easiest chapters to write in *Not Dark Yet* would be the story of my parents' travel in Asia. I was fascinated by the place of the 'overseas trip' in my parents' world. In 1963 they had visited Hong Kong, Thailand, and Egypt before flying on to Europe. It was their first overseas trip: 'Overseas' was important and of course required a diary. I had their travel diaries and lots of information. I thought, here are the documents I need in order to write my book. But as it happened, this story of my parents' travels, a story that had first appealed to me as relatively straightforward, based as it was on my parents' travel diaries, was one of the hardest chapters to write in *Not Dark Yet*. While the diaries explained where and when my parents travelled, what they saw and their responses, they also weighed my story down with excessive information. They impeded any imaginative rethinking of what travel might have really meant to them. In researching a family, there can at times be too many important-looking records and too much information. It soon emerged that all that information and that little pile of diaries pushed the writing towards summarising and documenting. The little pile of diaries, faithfully passed down and obviously treasured, can make it harder to see the bigger picture. It can make it hard to leave things out and to focus on what matters. I learnt not to let a plethora of detail get in the way of what I really wanted to say.

Reaching a point where one can look back

Bennett helped me to look at my own family in a more considered way and perhaps sowed one of the seeds for *Not Dark Yet*; even so, I was still a long way from embarking on my personal story. Two important changes laid the groundwork for a different approach to writing. First, I became older and in doing so discovered what most of us learn. When we are young and making our way in the world, we like to think of ourselves as free agents. We determine who we are and what we want to become. The family is something to escape rather than something to reflect on or understand. Yet as I grew older, I became increasingly aware that I was exhibiting traits and habits of mind that reminded me of my parents. I began to wonder about the competing influence of the mischievous Bournes and the respectable Walkers. Then, before I could really start understanding them, one by one they died. I found that in death, the mystery of their lives seemed to deepen and grow more tantalising. I began to wonder who these people really were.

I doubt that any of this alone would have brought me round to writing *Not Dark Yet*. The big jolt came in November 2004. As I read, straight lines began to wobble, bend, and warp. I trooped off to the eye specialist, hoping for good news. He had none to give that day, explaining that I had macular degeneration. The centre of my field of vision had collapsed. I left his surgery with a new label, a new identity. I was 'legally blind.' For a historian whose professional practice required close examination of archival documents, letters, and reports, it seemed that my days as an active writer were numbered. The words of a Bob Dylan song kept playing in my head: 'it's not dark yet, but it's getting there.' I no longer knew what the future held. Visiting the archives was now out of the question. I became aware of the rather disorganised archive between my ears.

Although my sight had disappeared, another kind of sight, the sort we call memory, consoled and tempted me. What had at first seemed to be a fatal limitation in piecing together a family story, my personal history, started to seem not such a problem after all. I was intrigued by all the ways we see, remember, and interpret the past. At one point in my book, I spoke about my eye condition; what it means to see and make visible was shaped by my experience of becoming 'legally blind' in 2004. In writing *Not Dark Yet*, it was not my purpose to write about disability, but seeing and not seeing, remembering and not remembering, all those gaps, spaces, and absences contributed to the telling of the story. While it might have helped to have more family letters and documents, I had come to realise that the language people use provides abundant clues if only we know how to decode them. Moreover, behind a glib phrase like 'middle-class' lies a particular and revealing set of practices, behaviours, and sentiments that help explain why people thought and acted as they did. It is possible to write a family history narrative that is an accurate record and a readable story by weaving family stories into the dry facts and gaps (Bennett). For me, this technique was another way of opening the door to speculation and imagination while also respecting the difference between speculation and outright invention. That jumble of memories, those stories inside our head, make us who we are and these, just as much as solid written evidence, need to be explored with confidence. In seeing but also not seeing, in remembering and not remembering, use can be made of all those gaps, spaces, and absences; they can all contribute to the telling of a story.

Placing the personal memory in wider historical context

I found that it is important to consider how absence may present ways of opening a door to speculation and imagination, though without crossing the red line to outright invention. I started by thinking about my mother. My mother had strange views about sight. Each of her three children was shortsighted, and I was the most shortsighted. She hated the idea of any of us wearing glasses. I had often wondered about her phobias and where they had come from. The digital revolution has now brought history into the home (see, for example, Archambault). In Australia, thousands are hooked on *Trove*, the free programme hosted by the National Library that has digitised hundreds of national and regional newspapers. Performing a quick search for phrases like 'race suicide' or 'threat from the north' and selecting a date range, such as 1921–29, will yield a host of articles and commentaries that illuminate the thinking of the times. In searching for background on family culture, such sources need to be used judiciously. Yet for an ordinary family, one should stick to sources they were likely to have read. Where it made sense to do so, I confined my searches to the *Adelaide Advertiser*, the paper that came daily into Glasson's home.

Digging into the literature, I found that in middle-class Australia in the 1920s and 1930s, there had been a lot of anxious speculation about 'racial fitness.' Social commentators at the time often speculated about whether the modern city dweller was becoming too cramped and constrained to enjoy a robust adulthood that was conducive to producing healthy children. Teachers with responsibilities for the mental and physical health of the rising generation were particularly vulnerable to concerns about defective populations and susceptible to the appeal of eugenic solutions designed to remove or limit the impact of those deemed racially unfit. This type of thinking led to some dark places in Germany, but as we now prefer to forget, that type of thinking also gained some currency in the United States and Australia. For Glasson, shortsightedness was not something to be corrected. It was a shameful defect to be hidden. Shame even led her to discourage my sister from having children. When my sister married and produced a bouncing boy, she was told by Glasson that one mistake was enough.

As Mark Twain said, 'A man's experiences of life are a book, and there was never yet an uninteresting life. Such a thing is an impossibility. Inside of the dullest exterior there is a drama, and a comedy, and a tragedy' (Rasmussen 164; Twain, *Mark Twain's Fables of Man* 197). Seemingly small details of personal history can provide illuminating glints of the nexus between individual lives and national culture. It was an area in which I had already developed an interest. I had also grown increasingly fascinated by the complexities of Australia's historical relationship with Asia. I began to be intrigued by what was emerging from my family, caught as they were in the web of history. I became intrigued by arguments put forward in 1900 and into the 1930s on the question of racial theorising. From the late 19th century onwards, there had been considerable speculation about what Australia's proximity to Asia might mean for the future. The common answer was 'nothing good.' Many people were anxious about the possibility of a 'yellow peril' invasion. To make matters worse, as Australia industrialised, women were having fewer children. How then would Australia raise an army? Stern warnings were given by the government bodies about 'race suicide,' a particularly terrible prospect for an empty continent like Australia, imagined as vulnerable to Asian invasion. In this context, women who produced somewhat blemished offspring could be pictured as unpatriotic. Glasson surely feared that her shortsighted children would be of little use in the event of a threat from the north. Here, a personal story about a mother's phobias connects in a revealing way with the wider historical context. Social currents in far-off countries are seen to have ripples influencing whether a small boy in rural South Australia is allowed to wear glasses and whether his sister should have children.

My mother, naturally, never spelt out her concerns in important speeches at the kitchen table. She left no letters discoursing on the perils of race suicide or the threat from the North. But as a cultural historian who could place her concerns in a wider context, I had something more challenging and satisfying. I had many memories of things said, of phrases used, that confirmed for me that questions of race, identity, and national survival indeed mattered to her. Where I had once thought that my very ordinary family had lived their lives outside of history, I came to see that I had not examined closely and with sufficient care the fragments that I had been given. I may have been legally blind, but I was at last seeing some things more clearly. As I discovered, in writing personal history, valuing your memories of ordinary family speech and seeking out phrases that capture contemporary concerns are important—phrases that can link the person to the national narrative. The language of ordinary speech and the phrases that capture contemporary concerns are rich sources for the writer on a historical quest.

Freedom in writing

I had a different experience when my thoughts turned to the family car. I was about six years old when, in 1951, my father brought home a brand-new, black Vanguard. In *Not Dark Yet*, I wrote what became a chapter about the family car. It started life as a paragraph or two. Apart from some newspaper advertisements from the 1950s, I had no documents about the car. Yet it was the absence of records that allowed me to write more freely and speculatively about the central place of the car in our suburban lives and what that said about the family. Yes, there were some wonderful advertisements, easily found on *Trove*, the National Library of Australia research engine, but there were no other written records. But as I got into the story, all sorts of memories came back to me of family holidays in the Grampians in Victoria, of the car overheating as we drove into the Adelaide Hills and of culture wars over whether the Australian-made Holden was a better car than the British-made Vanguard. I recalled that the Holden was thought to be on the tinny side and somewhat unstable when cornering, whereas the Vanguard was a more solid object, a fine example of dependable British engineering and British steel. I remembered that my mother wanted to learn to drive. Off we went, we three children in the back seat, with my father, the instructor, sitting alongside my mother in the front. After a good deal of dangerous lurching and some near misses, her driving lessons were hastily abandoned. My mother never learnt to drive and regretted it for the rest of her life.

The absence of documents here was rather a blessing. While I stayed close to the truth of my experience, writing about the 'Vanguard' proved an invitation to speculate and write more playfully and freely, released from the demanding presence of documents. My job here was to write what I knew, unconstrained by wise advice and important precedents.

Ordinary lives

I was fighting my way through the two-volume *Encyclopedia of South Australia*, a mighty publication that carried entries on various worthies in business and public affairs. These people often paid for the privilege of having their stories told, and there was an entry on Walker and Sons of Burra. Apparently, they had imported and sold Japanese fabrics, presumably to some of the wealthier business people and pastoralists. Those few lines in the *Encyclopedia* threw a new light on my family. Suddenly they appeared more modern, culturally curious, and experimental than I had imagined. I had been wrong to presume that I knew anything about them and wrong to presume that their lives were too dull to interest a person such as me, a cultural historian.

While too many records can pose problems, so can too few. In the absence of documents, using personal history to illuminate a historical period can fill gaps left in the narrative. When writing *Not Dark Yet*, many fragments of family history came to light in old copies of the local newspaper, the *Burra Record*, a repository of all kinds of stories and recently lovingly indexed by members of the Burra Historical Society. Whenever I visited Burra, I became one of them. I learnt that the family had settled in Burra, a small mining and pastoral town on the edge of the Goyder's Line in the arid north of South Australia. My great-grandfather had moved there in the 1870s to establish the family business. I knew nothing at all about him. But I soon found out that he had fathered thirteen children and had quite a flair for giving them important-sounding names. Once again, I would have to discard the patronising tag of the 'ordinary' if I were ever to get some sense of who this fellow was. I learnt that at the age of four, he had been involved in a terrible accident which had broken both his ankles. He had become disabled, spending the rest of his life on crutches. I now recalled and understood an oblique comment of my father's, not a man given to risqué humour, that his grandfather, with all those children to his name, 'could not have been too injured.'

Gradually, stories came through to me from across the family, stories of him painting the house and maintaining a large garden. He was said to have been a deadly shot with the rifle. Handling a rifle was a country skill and not one confined to the men. My grandmother had been no slouch with the rifle either and had shiny trophies to prove it.

On close inspection, the *Burra Record* was like a giant antique shop, crammed with wonderful curios. As a historian, I had long been interested in the late-19th-century fascination with Japanese arts and crafts. Called 'Japonism,' this enthusiasm had swept across the Western world, shaping modern art, design, and aesthetics; it reached Australia in the 1890s. I knew, or thought I knew, that the heady excitements of 'Japonism' were a world away from my dull old family. But the fascination with all things Japanese was evident in a photograph of women and girls from the local Methodist church where members of my family worshipped. My grandmother and her sisters would surely have been there. It was a good cause, a fundraiser for a new church building. There they were, all dressed up in Japanese style with kimonos, parasols, and dainty fabrics sourced, as I imagine, from Walker and Sons, the centre of Japonism in Burra and district. Knowing how to use this information in my writing depended on knowing the wider historical context that explained the timing, appeal, and impact of Japonism. This same principle can be extended to cover the full range of new technologies that get people so excited. Knowing the historical context is always key.

A photograph marked 'our Molly,' showing a little girl with her hair in ringlets and with the sweetest of smiles, graces the cover of *Not Dark Yet*. In 1907, in the Methodist church in Burra, Molly Day married my great-uncle Alfred. The ceremony was recorded in loving detail by the *Burra Record*. It was all there. Or was it? The report said that Molly was given away by a gentleman called Luke Day, her stepfather. He threw a wonderful banquet to celebrate the occasion, one of the finest that Burra had seen. As a young man, Luke had found Molly abandoned by the side of the road and had adopted her. While it is now hard to determine whether Molly's adoption was formal or not, she grew up as the much-loved child of Luke and his European wife, Hester. It was clear that he had been respected as a local business person and person of good character. Why had this detailed account of Molly's wedding in the *Burra Record* not mentioned the small fact that Luke was Chinese?

Given the time distance from the event and the lack of documentation on the matter, it is impossible to actually know what happened, but in my book, I can speculate a little. What I know from a much earlier issue of the *Burra Record* is that a few years before Molly's wedding, the paper had mocked Luke Day (though not directly by name) as a shifty

'Chinaman' with a poor grasp of English. At a time when the Chinese were often the butt of much prejudice, Luke sued the paper for defamation and won. Under these circumstances, the *Burra Record* might have felt that it was best not to go near Chinese references in any future story involving Luke Day. Until I found these things in the *Burra Record*, I had not known that a Chinese person appeared in the middle of my Burra family. Yet I still do not know much about Luke, including how he came to Australia at around age fifteen, where he came from in China, or his Chinese name. Until I have his name in characters, he will remain something of a mystery.

Using personal history to illuminate a historical period

The pinnacle of my grandfather's achievements appears to have been a giant record-breaking 1.2 kg onion. It was 1917. History had been made. It was put on display in a Burra shop window. Oswald's horticultural exploits reached the local newspaper. How should one weigh up the small events of day-to-day life against the big events of history? In a year when Russia's momentous bloody revolution created the world's first communist state, a year also when grotesque battles were being fought on the Western front during WWI, there was surely no place for a celebrated onion, big as it was.

My initial response to Oswald's onion was one of perplexity. In the great scheme of things, this was a small event. But it spoke to a world of gardening, self-sufficiency, and the communal rituals that were so vital to country towns. It raised questions about how people conducted ordinary lives against a background of war, destruction, and grief. While the historian in me was pleased to come across the story of the onion, it was the writer seeking to interpret and understand how we connect small events with large ones that welcomed the chance to speculate about how we might frame lives and tell stories.

The world and the turmoil of WWII quickly caught up with my family in Burra. My uncle Laurie Walker was sent to the island of Ambon (now part of Indonesia), as the Japanese moved rapidly south. Posted as missing in action, feared dead, it was not until 1946 that his parents learnt of his fate. It was a death that haunted the family. While the sequence of events that led to Laurie's death were known, the family somehow constructed and passed down a different and far from accurate history. One of the great strengths of writing a narrative 'personal history' as a mixture of memoir and history is that it can restore the emotional impact to the story of what might otherwise be yet just another military casualty. Tragic events can be found in all families. In an unusual narrative mix of memoir and history, the personal can speak to all of us.

It took some time before I understood that I might be writing a book. In the aftermath of becoming 'legally blind,' I was writing as a therapeutic exercise. An essay on my memories of my family, published almost as soon as it was submitted. The publisher surprised me by asking for another. After this second essay, I knew I loved the thrill of the chase for the memory or photograph that explained something that I had not understood.

 ACTIVITY

Exercises to practise writing a family history narrative that has difference

1. Using speech, dress, and manners as 'historical documents,' draw up an account of what the conduct of your parents says about them as individuals and their social situation.

2. The photograph is a document that at once reveals and conceals. Using a photograph from your own family history, consider how it might be interpreted, noting what can and cannot be said. How might the things that cannot be said or known help in the telling of a story rather than diminish the story?

3. Taking your earliest childhood memory, tease out what is important in this memory and the extend to which you can know whether it is your memory or a story often told that may reappear as memory.

 ## Recommended Reading

Bennett, Alan. *Untold Stories*. Faber and Faber, 2005.

Hirsch, Marianne. *Family Frames: Photography Narrative and Postmemory*. U Harvard P, 1997.

Long, J. J., and Anne Whitehead, editors. *W. G. Sebald: A Critical Companion*. Edinburgh UP, 2004.

Walker, David. *Not Dark Yet: A Personal History*. Giramondo Publishing, 2011.

Watson, Richard A. *The Devil's Race-Track: Mark Twain's Greatest Dark Writings, the Best from Which Was the Dream? and the Fables of Man*, introduction by John S. Tuckey. Paperback ed. U of California P, 2005.

 ## Works Cited

Archambault, Michael. '20 First Photos from the History of Photography.' 23 May 2015. Blog. petapixal.com/2015/05/23/20-first-photos-from-the-history-of-photography/. Accessed 7 Dec. 2017.

Bennett, Alan. *Untold Stories*. Faber and Faber, 2005.

Hirsch, Marianne. *Family Frames: Photography Narrative and Postmemory*. U Harvard P, 1997.

Long, J. J., and Anne Whitehead, editors. *W.G. Sebald: A Critical Companion*. U Edinburgh P, 2004.

O'Connor, Flannery. *Mystery and Manners: Occasional Prose*, selected and edited by Sally and Robert Fitzgerald. Farrar, Strauss and Giroux, 1961.

Rasmussen, Kent, editor. *The Quotable Mark Twain: His Essential Aphorisms, Witticisms, and Concise Opinions*, foreword by Shelley Fisher Fishkin. 1st ed. McGraw Hill Education, 1998.

Sebald, Winfried Georg. *The Emigrants*, translated by Michael Hulse. New ed. Random House, (1992–93) 2002.

———. *The Rings of Saturn*, translated by Michael Hulse. Random House, (1995) 2011.

———. *Austerlitz*, translated by A. Vigliani. Adelphi, (2001) 2006.

Twain, Mark (1905). *Mark Twain's Fables of Man*: Mark Twain Papers (Book 7), introduction by John Sutton Tuckey, edited by John Sutton Tuckey et al. U of California P, 1972.

———. *Mark Twain's Notebooks: Journals, Letters. Observations, Wit, Wisdom, and Doodles*, edited by Carlo de Vito. Notebook Series. Paperback. 1st ed. Black Dog & Leventhal, 2015.

Walker, David. *Not Dark Yet: A Personal History*. Giramondo Publishing, 2011.

Ward, Simon. 'Ruins and Poetics in The works of W. G. Sebald,' in *W.G. Sebald: A Critical Companion*, edited by J.J. Long, and Anne Whitehead pp. 58–74. Paperback ed. U of Aberdeen: U Edinburgh P, 2004.

Watson, Richard A. *The Devil's Race-Track: Mark Twain's Greatest Dark Writings, the Best from Which Was the Dream? and the Fables of Man*, introduction by John S. Tuckey. Paperback ed. U California P, 2005.

4 REVEALING WHAT IT MEANS TO BE HUMAN: THE NATURE OF LITERARY DOCU-MEMOIR[1]

Jo Parnell

Pioneered by the British writer Tony Parker, literary docu-memoir is a rare form of creative non-fiction as life-writing—a mix of fact, lyric, and story. It involves the writer interviewing and audiotaping ordinary people for their unusual experiences and their thoughts and feelings as the resource material for a literary production. In everyday conversation, people use a language of their own to make sense of their experiences for themselves and the person or people they are talking to. Literary docu-memoir brings out a deeper level of meaning in the speech and reflections of the subjects, as elicited by the literary docu-memoirist. In this chapter, I tease out the key aspects of literary docu-memoir[2] and discuss Parker's innovation. I take a brief look at *The Seamstress: a memoir of survival* (1999) by Sara Tuvel Bernstein et al. and offer my own work, *See Saw Margery Daw* (2012), for consideration as a new way to write a work of literary docu-memoir.

Key points

Caroline Forché and Philip Gerard define creative non-fiction as 'factual prose that is also *literary*': it is 'storytelling of a very high order' (1). Its 'very *literariness* distinguishes' it from 'deadline reportage' and 'daily journalism' (1–2). Unlike fiction writers, creative non-fiction writers cannot work from imagination and memory alone (Cheney 196). Literary docu-memoir involves the writer researching deeply and immersing themself in the subjects' lives. Theodore A. Rees Cheney writes, 'the highly involved research effort' requires the writer to 'conduct their research out in the real world,' to 'move in on the lives of complete strangers and to dig deep into those lives,' and to be willing to 'stick with a story' for weeks, months, or even years (196).

Literary docu-memoir blurs the boundaries between life-writing and life narrative and straddles literary memoir and literary documentary. The memoir component is the self-remembered true-life experience of the subject, as told by that subject to the creative non-fiction writer. The writer does not tell or explain the subject's story but rather creates a literary space in which to introduce the subject to the reader. Literary docu-memoir uses first person and is written in such a way that the subject speaks for themself about their experience. Unlike biography (for a comprehensive discussion on biography, Smith and Watson), in literary docu-memoir, matters of time and timing *do* matter; the subject is living at the time of writing—the death of the subject is definitive even though the work may be published posthumously. The documentary component can take the form of illustrations and images, such as photographs and documents inserted by the writer to lend credence to the text. The documentary component can also include factual elements which the subject mentions naturally in conversation about their experience, which produces a documentary-type effect in the subject's narrative on a personal and affective level.

This is a specialised form of writing that demands that the writer aspires to be as non-judgemental of the subjects as possible and to write with reflection and understanding. This necessitates that the writer feel empathy with the subject and convey that in writing to share with the reader another person's feelings or emotional experiences as if those experiences were their own. Affective resonance, how we internally 'mirror' ('see' and 'feel') affective states that are those of some other and relate to that person through unconscious recognition, is key to the process of empathy (Margulies 181–83). Alfred Margulies notes the psychiatrist's dilemma in providing descriptors for the subtleties and extraordinary nuances in the various in-between states or complex amalgams of some other's emotional experiences: 'in our attempts to feel into another person's' emotional experience, 'we come up against our inherent limitations of language and meaning' (181–82). Equally, words are the writer's sole tool to convey to the reader some other's complex and subtle affective states.

Being creative non-fiction, literary docu-memoir permits the writer's use of some novelistic techniques. Sondra Perl and Mimi Schwartz argue that even though 'the world of creative non-fiction is not invented,' the 'reality is mediated and narrativized': 'the particular subjectivities of authors are crucial and should be textually embodied,' because 'language and form must have a surface and texture that remind readers that the work is artificed,' because by its nature, creative non-fiction is 'not reserved for a narrow specialist audience' but rather aimed at the general reader (4–7). The further implication for literary docu-memoir is that to best convey a sense of the subject's experience, the writer must choose which threads to follow from the wealth of detail granted in audiotaped interviews.

Memoirists, and so literary docu-memoirists, are bound by a strict code of ethics that novelists are not. G. Thomas Couser posits that ethical dangers for memoir stem from the fact that it is 'rooted in the real world and therefore makes certain kinds of truth claims' (*Memoir* 9–10). While 'utter fidelity to truth' is neither possible nor desirable in a memoir, the writer assumes 'two distinct kinds of obligations': 'one to the biographical and historical record, and one to the people they depict' (Couser, *Memoir* 10).

Literary docu-memoir exists in a liminal space. It lies in the interstices of oral and social history and in life narrative and life-writing, and it crosses boundaries into other disciplines, such as psychology and sociology, and can also incorporate elements of survivor narrative, trauma narrative, and witnessing. But it is different from all those forms by the fact that it is essentially a work of literary memoir. Moreover, the creative approach to the crafting of the oral narratives, while maintaining their integrity, distinguishes the literary docu-memoir from other forms with which it might be confused.

Parker's legacy

Parker was a convinced socialist, atheist, and pacifist (Thompson 64–73). In his desire to help fight against what he saw as social injustice, he became a volunteer prison visitor. He had a chance meeting with a BBC radio producer that led to a broadcast of his tape-recorded interview with a serial offender and to being asked if he would write a book about the prisoner (Thompson 64). Parker wrote the book, his first, and every one of his twenty-two books thereafter using the method taught to him by the radio producer: 'Take the questions out, and try to make it into a consecutive piece' (Thompson 65). Parker seems to be the first creative non-fiction writer of literary works to craft his books entirely from extended interview material, from which he edited out most of his interview questions.

Parker's aims in interviewing were 'always directed at producing books forged from the interview material,' and he never interviewed for any other reason (Smith, Lyn, 244). He saw his writing as a way to give people on the margins of society a voice (Smith, Lyn, 247). Parker's stated purpose in writing was to show the ordinary person in the street to the ordinary person in the street to foster understanding of others (Smith, Lyn, 253).

The 'unseen' presence

When Parker sat down to write, he transcribed the interviews and waited to see what theme would emerge: 'I always regarded myself as a blackboard for people to write on' (Thompson 67). When asked if when he was dealing with a community rather than a single informant, he saw the problem of editing to be different, Parker replied, "Yes. Because you've always got to think, 'What gives this unity?'" and he named *Lighthouse* (1975) as an example of a successful work (Thompson 67). To research for *Lighthouse*, Parker lived amongst the lighthouse community and stayed out on the various lighthouses with the lighthouse keepers (*Lighthouse* 13, 18, 21, 30–283).

Lighthouse is crafted mostly as a series of interviews and conversations that begin with brief but vivid introductory descriptions of the individual informants. These short passages place the informants in their homes or places of work (lighthouses) and so provide an ordinary and 'normal' setting for the interviews. Parker has his subjects move, talk, and act as would ordinary people in actual life. Parker brings the informants and their stories to life on the page for the reader (Smith, Lyn, 251). Yet these introductions in *Lighthouse* do not employ the first-person pronoun, 'I.' The visiting writer-interviewer-researcher to the lighthouse community (Parker) is mostly an 'unseen' presence yet is nevertheless subtly evident throughout the book. Cheney argues a writer's positioning: 'creative nonfiction writers may well bring themselves into a story, either overtly or subtly, believing it only fair to let the reader gauge the writer's credibility and thus the accuracy of the facts presented' (197). For the main part, in *Lighthouse*, the visiting writer's presence is implied through only the lighthouse communities' conversations. Parker also demonstrates his use of creative empathy through the informants' conversations. The various members of the community understand what others in the community are going through and generally empathise with each other.

Revealing character

In *Lighthouse*, Parker takes a realist's slant and a sympathetically objective stance. The seeming oxymoron 'sympathetically objective' is an
accepted term used by sociologists and psychologists—one example of
how it is used is in *Becoming Good Parents: An Existential Journey* in
(2002) by James Hannush Mufid. Mufid describes parents who 'tend
to remain sympathetically objective towards their children' as 'secure
autonomous' adults, 'They are self-reflective and empathetic towards
themselves and others'; they are 'open to the point of view of others';
they are 'proficient perspective takers'; they 'have attained balanced
objectivity in the way they view' their own stories and the stories of
others 'with understanding and forgiveness'; and 'they have gained distance and are able to place things in perspective' (134). The term is also
employed by some writers. William Veeder and Susan M. Griffin, the
editors of the 1986 edition of Henry James's book *The Art of Criticism:
Henry James on the Theory and the Practice of Fiction*, provide one example. Veeder and Griffin paraphrase George Sainsbury's explanation of
why James's essays on Sand and Balzac were said by leading journals to
be 'admirable' and 'the best' (Veeder and Griffin 93). 'James' method-
ological preference for the sympathetically objective stance' allows him
'to praise and to criticize judiciously' (Veeder and Griffin 93). Veeder
and Griffin remark that James's 'matter of fact, external way of looking
at it [his subject] has its advantages' (93). His technique allowed him to
view his subject in a clearer light, get close to his subject, and understand
his subject (Veeder and Griffin 93). This technique as used by Parker
in *Lighthouse* allows Parker's persona (the interviewer-writer-researcher),
together with his informants, to question the deeper meanings of life.
For example, 'Assistant Keeper Alf Black' of the sea-rock tower is a too
heavy drinker, a senseless and uncaring drunkard when he is on shore
leave (191–95). Out at sea on the lighthouse, where drink is forbidden
and unavailable, he is sober and sensible and caring (195). Alf, a self-ed-
ucated man, listens to opera, reads Shakespeare, and ponders the words
of a religious writer whose name he cannot remember (194–98). In talking to the implied visiting presence about these things, Alf employs
metaphor to explain his philosophical concepts. He describes humankind's spiritual being as various forms of 'light' gained from some outer
source, compares the unreliable light given off by a match to the steadier
light of a candle, and likens the light of a candle to that of a lighthouse:

The lighthouse is a sort of fixed point isn't it, that helps with navigation? And what I'm doing is to keep the light going for people to make their way. But it's the fixed point in my life too … . Out here's the sort of light and ashore it's the sort of dark. So long as I keep coming the candle's still glowing for me. (197–98)

Alf adds: 'Crikey, Tawney, I haven't half got myself in deep water … . it'll go on in my head a bit now, will that' (198). In one way, Alf is only talking in an apparently honest manner about how life in the service affects him personally.

Noticeably, Alf addresses Tony Parker's persona as 'Tawney' (155, 161, 187, 189, 194, 198). Mark Kramer and Wendy Call say that when a writer records a person's dialect and speech patterns, it lets that person's 'voice' come through to the reader (108). Used in moderation, the technique of dialect in a creative non-fiction work can detail 'the flavour of the person you are portraying' and convey the essence of that character to the reader (Cheney 88, 137). Parker's sympathetic objective realism, and his treatment of his informants, suggests that Parker is showing the surface and the deeper levels of Alf's psychology to convey to the reader a sense of Alf's essence—and hence a sense of what it means to be human.

Two masters

Lighthouse is written so that the reader is encouraged by the text to believe that what they are reading is accurate in every detail. But at the end of the book, in the acknowledgements, Parker tells the reader that because of his personal promise to his informants, he masks their identities and all of their other identifying factors (287–88). He further reveals that the lighthouses are composites of the actual and that the informants are also composites of the real, and, he says, 'Additionally, the interviews themselves are composites of conversations with different people, transcribed from tape-recordings. But this is what was said; and I hope it conveys some impression of the world of those in the lighthouse service' (287–88). These sudden revelations highlight elemental flaws in the narrative.

According to Lyn Smith (and numerous others), Parker, a man of self-imposed ethics and strong personal principles, was 'determined to be faithful to the person and setting' and equally determined to adhere strictly 'to his principle of confidentiality' (245, 252–53). In keeping with his principles, Parker kept detailed resource books on each informant's physical features and characteristics, but when crafting his books, he would change each informant's height, hair, and eye colour' and 'hone these pen-portraits to economic perfection'; he called this method 'composing' (Smith, Lyn, 245–51). For the informants, Parker 'was looking for the essence of each person and to give them the opportunity to express this essence' (Smith, Lyn, 247). For his art, Parker's aim was to capture the essence of a marginalised life in a work that was both enjoyable and informative for the reader (Smith, Lyn, 252–53). By drawing his reader into the world inside the lighthouse community, Parker allows the reader access into the mysterious unknown. Yet his methods of 'masking' create a sense of mystery and a certain romance about a closed community that he is attempting to demystify.

In *Lighthouse*, Parker uses composites in such a way that they somewhat fictionalise a work of supposedly non-fiction. His methods create problems for the integrity of the voice because what was said by one informant could have been equally 'said' by others. Perl and Schwartz say that by using composite characters, a creative non-fiction writer puts their 'credibility at stake' (171–72). One solution would be for the writer to let their readers know what they are doing and why, upfront in, say, a preface (171–72). For Parker, these ethical concerns were simply not a consideration:

> This is what I do and what I want to do, and if it doesn't fit with any neat methodology—no problem for me … . I'm not appealing to scientists and academics. I'm trying to get through to your ordinary everyday reader. (Smith, Lyn, 253)

Ultimately, *Lighthouse*, a seemingly straightforward, honest, and compelling work, presents the reader with a dilemma in that it is written based on the personal ethics of an author who attempts to at once open a closed community to public view and protect his informants' privacy. In his need to find a solution, Parker inadvertently pioneered the literary docu-memoir. Lyn Smith writes that Parker 'had no role model; his style was entirely his own invention' (250). For the writer of literary docu-memoir, Parker's work is a treasure trove of techniques. Yet to fully adopt Parker's experimental approach could possibly result in a work that is potentially ethically questionable.

Stitching

The Seamstress (1999) is an unusual Holocaust narrative, written by Sara Tuvel Bernstein with her daughter-in-law Louise Loots Thornton and her daughter Marlene Bernstein Samuels. Edgar M. Bronfman, in his introduction, calls the work autobiography (xxv). The book's title describes it as 'memoir.' *Seamstress* can also be identified as literary docu-memoir.

In her preface, Thornton reveals that when Bernstein first asked her to listen to an audiotaped monologue by a Holocaust survivor, she did not know who the speaker was, but she learned that it was Bernstein herself (x). Later, Bernstein showed Thornton a journal in which she had recorded her experiences, and Bernstein asked her to write her story. Thornton notes that 'the lack of emotion' in these written and audio-taped accounts puzzled her: '*What happened to her feelings* . . . . Did she have to suppress them in order to survive?' (xi). 'I decided to see if I could write the book the way Sara envisioned. Taking a small paragraph from the transcription of the tape, I expanded it … writing in the first person, as if I were Sara, as if I were in the camp': Sara read the work and said, 'It's very good! . . . . It's just like it happened' (xii). Thornton then inter-viewed Bernstein for her story, audiotaping the discussions, and using the same technique as she had previously, she began writing from the interview transcripts (xii). Thornton discovered that she could not make the work 'line up' with the time frame she had constructed; Bernstein later admitted to failing to disclose certain facts important to her story (xiii–xiv). After Bernstein's death, Samuels found the 'dishevelled' man-uscript, and believing that her mother had written a book, she placed it with a publisher, carried out some extensive research, edited the work, and filled in the missing gaps partly from her researched material and from her own memory (xxii–xxiv). Later, Samuels duly acknowledged Thornton's authorship.

Thornton and Samuels use artistic licence to add what Bernstein did not divulge, to make her experience into what Bronfman asserts is a 'bril-liantly told story' (xxv). By adding into the story what Bernstein did not divulge and by 'writing in the first person,' as if they were Bernstein, and they themselves 'were in the camp,' Thornton and Samuels inadvertently allowed their own subjectivities to inform or shape Bernstein's personal 'truths'—at least as shown in the book. As Margulies advises,

> Empathy is by its very nature projective … . Our own experi-ence, even if powerfully and incontrovertibly in resonance with the other, must remain our own experience of the other's experience. We can share with, but can never be, the other … . We can only approximate another's experience from within the framework of our own. (183)

See Saw Margery Daw

See Saw Margery Daw focuses on the Forgotten Australians. These people, of whom I am one, are of mainly Anglo-Celtic heritage. Like the Australian Indigenous children of the Stolen Generation and the British and Maltese child migrants (the Forgotten Children), the Forgotten Australians spent part, or all, of their childhood in foster care or Children's Homes during the middle part of the 20th century. As innocent children, nearly all suffered severe hardship and horrific, unprecedented psychological, physical, and sexual abuse. There are thousands of Forgotten Australians, but not many write, or even tell, their stories. A few others would like their stories to be known, but for various reasons, they feel unable to write to publication. Some of these people asked if I might write their personal stories 'true' in a literary work and honour them by acknowledging their true identities.

Boundaries

The problem for me as a writer was how to approach the task ethically; how to stay true to the facts to honour my contract with the reader and with the subjects whose personal stories would be made public in a literary work; and how to manage this without imposing my own views on these people's stories. One way to meet the challenge would be to write a literary docu-memoir in which the subjects could speak for themselves. I decided to try and evolve the form, adapted from that pioneered by Parker, to fit my work on the care leavers.

Before I could begin, because I was dealing with living people, I needed ethics approval. The Ethics Committee required that I write participant information statements and consent forms tailored to my potential participants. These people had been carefully selected based on perceived suitability for the proposed project. Taking a lesson from Parker, to help make these potential participants feel more at ease, I arranged to interview each of them at a time and place of their choosing. As Parker advises (Soothill 237–40) and as per my training, in interviewing and writing, I have found it best to try to be sympathetic, non-judgemental, and empathetic of the subject while remaining as objective as possible; this stance allowed me to probe deeply but gently, listen well, observe the participant's facial expressions and body language, and quietly take notes without interrupting the flow of 'conversation' but still keep the participant on track. As was made clear at the beginning of the interviews, on tape, the decision to stay with the project or not was always the participant's. This is not to say that I did not suggest breaks in the interviews when needed.

In the interview sessions, a few things somewhat surprised me: almost at the start, each of the participants freely said on tape that they were speaking with me only because they felt that I would understand and could be entrusted to present their stories. This made me aware of possible power positions and ethical boundaries. A few minutes into each participant's interview session, the participant seemed to suddenly forget the tape recorder and began to speak freely of their experiences and thoughts and feelings. At the end of their interview sessions, while the audiotape was still running, each of the participants thanked me for a lovely chat and wanted to keep going. I have no real explanation for these things, only conjecture. But when crafting my book, I knew for certain that I could not possibly disclose to the reader everything that had been said in the interviews, even though they were said on tape. I had to be vigilant to include nothing that could betray any participants' trust in me and to decipher the meanings in their words as truly as is possible. To tell too much in a literary work could well prove intimidating for the reader. To best convey a sense of the subjects' experiences, I had to choose which threads to follow from the wealth of detail granted in the interviews which had been conducted over many hours and days, and I had to write just enough to inform potential readers and satisfy my subjects that I was telling their stories 'true.' Even so, some critics might question whether I tell too much. My answer is that as a writer, as a Forgotten Australian who has spoken with many other Forgotten Australians, and as one who understands the associated problems, not to reveal the truths of their stories would be condescension and betrayal and to once again humiliate these people and deny them a voice.

Ethical dangers

As Couser warns, there are ethical dangers inherent in writing the lives of others (*Vulnerable Subjects: Ethics and Life Writing*). One such danger is misleading the reader, another is misrepresentation of the subject, and yet another is (mis)using a vulnerable subject. Couser offers John G. Neihardt's *Black Elk Speaks* as an example of these dangers. Black Elk tells his story to Neihardt through an interpreter (*Vulnerable Subjects* 42–43). Couser names the work as an influential depiction of the Lakota culture and Black Elk himself, but he finds that Neihardt imposed his own agendas and interpretations on the interview transcript text (*Vulnerable Subjects* 42–43). Sidonie Smith and Julia Watson cite *Black Elk* as an example of the as-told-to narrative—one process of collaborative life narrative (264–65). Another process of collaborative life narrative is the ghostwritten narrative of a celebrity, and yet another is a 'coproduced or collectively produced narrative in which individual speakers are not specified or in which one speaker is identified as the representative of a group' (264–65). All three processes of collaborative life narrative face ethical dangers through being altered. Quite often they are subjected to being multiply mediated by 'two or more parties' in 'the production of the published story' (265).

When considering a potential subject for a project, the researcher-interviewer-writer must necessarily take great care not to influence that person and indeed avoid even so much as the appearance of coercion. I do not see the people who appear in my work as the vulnerable subjects of whom Couser speaks (*Vulnerable Subjects*; *Signifying Bodies*), nor do I see literary docu-memoir as a work of collaborative life narrative so defined by Smith and Watson (264–65). The subjects in my work are not diseased or disabled and do not suffer other anomalies, and they are not culturally, racially, or ethnically different from the society in which they live. Nor are they celebrities, or a tribe or a collective, and they do not rely on a translator and are not represented by one chosen speaker. Each of them chose to take part in the project of their own free will, and they each speak for themselves as they so wish. They are ordinary people who live ordinary lives, private individuals who are undifferentiated in their society. They are marginalised only by dint of being people with a history of having survived traumatic childhoods, but most of these people do not know, or know of, each other. According to the participants' expressed wishes, the only two people involved in the interview sessions were the researcher-interviewer-writer (me) and the participant in question. These interviews were conducted on an equal footing and with mutual respect. Moreover, all the participants were fully informed before the commencement of the project as to what was involved. All these people demonstrated that they were intelligent adults well able to understand the project's purpose and to make their own decisions, and they gave their informed consent of their own free will to participate in the project.

I suppose that when writing lives, it is virtually impossible to eliminate the ethical dangers inherent in the form altogether, but to try and minimise those risks, after transcribing the interview tapes word for word, I forwarded these texts to the individual subjects for their approval before proceeding further. Also, each subject was promised a copy of the published book. As well, in my book, I fully inform potential readers about my intentions, purposes, and methods of writing upfront, in the introduction to the work and also in the text. Even so, Couser's findings (*Vulnerable Subjects*; *Signifying Bodies*) have ramifications for a literary docu-memoir on the Forgotten Australians. This is partly because this is a story which has not been previously told from inside the ranks of the Forgotten Australians in a literary work aimed at the general reader, and it could seem to provide an influential depiction of an overlooked people in Australian society.

Crafting

To begin with, like Parker, other than to determine the focus of my work, I did not plot a theme for each of the subjects' stories. I could not. I did not know what any of my subjects would have to say about their experience; I did not know their personal 'truths.' Like Parker (Thompson 67), I waited to see what themes would emerge. Literary docu-memoir gives the subjects the opportunity to express some of the deeper realities they inhabit but may not have consciously plumbed in their ordinary everyday conversations. For example, M describes himself in ordinary life and in his taped conversations, and so his transcripts and in my book, as an ordinary person and as 'nobody special,' but because the taped conversations are intended as resource material solely for a literary production, M has been given a specific context in which to discuss his experience. As a result, M freely expresses himself in a philosophical way that he most likely would not do in ordinary, everyday conversation. He observes that sometimes in life bad things just happen and that reflection can bring a form of resolution. He then voices his childhood experience as the source of his bouts of depression:

> So my reality is all I've got and it's made me what I am and I figure I could be a lot worse, but with people like us … you have to accept you'll always have that monkey on your back. You can't throw it off because it'll just jump straight back on … so you've got to learn to try and carry it with dignity. *(See Saw)*

In *See Saw*, similarly to Parker in *Lighthouse*, I situate my subjects in the ordinary world, in their actual homes and place of work, as they go about living their daily lives. To bring the subjects into three-dimensional life for the reader (hopefully), I have them move and speak as ordinary people. I believe that writing of this type could allow readers to identify with the subjects and allow the subjects a literary space in which to claim a sense of identity—something they did not have as children. Differently to Parker and his persona in *Lighthouse,* I openly include myself in my book as a lead into the work and as a part of the action, as the interviewer-writer-researcher and observer. My intention is to provide a point of reference for the reader and a framing device for the story—and hence a setting for the individual stories—and to lend credibility to the work as a whole. I begin *See Saw* with my true story of my traumatic childhood, and I begin the subjects' stories with my true experience of battling floods to gather these stories. I end with an equally true story: on the hot March day when I finished collecting the data for my work, as I made my way home, a welcome storm broke the sweltering heat, and the after-storm light bathed the landscape with a surrealistic golden glow. I intend the story of my interviewing journey, a journey that is both physical and metaphysical, to foreshadow the drama of the tragedies in the subjects' stories. I also intend this outer shell to highlight the temporal by situating the subjects' stories within a given time frame and anchoring them in a text to create a sense of continuity—something the subjects also did not have as children.

Somewhat differently to Parker, in *See Saw* in my more creative story (the inner framing narrative about my interviewing journey), I step outside the interview situation at times and view the world through the lens of my own subjectivity. In this, my intention is to add validity to the work by providing the reader with information they can use as further points of reference. Within the framework of the interview process, I frequently interrupt the subjects' narrations with 'smaller' stories that refer to life in general and tie back to the deeper meanings in what the subjects are saying. Some of these smaller stories are about my own experiences, present and past. I tried not to overbalance by going into competition with the subjects but rather to write in a way that these smaller stories at once displace, frame, and support the subjects' stories yet take second place to the subjects' stories, so that as soon as the subjects' conversations are reinstated, their stories displace and reframe these smaller stories. This technique allowed me to create in the work a sense of place, displacement, place, and displacement that is in keeping with the subjects' childhood experiences.

Similarly and yet differently to Parker, also, in crafting, I chose selections from the interview transcripts that would balance the work and edited them without compromising the integrity of what the subjects have actually in their interviews, and then I moved these 'edited' lines around to create a readable story. Some critics might argue that this is in itself a fictionalising process. Others might say that fictionalisation begins the moment the writer begins crafting from the interview transcripts. Nevertheless, if one were to directly insert interview transcripts into the written work without removing nearly all the neutral vowel sounds (filler pauses or discourse markers), natural in spoken conversations, and without moving the edited interview material around to create a sense of flow and engender continuity in sometimes discontinuous memories, the reader would without a doubt find the written work too arduous to contemplate. But over the course of this 'composing,' I do not alter what the subjects have said in their interviews and transcripts, and I assign what has been said to the original speaker so that, in the text, each of the subjects only ever says what they have actually said in real life. To make it clear to the reader where the boundary lies between creative 'non-fiction' and fact, I use italics to indicate my actual interview questions, as lifted from the transcript text, and I sandwich the edited and verbatim transcript material in between the more creative work, which also includes snippets from the actual audiotaped conversations.

With my work, because of my participants' histories as care leavers, I believed that to mask and confuse my subjects' identities, as Parker does, would be an act of condescension and betrayal. To show each of my subjects as living people and to keep the reader fully informed upfront as to what they are reading, I begin each story with a short introductory passage about the subject and follow this with a photo of that subject which was taken by me with the subject's permission at the time of interviewing, for use in *See Saw*. As children, most Forgotten Australians were dehumanised and stripped of their identity. Often their names were changed by those in charge, and most of their childhood records were either lost or destroyed by the authorities. Rarely do they have photos from their childhood. Few photos were taken, but quite often, some photos were destroyed by care leavers themselves. Many care leavers experience anger, flashbacks, and horror in seeing images of themselves as children in care. In the main, all that these people have to show to prove that they existed as children are their memories. Many call themselves 'ghosts.' In my book, hopefully this double act of introduction and photo serves to show the subjects as people who actually exist, helps the reader feel that they are meeting them, and refers the reader back to the subjects' stories.

In *See Saw*, I try to create 'colour' to give the work a cinematic quality in order to highlight the affective content in the stories. Ivan Magrin-Chagnolleau posits that the use of 'colour' in theatre and film can produce multiple effects that influence emotional responses in the audience (1–5). With literary works, all a writer can use to create 'colour' are words and the imagery suggested by contextual placement of these words, and perhaps images such as photographs that may draw the viewer on an affective level. In *See Saw*, to encourage the effect of affect, I use words, imagery, and photos in conjunction. When crafting, I looked for the poetry in the interview transcripts, to use in my book. For example, in G's interview, so in his transcripts and so in *See Saw*, he said of one place in which he had lived as a child,

> Port A—was blue skies even when it rained sort of thing, and in the summer the city came to a meeting of the town and the country by the sea…. visitors in the summer, colours every-where, a juke box in the shop down the road, fish and chips, picnics, and lemonade, and me catching pigeons and trying to sell them. *(See Saw)*

In *See Saw*, to induce 'colour' into the work, I also inserted photos, if any, from the subjects' own collections, into their stories: black-and-white photos and monochrome photos to refer the reader to the sub-jects' childhood and colour photos to refer the reader to the subjects in the present day. In the more creative sections of the work, I marshal the affective thread in these people's stories and harness it to the imagery suggested in the framing narrative, then I braid this into the narrative thread that I weave throughout the work. G's three gardens will serve as an illustration. These gardens really do exist, and they are as described in *See Saw*. One of these gardens has a strange fairy tale atmosphere. In actuality, and so in my book, I find it fascinating and somewhat appealing, but equally, G describes it as a 'mess.' Likewise, another of the gardens is a wasteland and has an eerie, foreboding quality:

> 'It's my problem area. I don't quite know what to with it at the end of the day. So I hang my washing out here.' We stare at the would-be place. I have nothing to say. This garden does my head in, and I shiver. *(See Saw)*

The other, G's narrow back garden, provides the viewer with sharp contrasts of deep shadow and unreal light when the late afternoon sun angles obliquely down. My intention is to show these gardens slant, as real but not real and as a reflection of G's emotional experiences. In much the same way, in the story of my visit, I am me and not me—I am the researcher-interviewer-writer in the work; the literary docu-memoirist in fact; and the one who in the story wears a fictional cloak.

Conclusion

I believe that literary docu-memoir occupies a territory that has immediate access to the real human story. It takes the emotional field to access the facts: history is to each of us what we experience on a personal and affective level. At the core of the literary docu-memoir is the myth that carries the meaning of what it is to be human. In this instance, myth is the essential learning from the past. It is the way each of us makes sense of our experience and which is never just an experience but rather 'truth'—a mixture of our lived life (the actual or factual experience) and our myth life (our memories and how each of us chooses to interpret our story). All any of us really has that is truly our own is our story.

 ACTIVITY

Exercises for practice

1. Interview on audiotape someone you know and who is willing about one of their more unusual life experiences.

2. Do not lead the interviewee, but gently keep the interview on track.

3. During the interview, also take notes by hand, recording your observations of your subject's facial expressions and body language. Listen deeply, and try to place yourself in the subject's shoes; empathise but try to be as objective as possible, and probe your subject deeply for their story and their thoughts and feelings.

4. Transcribe the audiotaped interview word for word, listening for the poetry in the subject's words.

5. Choose which threads in your subject's story you are going to follow in your piece of creative non-fiction.

6. When crafting, attempt to edit without compromising the integrity of what the subject has actually said, and work what has been said into a piece of creative non-fiction as life-writing.

Recommended Reading

Ablon, Steven L. et al, editors. *Human Feelings: Explorations in Affect Development and Meaning*. Analytic Press, 1993.

Alcoff, Linda, and Laura Gray. 'Survivor Discourse: Transgression or Recuperation?' *Signs,* vol. 18, no. 2, Winter, 1993, 260-290. U Chicago P. *JSTOR*. www.jstor.org/stable/3174976.

Bathurst, Bella. Afterword. *Lighthouse*, by Tony Parker, pp. 289—96. Eland, 2006.

Bernstein, Sara Tuvel, Louise Loots Thornton, and Marlene Bernstein Samuels. *The Seamstress: A Memoir of Survival*, edited and with introduction by Edgar M. Bronfman. Berkley Books, 1999.

Gutkind, Lee, and Hattie Fletcher, editors. *Keep it Real: Everything You Need to Know About Researching and Writing Creative Nonfiction*. W. W. Noron & Company, 2008.

Harrington, Walt. *Intimate Journalism: the Art and Craft of Reporting Everyday Life*. Sage, 1997.

Margulies, Alfred. 'Empathy, virtuality, and the birth of complex emotional states,' in *Human Feelings: Explorations in Affect Development and Meaning*, edited by Steven L. Ablon et al., pp. 181–202. Analytic Press, 1993.

Parker, Tony. *Lighthouse*. Eland, 1975.

Parker, Tony. 'Principles of Tape-Recorded Interviewing,' in *Criminal Conver sations: An Anthology of the Work of Tony Parker*, edited by Keith Soothill, introduction by Terence Morris. pp. 237-242. Routledge, 1999.

Veeder, William, and Susan M. Griffin, editors. *The Art of Criticism: Henry James on the Theory and Practice of Fiction*. U of Chicago P, 1986.

Wolfe, Tom. *The New Journalism. With An Anthology,* edited by Tom Wolfe and E. W. Johnson. Harper & Row, 1973.

 Works Cited

Bernstein, Sara Tuvel, Louise Loots Thornton, and Marlene Bernstein Samuels. *The Seamstress: A Memoir of Survival*, edited and with introduction by Edgar M. Bronfman. Berkley Books, 1999.

Black Elk. *Black Elk Speaks: Being the Life Story of a Holy Man of the Oglala Sioux as Told through John G. Neihardt (Flaming Rainbow): Annotated by Raymond J. DeMaille; with Illustrations by Standing Bear*. Excelsior Editions, U State of New York P, 2008.

Cheney, Theodore A. Rees. *Writing Creative Nonfiction: Fiction Techniques for Crafting Great Nonfiction*. Ten Speed Press, 2001.

Couser, G. Thomas. *Vulnerable Subjects: Ethics and Life Writing*. U Cornell P, 2004.

———. *Signifying Bodies: Disability in Contemporary Life Writing*. U Michigan P, 2009.

———. *Memoir: An Introduction*. U Oxford P, 2012.

Forché, Caroline, and Philip Gerard, editors. *Writing Creative Nonfiction: Instruction and Insights from the Teachers of the Associated Writing Programs*. Story Press, 2001.

Kramer, Mark, and Wendy Call, editors. *Telling True Stories: A Nonfiction Writer's Guide from the Nieman Foundation at the Harvard University*. Penguin Group, 2007.

Magrin-Chagnolleau, Ivan. 'The use of Color In Theater and Film.' AIC Conference. Newcastle-on-Tyne, England. 8–12 July 2013. www.academia.edu/3522822. Accessed 6 July 2014.

Margulies, Alfred. 'Empathy, virtuality, and the birth of complex emotional states,' in *Human Feelings: Explorations in Affect Development and Meaning*, edited by Steven L. Ablon et al., pp. 181–202. Analytic Press, 1993.

Mufid, James Hannush. *Becoming Good Parents: An Existential Journey*. State U New York P.

Neihardt, John G. (Preface 1932). *Black Elk Speaks: Being the Life Story of a Holy Man of the Oglala Sioux as Told through John G. Neihardt (Flaming Rainbow): Annotated by Raymond J DeMaille; with Illustrations by Standing Bear*. Excelsior Editions, U New York State P, 2008.

Parker, Tony. *Lighthouse*. Eland, 1975.

Parnell, Jo. *See Saw Margery Daw*. PhD diss. 2012. NOVA. U of Newcastle, Australia, Digital Repository, 2013. hdl.handle.net/1959.13/1039417. Accessed 6 July 2014.

Perl, Sondra, and Mimi Schwartz. *Writing True*. Houghton Miffin Co., 2006.

Smith, Lyn. 'Only listen. Some reflections on Tony Parker's methodology,' in *Criminal Conversations: An Anthology of the Work of Tony Parker*, edited by Keith Soothill and introduction by Terence Morris, pp. 243–54. Routledge, 1999.

Smith, Sidonie, and Julia Watson. *Reading Autobiography: A Guide for Interpreting Life Narratives*, edited by Louisa Castner, 2nd ed. U Minnesota P, 2010.

Soothill, Keith, editor. *Criminal Conversations: An Anthology of the Work of Tony Parker*, introduction by Terence Morris. Routledge, 1999.

Thompson, Paul. 'Tony Parker: Writer and historian interviewed by Paul Thompson.' *Oral History,* vol. 22, no. 2, 25th Anniversary Issue, Autumn 1994, pp. 64–73. *JSTOR.* www.jstor.org/stable/40179366. Accessed 3 Aug. 2010.

Veeder, William, and Susan M. Griffin, editors. *The Art of Criticism: Henry James on the Theory and the Practice of Fiction*, by Henry James, edited by William Veeder and Susan M. Griffin. U of Chicago P, 1986.

Notes

1. This chapter contains some material from my essay 'Literary (Creative Nonfiction) Docu-Memoir: A Different Way of Writing a Life,' originally published in *European Journal Life Writing*, vol. 3, pp. C87–C104, October 2014. ISSN 2211-243X. dx.doi.org/10.5463/ejlw.3.136 ejlw.eu/article/view/136.

2. To the best of my knowledge, other than for my own work, there is no existing research or definition of *literary* docu-memoir.

5 THE STRUGGLE IN KARL OVE KNAUSGAARD'S *MY STRUGGLE*

Michael Sala

The conflict that drives Karl Ove Knausgaard's *A Death in the Family: My Struggle: Book 1* (2012) (written in two parts and first published in Swedish as *Min Kamp 1*), is not the quotidian project emphasised by many critics and reviewers—the protagonist, Karl Ove Knausgaard, struggling to deal with the painstaking trivialities of parenthood and his own adolescence—but rather one that relegates these aspects of the book to a preliminary role in the writer's intricately staged confrontation with a more fundamental question: How can one write about what is most difficult to relate in one's own life? For Knausgaard, this becomes the struggle to write about his relationship with his father. The climax of Knausgaard's book, the account of cleaning the house in which his father died, symbolises the transgressions and transformations inherent in this struggle, operating both as a vehicle to depict the self-destruction of his father and as a metaphor for the nature of the transaction that occurs between the autobiographical writer and the reader. It operates simultaneously on a literal level: we follow the author/protagonist in visceral detail as he prepares the private space of a family home for public consumption, and in the literary sense, we see how private material is staged to become a public currency.

Knausgaard's work echoes and ultimately combines contrasting literary autobiographical traditions: the stylistic earnestness and apparent spontaneity of Jean-Jacques Rousseau's *Confessions* (1782) and the structural sense of play and premeditation of Vladimir Nabokov's *Speak, Memory: An Autobiography Revisited* (1989). By doing so, Knausgaard problematises how the basis of autobiographical currency, its private as opposed to public nature, is inverted as part of the literary transaction. With profound consequences for writer, subject, and reader, autobiographical currency draws its power from what it no longer *is*. Knausgaard's contribution to the autobiographical genre is to lay bare the tension generated by this contradiction as never before and to invite the reader into the interpretative heart of the problem. The autobiographical transaction's public nature is set against the author's private desire to confront himself. This becomes the defining struggle for Knausgaard's book, which draws the reader into the act of interpretation both stylistically and through its patterns and repetitions, and in doing so, it ultimately disintegrates the boundaries between autobiography and novel. Knausgaard's experimental approach to writing lives thus models an unusual form of life-writing lying outside the conventional auto/biography[1]text corridor. In an article in *Auto/Biography Studies* (2016) Arnaud Schmitt and Stefan Kjerkegaard say that '[a]lthough *My Struggle* can be read as memoir and novel, and even as autofiction, Knausgaard is aiming at a higher truth, where the genre label does not undermine the autobiographical quest but supports it' (1).

The literary window: objects as entry points to the story

Towards the end of *A Death in the Family: My Struggle: Book 1* (2012), the English translation of the first book in Karl Ove Knausgaard's six volume autobiographical series *My Struggle*, the narrator, Karl Knaussguard, relates an incident involving a bottle of vodka. He is sitting in the house sharing a drink with his brother Yngve and his grandmother. They empty the bottle, and without thinking, Karl places it on the windowsill. When both his brother and grandmother react, he quickly removes it. He explains the situation thusly:

> In this house where we had always been so careful to prevent others from prying ... the closest you could come to the absolutely unthinkable was to exhibit a bottle of booze in a brightly lit window. (355)

The house is the location where part of Knausgaard's adolescence played out. It is also the site of his alcoholic father's final isolation and self-annihilation. On a structural level, the portrayal of the house, which dominates the narrative in Part 2 of *A Death in the Family*, serves both as the nexus for the novel's key thematic conflicts to reach their climax and as a physical representation of Knausgaard's father—more precisely, of the most crucial conflict embodied in the book: Knausgaard's struggle with the act of writing about him.

Yngve and Karl have come to the house to clean it, to take on the responsibility that their father abrogated. There is a practical dimension to this. The plan, determined by Karl while he takes a break from cleaning to buy his grandmother sedatives, is to have the wake for their father's funeral in the house (274). The house must be cleaned anyway and then sold, because their grandmother is no longer in a state to look after it. Fused with this practical concern is the more symbolic: a redemptive project to counteract the impact on the family of their father's long, slow act of self-destruction. By cleaning the house, the traditional familial space defiled by their father, and preparing it for public consumption, Karl and Yngve will restore the dignity of the family. Writes Knausgaard, 'He might have ruined everything, but we would restore it' (274). The depiction of this decision is an ironic gesture—doubly so given what will, in the extratextual world, be the negative reaction of Knausgaard's extended family to its publication (Hughes)—and part of a pattern of ironic gestures that invite the reader into examining the implications of the autobiographical act.

If the goal is to restore the house, to remove the stain of their father's legacy, then the literary depiction of the act of cleaning it performs the *opposite* function. Structurally speaking, it is not likely the final state of the house that makes the strongest impression on the reader's mind but rather the defiled surfaces that must be cleaned, the soiled objects that must be removed, which dominate the second half of the book through their detailed rendering and often visceral nature: the excrement covered clothes and sofa (257), the vomit under a bed (261), and the enormous rotting pile of clothes in another room (262). Even as the home is cleaned, there remains Karl Knausgaard's grandmother, filthy and (in a word that he links to his family to denote senility) mentally 'unravelling' (381–82). She remains the dominant presence in the house, alongside their father's absence, so that the house, in both the physical and metaphysical sense, does not, by the end of the book, become restored. What happens instead is the literary representation of an inversion essential to the autobiographical project, the transformation of private experience into a public currency.

Commodifying the self

Linda Anderson identifies the act of 'debasing the self by commodifying it' as a feature separating the popular memoir from its literary counterpart (7). One could argue, however, that the point Knausgaard is making through his portrayal of the house is that the self is *always* in a sense commodified in the autobiographical act and that it is the nature and purpose of this commodification—in particular how it intersects with a work's authority—that is at issue when determining the literary quality of an autobiographical work. Authority, here, denotes the means by which an autobiographical text establishes and exerts its credentials according to what Philipe Lejeune calls the autobiographical pact: the guarantee that the writer, narrator, and protagonist are the same individual and that the experiences of this individual in fact happened (14).

As G. Thomas Couser puts it, 'autobiography has a kind of 'authority' lacking in most forms of literary discourse—the authority of its grounding in a verifiable relationship between the text and an extratextual referent' (15). Alongside this term, I deploy commodification in a broad sense as the use of one's self (or at least a publicly constructed and staged self) and the experiences that it contains to gain something. The most easily measurable end in the publication of a memoir is financial gain, making a profit through publication. Nevertheless, for most if not all memoirists, there are less tangible but far more pressing objects in tension with these pragmatic concerns—for instance, the desire to work through a problem or gain or deliver an insight or for the literary autobiographical writer to gain artistic ambition, the desire to establish an enduring presence in the literary domain through a work that can be identified as authentic or truthful and as making a contribution to the genre. While insight for both reader and writer is an important factor that might be gained through the commodification of the self in any memoir, for the literary writer, this insight must come in part through a self-reflexive engagement with form—that is, with the very processes and structures that enable autobiography to be written in the first place. When an autobiographical work reflexively negotiates its own processes of commodification, it problematises its own authority, enabling it to operate 'as a site for negotiating and challenging the different ways meaning is given to the self' (Anderson 16). In this way, Knausgaard's portrayal of the act of cleaning is an indicator of the problematised status of authority in *A Death in the Family* and combines with the structural features of the book to model an important means by which a writer can stake a claim on the literary side of autobiographical writing.

Creating dramatic power: structural resonance

The symbolic confrontation with the house in Knausgaard's book, *A Death in the Family*, draws much of its dramatic power from the intense structural resonance between the two halves (Part 1 and Part 2), of the book. The writing is not divided into chapters but rather flows on page after page until the decisive break between the two sections (the break between Part 1 and Part 2), creating a stylistic effect (entrenching the literary illusion) of spontaneity and accentuating the dichotomous relationship between the two sections. Both parts of *A Death in the Family* adopt the pattern of approaching Karl Knausgaard's father via a seemingly random philosophical digression that unexpectedly thrusts the reader into the first encounter. In Part 1 of *A Death in the Family*, the father makes a distant figure, self-contained, decisive, in opposition to the self-doubting Karl, and he is subtly framed from the opening scene (where he stands, all seeing and all hearing, hammer in hand, alongside what might be mistaken for an open grave) with old Norse mythological elements (7–11). In Part 2, of a *Death in the Family*, this image of the father is not only dismantled but also fractured between the father and Karl himself, who echoes and diverges from his father when he finds himself at a similar point in his life. That point in time extends through at least six years and emerges in Part 1 from the initial encounter with Karl Knausgaard's father, when the narrator's present vantage point as a parent and adult is carved out in relation to the events with which the novel is concerned (8–34). Karl Knausgaard's father is thirty-two years old in this first scene; Karl Knausgaard the protagonist of the memory is eight; and Karl Knausgaard the narrator is thirty-nine. The reader is told the exact point at which he is writing a certain passage in this sequence: '27 February, 11.43pm' (22). It is as if the reader is present, looking over Knausgaard's shoulder as he writes. By this stage in his own life, Karl Knausgaard has left his first marriage and fathered three children in a new union. He struggles with parenthood, is socially isolated, and avoids alcohol because he blacks out and 'completely lose[s] control' of his actions (23). Writes the narrator about his father, 'I see him as a peer through whose life time is blowing' (10). A little later he says, 'When my father was the same age I am now, he gave up his old life and started afresh' (34).

In contrast to the discursive meandering through time in Part 1, in *A Death in the Family*, most of Part 2 portrays a focused period in which Karl Knausgaard, still married to his first wife, cleans the house in which his father died. It opens, however, with scenes from the narrator's later life: with his second wife on the eve of the birth of their first child (167–202). The conflict established in this opening sequence is simple: Karl Knausgaard has finished a novel that he is not satisfied with, and he is unsure about what to do next. He is searching for meaning. Something is holding him back from writing about what really matters. The sequence in which this is laid out is structurally disruptive. It serves as a causal link between the past that the novel recounts and the present point from which it is narrated. Karl Knausgaard the protagonist is awaiting two births that Karl Knausgaard the narrator has already experienced: that of his first daughter and that of his new autobiographical writing conscious-ness. These opening sequences of Part 2 in *A Death in the Family*, there-fore occur before Karl Knausgaard the protagonist gives birth to Karl Knausgaard the narrator; the moments before the elements of Philippe Lejeune's autobiographical pact fall into place, transforming Knausgaard from a writer of fiction into a writer of his own life (Gudmundsdóttir; Sala, *The Last Thread*; Sala, 'Knausgaard's my struggle: The interplay').

The reader is in a position to know all this not just because the nar-rator in Part 1 of *A Death in the Family* already has three children but also because the tangible artefact of the book, with its numerous finely rendered scenes of childhood, indicates that one of the protagonist's key struggles enunciated in this opening sequence of Part 2 of the book—to write in detail, or indeed remember, his childhood—has been overcome. 'Writing,' Knausgaard says, 'is drawing the essence of what we know out of the shadows' (172). It is, as he depicts it, a state of being, an ongoing process, rather than an end point. When relating the protagonist's dreams of childhood, he refers to a feeling of 'near constant humiliation' and describes 'a barely perceptible hint of aversion' towards actively remem-bering his childhood (180–1). For the protagonist, it is debilitating, a boundary he struggles to cross; yet Knausgaard later declared in an inter-view, 'I thought of the most shameful thing I could and started writing' (Liveshorts). Thus shame is established in this opening sequence of Part 2 of *A Death in the Family* as the potential obstacle to the autobiographical writing act but also as the means to access the memories on which it relies.

Harnessing emotion

Knausgaard is preceded in this shame-based relationship to the autobio-graphical writing act by one of the progenitors of modern memoir, Jean-Jacques Rousseau. Rousseau's *The Confessions* opens with a hyperbolic commitment to autobiographical representation: 'I have entered upon a performance … whose accomplishment will have no imitator. I mean to present my fellow-mortals with a man in all the integrity of nature; and this man shall be myself' (12). Rousseau begins the narrative with a por-trayal of his childhood that centres on an incident in which he is spanked by his nanny. He relates how, ever since then, he has secretly yearned to be spanked by the women he has sexual relationships with, although he has always felt too ashamed to ask (24). Not having the courage to confess it to any other person, Rousseau discloses to the reader and stages himself in the act of confessing (see also De Man):

> I have made the first, most difficult step, in the obscure and painful maze of my confessions. We never feel so great a degree of repugnance in divulging what is really criminal, as what is merely ridiculous. I am now assured of my resolution, for after what I have dared disclosed, nothing can have the power to deter me. (27)

Confronting the problematic nature of autobiographical authority—that it is wielded by an individual, the author, whom the reader has no reason to trust—Rousseau demonstrates his solution. He presents his shame as both subject matter and signifier of authority—hence indicating that he can be trusted as a narrator because he is willing to bring shame on himself. J. M. Coetzee provides a neat summation of Rousseau's approach: 'The immediacy of the language Rousseau projects is intended as a guarantee of the truth of the past it recounts. ... it is a naïve language that reveals the confessant in the moment of confession in the same instant that it reveals the past he confesses' (209). The use of present tense and the portrayal of the author and narrator struggling with his material in the act of narrating it (performative elements that feature in Knausgaard's work as well) are fictional techniques that create an impression of veracity and intimacy; after all, it is only in the illusion that the reader has entered a private space that the dramatic effects of shame can find their traction.

Thematic design: counterbalancing emotional currency

Whereas Rousseau begins his work with the most shameful scene, or one that could be characterised as such, Knausgaard does not. The first autobiographical scene in *A Death in the Family* features a face in the water. Karl believes that he sees it, so he tells his father, but his father is not entirely receptive (7–12). While there is an element of shame depicted here (his father's dismissive approach and his brother's humiliation of his pronunciation), this is not the sort of shame that conveys to the reader a sense of audacity or risk that adds heft to a promise of uncompromising honesty. The first real moment of autobiographical revelatory audacity, the sort that offers traction in the contemporary context, occurs with Karl Knausgaard's admission that sometimes he gets so frustrated with his daughter that he shakes her (24). Yet the most sustained engagement with shame does not occur until Part 2, of *A Death in the Family*, with the cleaning of the house, a space that Karl Knausgaard identifies as private and that features the intersection of Karl Knausgaard's shame with that of his father and, ultimately, because of his literary portrayal, that of his entire family. In Knausgaard's work, the deployment of shameful detail as a signifier of veracity, of honesty, and therefore of autobiographical authority is evocatively renegotiated by another less overt element that tests the borders of genre by negotiating its authority differently from that in Rousseau's work.

Vladimir Nabokov's *Speak, Memory* (1951) presents a take on the autobiographical mode that is as performative as Rousseau's approach but that is also its antithesis. Nabokov's project is encapsulated in a statement he makes in chapter 2: 'As far back as I remember myself (with interest, with amusement, seldom with admiration or disgust), I have been subject to mild hallucinations' (34). In contrast to Rousseau and Knausgaard, Nabokov seems to deliberately downplay shame, or any demonstrative emotion, and also his own authority; more restrained attitudes of interest and amusement, underpinned by a sense of play, define Nabokov's relationship to his autobiographical self. Each of the chapters in *Speak, Memory* is intricately structured according to a theme, what Nabokov calls a 'thematic design,' which he identifies as 'the true purpose of autobiography' (27). The thematic design, as Nabokov conceives it, is a structural sense of play, the arrangement of detail and incident that simultaneously mobilises autobiographical truth and holds up its contingent nature: its reliance on the vantage point, the organisational vision, and indeed the seductively distorting potential of the autobiographical narrator.

This approach demands that the reader be active rather than passive in the encounter with autobiographical meaning. Any signifier of authority is both necessary and suspect and, for its own validity, cannot be allowed to hold the field of autobiographical truth alone: the reader must be mobilised and implicated in the autobiographical process as a means of bolstering its credentials. The mechanism of the thematic design, as evidenced throughout *Speak, Memory*, is exemplified by an incident in chapter 2 which is arranged around Nabokov's relationship with his mother. Nabokov portrays himself as recovering from an illness and watching his mother emerge from a shop with a servant carrying a pencil: he writes that he was 'astonished that she did not carry so small an object herself' (38). He then says that he also watched 'the familiar pouting movement she made to distend the network of her close-fitting veil drawn too tight over her face' before he says that as he writes that 'the touch of reticulated tenderness that' his 'lips used to feel when' he 'kissed her veiled cheek comes back' to him, 'flies to' him 'with a shout of joy' (Nabokov 38).

Notable in this moment is the intense and intimate detail in the depiction of Nabokov's mother. In a similar manner, in the opening scene of Knausgaard's *A Death in the Family*, the image feels so lifelike that the reader might be tempted to forget its context as the portrayal of an autobiographical moment from childhood, with all the difficulties in memory that that entails. With Nabokov's work, the context is particularly problematic in that he prefaces this recollection with the assertion that his childhood self was not in fact present at the purchase of the pencil: he apparently hallucinated the episode while lying on his bed at home. Yet the focus of the incident is on a less substantial sleight of hand: the visual impression of the pencil, an item which appears to be a normal size from a distance when carried by the servant seems to become absurdly large when his mother takes hold of it. Similarly to Nabokov's pencil, Knausgaard's bottle in the window in *A Death in the Family* becomes a potent signifier of the writer's self-reflexive autobiographical method and, through this, his relationship to authority. In *Speak, Memory*, Nabokov relates that he goes so far as to drill a hole in the pencil to test whether it is 'real,' thereby implicitly reminding the reader that the illusory bedrock of vantage point from which the incident is recollected remains unexamined and therefore stranded on the reader's credulity. Even as he plunges the reader into the compelling detail of the moment, he is playfully and performatively testing his own authority and inviting the reader into an interpretative stance in the gap between private experience and autobiographical depiction.

Despite the playfulness and the restraint, Nabokov deals with high stakes, particularly the loss of his beloved father, who was killed by assassins five years after the Bolshevik Revolution, by which time his family were also financially ruined and exiled forever from Russia. The father for Nabokov, and likewise for Knausgaard, serves as a gateway to the autobiographical project; he is the source of the most intense emotion and most pronounced thread of autobiographical meaning. Nabokov approaches the loss of his father from multiple directions, always tracing through its intersections with history and other private events—for example, foreshadowing it in the last sentence of the opening chapter, inserting the hint of it in chapter 2 (much as, years later, Knausgaard also talks of his father's 'fresh start' long before he fills in the details). Then, when a phone call at a precise date and time interrupts a conversation with his mother (49), Nabokov uses this to overshadow the conclusion of an account in chapter 9 of when his father challenges another man to a duel (193): Nabokov's childhood self spends an afternoon anticipating the possibility of his father's death only to arrive home to discover that the duel has been called off. But the moment is not allowed to exist untainted: 'ten years were to pass before ... my father ... was fatally shot .... But no shadow was cast by that future event upon the bright stairs of our St Petersburg house' (192). There is an evocative resonance between this moment in Nabokov's book and Knausgaard's account in *A Death in the Family* of cleaning the house. In both cases, there is an implicit significance in the act of depiction that runs counter to the substance of the portrayal, a playful staging of harrowing detail. Knausgaard's reflexive portrayal of cleaning the house entrenches its symbolic defilement; Nabokov's dismissal of the shadow anchors its symbolic presence within the narrative at that point in time as a signifier of the narrator's unshakeable and unassimilable grief. Grief, rather than shame, is at the heart of Nabokov's struggle to write about his father and, by implication, himself. Thus, while Nabokov's relationship to his autobiographical past may not be driven by shame (Nabokov's father was beloved and died a heroic death), it is nonetheless shaped by intensely intimate and private emotion that finds its locus in a merged identification between parent and child (see also De La Durantaye).

Nabokov engages in an intense structural negotiation with the subject of his father's premature death, and therefore his authority, precisely because he does not trust the illusory qualities of fictional techniques in the autobiographical mode; he does not trust the way these techniques can reduce the most private emotions into a public currency that is easily traded away to make a dramatic experience for the reader, one that inevitably overplays the writer's authority by virtue of the fact that its fictive qualities are concealed by the emotional currency. Nabokov expresses his grief most powerfully by emphasising an authority that balances emotional currency with artifice, one that deploys a range of intersecting literary techniques, interruptions, negation, foreshadowing, and indirect references, through a sense of play and arrangement that pit the traumatic event against the literary mechanisms of its presentation, thereby demonstrating both the dramatic potential of fictional technique and its limitations.

One might argue that this is about postmodernism in memoir. As Patrick Madden points out, features common to postmodernism, particularly the structural elements, can be found in many of the most literary works of autobiography (223), to which I would add Knausgaard's *A Death in the Family* and Nabokov's *Speak, Memory*. Further, Madden disagrees with G. Thomas Couser's position on postmodernism in memoir, particularly the contention that 'the open acknowledgment of the artifice of the text ... is inconsistent with the nature of memoir' (Madden 223), and Madden writes that 'There are many books that both acknowledge textual artifice and seek to understand experience' (223). The acknowledgement of the artifice of the text, along with a structural sense of play, does not belong to postmodernism alone, and regardless, it follows its own course in the auto-biographical genre, as it does in both Nabokov and Knausgaard, where the question of authority, underpinned by the relationships, tensions, and ambitions embodied in Lejeune's autobiographical pact, has always been different from that found, for example, in the novel as a genre.

The unstable nature of autobiographical currency

Importantly, while Knausgaard depicts the shameful detail in *A Death in the Family* to drive and validate his autobiographical quest, his anxieties (both in his identification with his father and in the transgressive nature of the autobiographical act) are embodied in its structural and symbolic features. One of the most obvious of these features in *A Death in the Family* is in Part 2 in its loop narrative design. The body of Karl Knausgaard's father is encountered near the beginning of Part 2 (202), then the narrative performs a leap back in time to the moment when Karl first finds out about his father's death. In broad brushstrokes, the narrative drives the reader towards this very same encounter with Karl Knausgaard's father's body, via the visceral and humiliating (for Karl Knausgaard, for his father, for his family) ordeal of cleaning the house and all that it represents.

By the time the body is encountered again (373), it has become inscribed with the images of the house, images of Karl Knausgaard's mother, and the stories of his father's relentless decline. A key image reiterated on several occasions is one of his father, who is covered in excrement, has a broken leg, and is refusing to leave the living room, both the most obvious victim and the incontrovertible agent of his own self-degradation. On the second instance, Karl Knausgaard's father makes the connection that the excrement he is covered in is both physical and metaphorical and that he might, by the action of others, be pushed 'deeper' into it (264). In relating this story, Knausgaard implicitly foregrounds his own role in the autobiographical process, his anxiety that he is pushing not only his father but also himself and his entire family 'deeper' into it.

The nature of the autobiographical act comes under further pressure with a focused rupture in the rhythm and structure of the loop narrative in the middle of Part 2: Karl, standing on the veranda of his grandmother's house discussing the next course of action with his brother, suddenly drops back in time and takes the reader through a sequence of incidents beginning in adolescence and ending in early adulthood, which portray his relationship with his brother. The sequence ends as suddenly as it begins, with the following sentence: 'All of this existed inside me as we stood there on the veranda' (308). Knausgaard does not allow the reader to become immersed in the projected reality of the narrative; just as it reaches the height of its intensity, he cuts it short, to bring the reader back to himself as he stands on the veranda, lost in contemplation about the 'realities.' By doing so, it also lays bare the fictional machinery underpinning Knausgaard's approach. In the space of a breath or two, standing in a kitchen, he (Karl) does not recall all of the events that take place across the twenty pages of digression. This technique invites the reader into examining the implications of the sequence of events and Karl Knausgaard's relationship to an occurrence: Is it remembered? Is he aware of it at that moment in time, or is it merely there as an untapped memory? Is this indeed the moment when Knausgaard is born into Lejeune's intersection of writer, narrator, and protagonist?

Buried in this memory sequence is an incident that functions as a key to answering these questions. Yngve takes a photo of Karl and exhibits it, without his permission, in a public space (the foyer of a local cinema). Karl Knausgaard admits to being confused and annoyed at the intrusiveness of the act: he divulges that he 'could never quite associate [the photo] with' himself, with the life he was living,

> 'which had a certain external, objective quality to it,' since, for him, the photo 'was connected in quite a different way to something that was intimate and hidden, first … the core family but also the person I would become.' (291)

This incident indicates that Knausgaard the autobiographical writer is aware of the implications of making things seen, indeed *driven*, by unpacking these implications and how they relate to the end product in the transformative process of private experience into a public autobiographical currency.

This seeming awareness is the thematic pinnacle of Knausgaard's approach to the autobiographical act in *A Death in the Family*: much like the body of his father becomes, through its literary depiction, both inanimate and inscribed with the significance of its former life as the narrator portrays it, the same literacy process determines that the house and the defiled objects within it, including Karl Knausgaard's grandmother and Karl Knausgaard himself, remain part of the public space of the book without losing their connection to a private domain. Knausgaard's achievement in *A Death in the Family* is to elaborately stage, using fictional techniques, the manner in which these objects are paradoxically inscribed with the status from which they have been wrenched, or excised, and how this inscription means that the unique state of autobiographical material and its vital connection to a referential reality that is in part private is therefore not only subjective but unstable. The vodka bottle in *Death in the Family* is removed from the window and yet remains there. It is in this context that 'the label 'novel' does not undermine the autobiographical quest but supports it' (Schmitt and Kjerkegaard 555).

Maria Di Battista and Emily O. Wittman write that 'Since Augustine's *Confessions*, the manifest paradox confronting the autobiographer within his act of textual composition has been his experiencing his past self as at once the same as his present self, continuous with it, and yet strangely, uniquely, as other to it' (7). The intersection of authority and the autobiographical process in the work of Knausgaard, Rousseau and Nabokov arguably offers a formulation of the same paradox, along a different vector or line of differentiation. That is, the so-called past self that Di Battista and Wittman refer to constitutes a private world that the reader can access only through a public self: the self that is projected by the author as narrator from the current vantage point of the autobiographical work—the present self. For that past or private self to have currency, it must be both continuous *and* other to the present self, or it must be both private and public. The irony in the deployment of fictional technique in autobiographical writing is that the fiction of a private space it creates between reader and writer masks the very paradox from which it springs.

Conclusion

Lying as it does outside the conventional auto/biography text corridor, *A Death in the Family* serves as a reminder of the potential impact of structure and other fictional techniques on autobiographical material when it comes to shaping meaning and authority and as a model for the memoirist in staking out a literary claim. Knausgaard, with his experimental method, has laid claim to Rousseau's and Nabokov's respective unique approaches and, through this, to the aesthetic territory of the novel and the memoir. By using structural and other fictional devices to problematise the authority that he gains from depicting his private, visceral encounters with shame and anxiety, he illuminates and evocatively tests the complex ways in which the basis of autobiographical currency, its private as opposed to public nature, is inverted as part of the literary transaction. In doing so, he invites the reader to examine the nature of the autobiographical process and opens up a vital practice-led space in the eroding border between the novel and the memoir that may be further broadened. For the writer, *A Death in the Family: My Struggle: Book 1* serves as a model for engaging in the complex web of interpretative play that literary memoir increasingly embraces to remain relevant in the 21st century and beyond.

ACTIVITY

Writing tasks for practice

1. Find a point where the potential story of your life could be divided into two halves that are in some way equal.

   For example, you might divide your life into the first ten years and the next twenty, arguing that what happened in the first ten was as significant as what happened in those that followed. Write notes about this fracture point, identifying it in terms of relationships and events.

   Write a page for all that led up to the fracture and one detailing what happens after.

2. Brainstorm the symbolic objects in your life.

   For example, brainstorm about an important book, a feature of someone else, a gesture, a house, a song, and so on. The object might be present in your life or remembered.

   Now compile a private list of symbolic objects that lead to a different shameful memory or secret (not necessarily your own). Note whether there is overlap between your two lists. Jot down possible conflicts and themes that may be connected to each object.

   Which of the objects in your second list would be the most difficult to write about honestly? Compile a final list of ten objects, using five from one of your lists and five from the other, and then write a sentence or two that evokes the significance of each object.

3. Use these ten objects as a personal essay, a story, or chapter titles.

   How would you arrange these objects in relation to one another to create a structured narrative?

   How would you stage each object within its relevant chapter to convey its significance?

   Write the first draft of each piece, exploring evoked memories.

Recommended Reading

De La Durantaye, Leland. 'The True Purpose of Autobiography, or the Fate of Vladimir Nabokov's Speak, Memory,' in *The Cambridge Companion to Autobiography*, edited by Maria DiBattista, and Emily O. Wittman, pp. 165–79. E-book. U Cambridge P, 2016.

Gudmundsdóttir, Gunnthórunn. *Borderlines: autobiography and fiction in postmodern life writing*. Rodopi, 2003.

Nabakov, Vladimir. *Speak, Memory: an autobiography revisited*. Vintage International, 1989.

Rousseau, Jean-Jacques. *The Confessions*, edited by Christopher Kelly et al. E-book. U of New England P, 1995.

Sala, Michael. *The Last Thread*. Text Publishing, 2017.

Schmitt, Arnaud, and Stefan Kjerkegaard. 'Karl Ove Knausgaard's My Struggle: A Real Life in a Novel.' *Auto/Biography Studies,* vol. 31, 2016, pp. 553–79. dx.doi.org/10.1080/08989575.2016.1184543.

 Works Cited

Anderson, Linda. *Autobiography*. Revised 2nd ed. Routledge, 2010. E-book, posted by Taylor and Francis. www-taylorfrancis com.exproxy.newcastle.edu.au/books/9781136845543. Accessed 24 Nov. 2017.

Coetzee, J. M. 'Confessions and double thoughts: Tolstoy, Rousseau, Dostoevsky.' *Comparative Literature*, vol. 37, no. 3, Summer 1985, pp. 193–232. *JSTOR*. www.jstor.org/stable/1771079. E-book, published by U Duke P on behalf of U of Oregon. doi.10.2307/1771079. Accessed 24 Feb. 2017.

Couser, G. Thomas. *Altered Egos: Authority in American Autobiography*. U Oxford P, 1989.

De La Durantaye, Leland. 'The true purpose of autobiography, or the fate of Vladimir Nabokov's speak, memory,' in *The Cambridge Companion to Autobiography*, edited by Maria Di Battista and Emily O. Wittman, pp. 165–79. Cambridge UP, 2014. E-book, published by Cambridge UP, 2014. doi.org/10.1017/CCO9781139235686.016. Accessed 26 Nov. 2017.

De Man, Paul. *The Rhetoric of Romanticism*. Columbia UP, 1984.

Di Battista, Maria, and Emily O. Wittman. 'Introduction,' in *The Cambridge Companion to Autobiography*, edited by Maria Di Battista and Emily O. Wittman, pp. 165–79. U Cambridge P, 2016. E-book, uploaded by Cambridge UP www.cambridge.org/ doi.org/10.1017/CCO9781139235686. Accessed 24 Feb. 2017.

Gudmundsdóttir, Gunnthórunn. *Borderlines: Autobiography and Fiction in Postmodern Life Writing*. Rodopi, 2003.

Hughes, Evan. 'Karl Ove Knausgaard became a literary sensation by exposing his every secret.' *New Republic,* 7 Apr. 2014. newrepublic.com/article/117245/karl-ove-knausgaard-interview-literary-star-struggles-regret. Accessed 26 Nov. 1017.

Knausgaard, Karl Ove. *A Death in the Family: My Struggle: Book 1.* (Originally published as *Min Kamp 1.* Oslo, Norway: Forlaget Oktober, 2009.) Translated to English by Don Bartlett. Vintage, 2012.

Lejeune, Philippe. *On Autobiography*, translated by Katherine Leary. U Minnesota P, 1989.

Liveshorts. 'Karl Ove Knausgaard: In conversation with Jeffrey Eugenides,' edited by Ben Rich, produced by Aisha Ahmed-post, directed by Paul Holdengräber. *YouTube*. Recorded at New York City Public Library, 6 June 2014. Uploaded by New York City Public Library on 19 June 2014. video.search.yahoo.com/search/video?fr=crmas&p=karl±ove±knaus-gaard±shame#id=2&vid=6cb895c771aa078b62990aff1c563543&ac-tion=click. Accessed 26 Nov. 2017.

Madden, Patrick. 'The new memoir' in *The Cambridge Companion to Autobiography*, edited by Maria Di Battista. and Emily O. Wittman. pp. 222–36. U Cambridge P, 2014. E-book, uploaded by U Cambridge P, May 2014. doi.org/10.1017/CCO97811392535686.020. Accessed 26 Nov. 2017.

Nabokov, Vladimir. *Speak, Memory: An Autobiography Revisited*. (Originally published, Victor Gollancz, 1951). Vintage International, 1989.

Rousseau, Jean-Jacques. *The Confessions* (1782), edited by Christopher Kelly et al., translated by Christopher Kelly. U New England P, 1995. Ebook, published by eBooks.com ReadHowYouWant, May 2009. www.ebooks.com. Accessed 26 Nov. 2017.

Sala, Michael. 'Knausgaard's my struggle: The interplay of authority, structure, and style in autobiographical writing.' *Life Writing,* 30 May 2016. dx.doi.org/10.1080/14484528.2016.1187989. Accessed 26 Nov. 2017.

———. *The Last Thread*. Text Publishing, 2017.

Schmitt, Arnaud, and Stefan Kjerkegaard. 'Karl Ove Knausgaard's my struggle: A real life in a novel.' *Auto/Biography,* vol. 31, Jan. 2016, pp. 553–79. dx.doi.org/10.1080/08989575.2016.1184543. Accessed 26 Nov. 2017.

Notes

1. For many years, the literary world argued about whether biography was life-writing or if it was some other form of writing. The world bench-mark-setting body the International Auto/Biography Association now acknowledges biography as being a life-writing genre that is on an equal footing with autobiography—hence the accepted term *auto/biography*.

PART
2

MOVING LIVES: RELOCATING IN TIME AND SPACE

6 MAPPING LIVES: (RE)MAKING PLACE

Sonya Huber

The notion of the wanderer, the map, and the act of making the map has been one of the most vital preoccupations of literature. In my own writing projects, I explore and describe mapped 'visits' to a landscape—which may be encapsulated in a walk but do not have to be—to sample this landscape and create individual and collaborative subjective maps of that landscape. The resulting picture of the map suggests new relationships.

Map-based essays have emerged for me as an adaptable way to locate life stories on a landscape in an accessible online and non-linear format that is easily shared with readers. I was first inspired to use a map as a creative platform after seeing Dinty W. Moore's hybrid map essay 'Mr. Plimpton's Revenge,' housed in Google Maps, and after seeing scholarly digital humanities work by colleagues who are collaborating to map Shakespeare's London. My work in progress at the time of writing this chapter uses a map of Fairfield County in Connecticut as a visualisation for analysing and writing about socio-economic inequality over time, through the first-person subjectivity of the essayist. Seeing the varied forms of mapped essays, and continuing to work on my own, made me begin to interrogate what about the maps could be useful for writers in general. It seems that they serve not just as a container for writing in the form of a finished piece but also as an engine for generating writing through the place-based connections that are revealed.

In this chapter, I discuss the effects of grounding personal writing in place rather than in time, exploring the implications of the notions of authorship and chronological life narrative and the notions of self and community. In this, I also draw a distinction between the walk as a narrative through line and the different results that emerge when the concept of a 'visit' to a landscape is explored as an alternative in a collaborative or individual and dynamic platform.

Mapping places: physical and metaphorical journeys

The account of a journey or pilgrimage is one of the oldest forms of oral and written storytelling: this assertion is evidenced by works of classical antiquity, from *The Odyssey* of the classical Greek times to *The Epic of Gilgamesh*, a poem from ancient Mesopotamia. As Professor of classics Chris Mackie points out, Homer's Greek epic poem *The Odyssey* 'tells of the return journey of Odysseus to the island of Ithaca from the war at Troy, which Homer addressed in The Illiad' (Mackie). Luke Mastin notes that *The Epic of Gilgamesh*, which charts 'the story of Gilgamesh, the mythological hero-king of Uruk' and his friend 'as they undertake a series of dangerous quests and adventures,' is 'among the earliest known literary poems in the world,' dating back to third or second millennium BCE (Mastin).

Some of the earliest autobiographical forms in Christian writing, such as *The Book of Margery Kempe* (early 15th century), among many others, trace a journey to a spiritual location as a means of proving devotion and purifying the soul, drawing on the iconography of a spiritual leader such as Jesus or such as Moses and his followers journeying in the desert. The journey may be said to be one of our central frameworks of narrative, and the pilgrimage tale was adapted into well-known works of fiction, including John Bunyan's *Pilgrim's Progress* (1678) and Geoffrey Chaucer's *The Canterbury Tales* (1476). A walk in nonfiction or fiction provides the suspense of a destination that grows ever closer, along with the episodic drama of what is encountered along the way. The form was then easily transposed into nature writing as the adventure of a person heading out into the wilderness on a vision quest, a personal test, or as a way to deeply observe the environment. Often the framework of nature or travel writing contains vestiges of the spiritual pilgrimage tale in that the walker emerges with some form of transformation or insight.

Place and space

Beyond the narrative of a specific journey, the figure of the walker, or flâneur, has been the object of persistent interest to artists and writers for centuries, a subjectivity that moves freely in a landscape, usually a city, reflecting and making meaning while transgressing boundaries. Thus, along with the figure of the wanderer, the map—and the act of making the map as one goes—has been one of the most vital preoccupations of literature (e.g., Livingstone and Gyarkye).

Guy-Ernest Debord, credited with coining the term 'psychogeography' in the 1950s, describes the field in 'Introduction to a Critique of Urban Geography' as 'the study of the precise laws and specific effects of the geographical environment, consciously organized or not, on the emotions and behavior of individuals' (1955). Rather than envisioning this as a hard science, Debord conceived of the field as encompassing findings including 'influence on human feelings, and even more generally to any situation or conduct that seems to reflect the same spirit of discovery' (1955). Wanderers influenced by psychogeography would record the interaction between the environment and the self, noting the unplanned routes and the associations that emerged.

Debord broadens out the walk or journey in at least two ways. In his framework, the subjectivity of the narrator has an interdependent relationship with the geography, allowing both present reactions to landscape and past associations triggered by the landscape to influence not only the account but also the physical path of the journey. This openness to associations within the subjectivity and the past of the narrator formally acknowledges what often happens in a journey or pilgrimage: there is a detour, an unplanned side trip, or an encounter that results in a changed notion of the journey. In a way, Debord takes a central engine of interest in the tale of the journey or pilgrimage and formalises it as a method in which every moment is open to detours and the goal of a journey is secondary to the experience of the path.

Influenced by the journey narrative and the field of psychogeography, writers have employed mapped narratives and map-making as a way to introduce others to movement in space as a form of expression and a site of investigation. As Michel de Certeau describes in *The Practice of Everyday Life* (2011), 'The act of walking is to the urban system what the speech act is to language or to the statements uttered' (97). Certeau sees walking 'as a space of enunciation' because the movement through a space creates several stories, including the multiple 'intersections' of the person with the changing reaction to the space itself (Certeau, *The Practice* 99, 115–18). Certeau also enunciates how a story based on a journey is composed of encounters with cast-off objects: 'Stories are makeshift things. They are composed with the world's debris' (107).

Pedestrian performers

In my own work, the debris of the world—'a story based on a journey is composed of encounters with cast-off objects' (Certeau 107)—has been a persistent interest. Carl Lavery, author of 'Mourning Walk' in

Walking, Writing, and Performance (2009), cites Michael Pearson and Michael Shanks's influential work *Archaeology/Theater* (2001) to draw out four types of pedestrian performer, each of whom is linked to a key cultural theorist: the walker, the flâneur, the nomad, and the rambler (Lavery 43). In Pearson and Shanks's typology, says Lavery, 'the walker is defined in terms of Michel de Certeau's notion of the 'user' of the city, an itinerant figure who escapes from the disciplinary grid (strategy) imposed by urban planners and architects by following his/her own ... inclinations (tactics)' (Lavery 42). To this, Lavery adds that Pearson and Shanks follow de Certeau when they argue that 'the errant 'desire paths' opened up by the pedestrian performer are ways of rewriting the city, of making place' (the environment) 'into space' (the pedestrian's own relationship with that environment) (Lavery 43). That is, the pedestrian transforms the street into their own space: 'We are drawn back' to places that have significance for ourselves, 'weaving them together in impro-vised narratives': 'Through memory and imagination, we can claim a measure of control' (Lavery 43).

Thus, in this scheme, the flâneur, Lavery explains, 'has come to stand as a metaphor for the contemporary urban dweller, moving through the flux of the city, as a mode of being in the world, in relation to the daz-zling consumer spectacles' (Lavery 47). Whereas the figure of the nomad 'refuses to stop and look, preferring instead the bodily joys' of con-stant motion, exercise, and 'shifts across the smooth space of the urban desert[,] using points ... to define paths rather than places to be, making the most of circumstance,' the rambler moves in pursuit of pleasure of experience (Lavery 47). 'Pedestrian performance,' as Lavery calls it, is valuable because it can 'highlight the essentially performative quality of landscape' (46). In addition, says Lavery, the act of focusing on a pedes-trian world can remake place in an era when we encounter place only by passing over it at high speeds, thus rendering 'the world placeless, a kind of virtual desert,' as described in the work of French sociologists and ethnographers such as Marc Augé and in Paul Virilio's many books, one example of which is *The Paul Virilio Reader* (2004) (Lavery 46).

Of the four types of walker as outlined in the findings of Pearson and Shanks, in my own mapping project, I would say that I seem to be a straightforward walker, aiming not primarily for pleasure but instead for understanding the landscape and hopefully making new meaning from a fractured landscape, thus sharing the goal of drifting to actively produce meaning. The walk, for me, often involves an encounter with cast-off treasures I find as I wander in urban and suburban spaces.

Since this is a practice I have engaged in since childhood, I find Certeau's statement about walking and childhood to be highly resonant: 'To practice space is thus to repeat the joyful and silent experience of childhood; it is, in a place, to be other and to move toward the other' (Certeau 109). To my mind, one of the most useful elements of a journey, large or small, is the way one can be returned to a childlike focus on the present by consciously detaching one's self from the necessity of accomplishing tasks in frequently inhabited spaces. This would seem to be in line with Gaston Bachelard's concepts. Lavery describes Gaston Bachelard's view of a walk as 'a synthetic act that combines a series of opposites in a dynamic dialogue: inner/outer, past/present, the poetic/real. Moreover, the point of that dialogue, as in Bachelardian reverie, is to open the subject to him/herself and to the world at large' (51).

Triggers

Using place as a trigger—even an unfamiliar place—can allow the writer to access what cannot be initially expressed otherwise. Richard Hugo writes in *The Triggering Town*, (2010), about the various ways any external trigger might influence a poet or writer. One of his many points of advice for writers is that the trigger can be associative and does not have to have a preset meaning. Yet a trigger comes from an obsession, and that devotion to place carries with it the danger of egotism in claiming to 'know' something as vast as location: 'It is narcissistic, vain, egotistical, unrealistic, selfish, and hateful to assume emotional ownership of a town or a word. It is also essential to writing' (14). Hugo also writes about how we cannot see the place we are from and cannot say the things we need to say about it, but the adoption of another location as trigger will accommodate those 'intimate hunks of self that could live only in your hometown' but that could not be expressed (18). Hugo sees the use of a triggering town to be a way to build strength to see, write, and confront: 'Finally, after a long time and a lot of writing, you may be able to go back armed to places of real personal significance' (17–18).

For a writer, the walk or the encounter with a location or landscape scattered with fascinating debris often brings up associations that lead to the scraps of future fictional stories and triggers for essays based on those experiences, as Hugo recommends in his book *Triggering Town*. Hugo thus broadens the notion of pilgrimage as a long, continuous journey that must be undertaken on foot, offering the potential of a 'visit' to an unfamiliar landscape as an equally valid way of engaging in pilgrimage or in place-triggered writing.

The varied landscape

The notion of the visit as opposed to the walk or pilgrimage is important as an option, especially for those with mobility challenges or other disabilities, because a continuous walk across a varied landscape is inaccessible for many. I confront this issue in my own work as someone with mobility issues. One way I have learned to work around and with this disability is to break a long walk into a series of much shorter walks over time to accommodate my energy and movement challenges. My map-based work in the field of creative writing has employed psychogeography married to the performance of Oulipo (ouvroir de littérature potentielle, or workshop of potential literature): a technique which was formulated in the 1960s by Francois Le Lionnais and others for generating writing with a repetitive element or constraint in real time (Turchi 206). For my own writing project, I mapped 'visits' to a landscape to sample this landscape and to create individual and collaborative subjective maps of that landscape. This life-writing method is open to a choice of a route that has personal significance for one's own life story or as a way to trigger new experiences. These visits may be part of a larger walk or series of walks, either leading to a set endpoint or with the goal framed by some other internal or external standard (such as 100 visits, or visits at all hours of the day and night, and so on).

I set myself an initial project of finding a way to write about socio-economic disparity in the wildly unequal location of Fairfield County, Connecticut. I researched a great deal on this topic, emerging with a head full of facts and figures that had been ably digested and relayed by many writers before me. I considered employing my journalistic background to interview people on the extremes of the divide between wealthy and poor, but I rejected that as a central organising principle because I believed that the case study approach has as a limitation the idea that one case becomes an abstraction or worst-case scenario that readers can easily distance themselves from. As I mulled over approaches, I saw that the crux of the problem was written on the landscape, embodied for me in my daily commute back and forth on Interstate 95 across the line that separated the city of Bridgeport from the town of Fairfield. As I drove past it each day, I began to think of it as a scar, a place that held and represented so much distance and such a history of racial and economic separation. That actual scar was unmarked, yet it functioned as a kind of invisible wall. In this way, I began thinking about tracing the line with my body, visiting it over time as a way to make visible through my attention to it the significance of the location as a representation of more abstract racial and class divisions.

In my own project, my impulse for locating a social justice issue on the landscape is also influenced by the long history of marches and activism that moves people's bodies to a visible point in order to make an argument for change. I began thinking about this project after Occupy Wall Street, an activist occupation of the financial centre in New York in the fall, on 17 September 2011. This protest action against wealth inequality and political corruption, with its physical and gradual construction of a tent city and functional village on the plaza of an urban and inhospitable landscape, brilliantly insisted on making concrete and visible what is considered to be the most abstract relationship of all: commerce and the stock market. Protest marches use this logic, tracking a route with a collection of people, moving in a performance between significant locations or showing up at homes of boards of directors and at meetings of shareholders, relentlessly attempting to make their own faces a concrete manifestation of what is too often considered an abstraction or collateral damage of capitalism. Thus, my first encounter with the landscape was not to visit it but rather to map it in preparation for the visit, because I did not at all know the territory I aimed to encounter. I used a Google Map to locate the municipal boundary between Bridgeport and Fairfield and then used markers in that map to trace it so that I could see it for myself and confront the issue of whether my intended subject was indeed walkable, especially for me. Peter Turchi describes in *Maps of the Imagination: The Writer as Cartographer* (2007) this part of the process as 'premapping: the desire, and so the attempt, to locate oneself' (38).

Continuing to map this territory for my chosen project has been as vital to me as walking it. I began to see that some parts of this municipal territory were explicitly walkable and appeared to have sidewalks, whereas other parts were explicitly or implicitly off limits, with blank spaces that suggested a tangle of private property and untraversable highways, waterways, and restricted municipal areas. The lack of walkability and accessibility thus becomes part of the story. Throughout this project, I encountered many blanks on the map as well as what critical cartographer J. B. Harley names 'silences': 'the intentional or unintentional suppression of knowledge in maps' (Harley, qtd. in

Turchi 74). Harley's essay 'Silences and Secrecy,' quoted in Turchi, describes the silences of a map as necessary for the contents of a map to be intelligible (133). Each mapmaker must decide what to include and what to leave out (133). Turchi thus describes map-making as a subjective, not objective, endeavour, as 'every map intends not simply to serve us but to influence us' (133). With my challenge of walking a specific boundary line over time along an uncertain path, I had a large self-imposed constraint, which Oulipo practitioners believe can lead to creative output. I also had concrete evidence of how the boundary and divide between two cities was erased both on the map and on the landscape itself.

After I plotted the boundary line, I decided that I would start at the top of the 7.3-mile boundary and walk it to the bottom, in increments as short or long as they needed to be based on the difficulty encountered and time constraints of my schedule and energy level. I decided I would take a journal with me and make notes as I went, that I could pick up objects, and that I would also take photos on my phone as references for later writing. Initially, I worried that I would be done too quickly, but as the line became more difficult and tangled, and as it led me off on research tangents, I found that even tracing the basic spine of the territory took three years, with repeated pauses for other responsibilities and with limitations due to weather. What quickly emerged, however, was that my map became as important as my walking. I discovered that in order to do justice to a single city block, I had to research the history of the landscape I was walking on. I contained the research with reference points on the Google Map. Every time I read a piece of history about Bridgeport or Fairfield, I recorded any specific locations on the map that I could find. Thus, as my walk progressed south, I also proceeded into areas that had more historical resonance, and I began to have a unique and rich reference point for events in time as tied to locations in space. By the time I had proceeded down to the middle of the map, I knew a neighbourhood so well through historical research that I could locate, for example, where a factory had once stood that had engaged in the manufacture of wigs and shoes for dolls. My research was as freewheeling as any associative psychogeographic jaunt, and questions framed by the past and present of a place led me to inquire in archives and through my walking, what happened here? All information was plugged into my map, and the walking became informed and infused by the research.

In a way, then, the walk was not merely a walk but a performance. Each walk began at a certain point and ended wherever I felt it should end, based on constraints of obstacle, energy, distance, or other limiting conditions in a decidedly unwalkable landscape. As I wrote and continued to write, the walking experience formed the narrative spine of my project, although the bulk of the chapters in that narrative often contained a history of the places I traversed and led to locations and stories branching into contexts from my walk. The open-ended nature of the walks required encountering the landscape, and each walk's performance of success, happenstance, association, and encounter with history and the map was recorded for reading by others. This type of activity for a project, as undertaken by me, comes under the remit of performance studies. The field of performance studies is described by Laura Marcus, as noted by Roberta Mock in the introduction to *Walking, Writing, and Performance* (2009), as including the 'valorisation of personal histories, a stress on the positional, a certain anti-theoreticism, a sense of importance of 'speaking out' as a way of authorising identity, while at the same time identity is said to be performatively constituted rather than pre-discursive' (Mock 14). The 'stress on the positional' in my own walking project creates a way into the impenetrable subject of socio-economic inequality as enacted on the landscape and at the same time a way of 'speaking out' against the silence that the landscape has been forced to record and hold.

In Lavery's chapter 'Mourning Walk,' he describes his walk as a time when he had 'the impression that past and present had entirely collapsed,' and he says that he 'had magically returned to other landscapes which, for some reason or other, had, until that moment, remained hidden and out of reach' (10). This notion of return to other times through the portal of space echoes accounts in Dakota scholar Vine Deloria Jr's description of Native American creation stories as maps which are 'more concerned with geography and spatiality, 'what happened here,' than with chronological origins and temporality, 'what happened when'' (Brooks 41). I found in the practice of my walks that looking at landscape as embedded history, as 'what happened here,' allowed the landscape to be populated with the living and the dead in my subjective imagining. Phil Smith in his chapter 'The Crab Walks', in *Walking, Writing, and Performance* (2009), similarly finds time unhinged in his performative walk, the walk bringing his own wonder to the forefront of his consciousness. Because the ground moves, the wonder becomes a kind of separate presence: 'the wonder looks back at you, looks into you, and you look back at it' (Smith 78, 119; Mock 10). But this is not merely a return to the wonder of childhood or an immersion in nostalgia, as the wonder is more an experience of newness or altered perspective. Writers who employ mapping, walking, and visiting may experience what Jennifer Ladino terms 'counter-nostalgia' to denote a return to a landscape that is 'layered, fragmented, and complicated' (Lavery 41). Svetlana Boym describes 'reflective nostalgia' as that which returns and 'cherishes shattered fragments of memory and temporalizes space' (Mock 11). I found myself in the grip of this reflective nostalgia as I traced and became familiar with a landscape that was not mine; in the act of walking and visiting it, it became a familiar I felt affection toward, and yet it revealed itself as both endlessly unknowable and worthy of respect. The process of walking along the line led me to understand and see that every step I had taken was also onto a path that so many others had walked before, that this inaccessible line was part of a path worn by homeless people looking for refuge. The concrete manifestations of their presence— cigarillo wrappers, tents, crumpled chain-link fences—decentred me as the sole walker and allowed me to see myself as one point along a long line of urban walkers in an inhospitable location that was nonetheless a kind of home.

Conclusion

In my experiments and investigations, I have found that the resulting map itself, as it has accumulated through research, visits, walks, and reflection, thus suggests new relationships to place based not on the time-bound narrative of a journey through the landscape but rather on strictly the relationship to place itself as encountered by narrators over time. I suggest that writers who participate in individual or collective map-making exercises may find that their sense of relationship to the landscape changes as their own experiences, photos, and memories are embedded in that landscape and claimed in a public performance of experience on that landscape in its online representation. I also found that the experience of mapping research and questions onto a map creates for the writer an alternative form of story that pushes at the bounds of narrative, suggesting endless beginnings and endings.

ACTIVITY

Practice exercises

1. Make a blank map of a place you have already visited, and use the spaces in the map itself to tell a story about your visit or journey. What understanding about the narrative emerged through presenting your story as a map? Is indicating steps or chronology on the map itself useful? How does the writing and reading experience change when chronological markers are removed?

2. Find a location that you would like to 'map' with a series of walks or visits, and plot a possible route. Import into this map text and images from your walk, as well as the detours from and changes to your planned route.

3. Make a collaborative map of a location based on either individual or shared experiences, using multiple voices and inputs as well as map icons and links to represent specific categories of experiences, impressions, and information related to the map topics and tangents.

 ## Recommended Reading

Augé, Marc. *Non-Places: An Introduction to Supermodernity*, translated by John Howe. Paperback, 2nd ed. Verso, 2009.

Certeau, Michel de. *The Practice of Everyday Life.* U of California P. 2011.

Debord, Guy-Ernest. 'Introduction to a Critique of Urban Geography.' *Les Lèvres Nues*, 1955.

Hugo, Richard. *Triggering Town*. W. W. Norton & Co., 2010.

Mock, Roberta, editor. *Walking, Writing, and Performance: Autobiographical Texts by Deirdre Heddon, Carl Lavery, and Phil Smith*, edited by Roberta Mock. Intellect Books, 2009.

Turchi, Peter. *Maps of the Imagination: The Writer as Cartographer*. U Trinity P, 2007.

Works Cited

Augé, Marc. Non-Places: *An Introduction to Supermodernity*, translated by John Howe. Paperback, 2nd ed. Verso, 2009.

Bachelard, Gaston. *The Poetics of Reverie: Childhood, Language and the Cosmos*. Beacon Press, 1971.

Brooks, Lisa. *Indigenous Americas: The Common Pot: The Recovery of Native Space in the Northeast*. U Minnesota P, 2008.

Bunyan, John. (1678) *Pilgrim's Progress*, edited by W. R. Owens. U Oxford P, 2003.

Certeau, Michel de. *The Practice of Everyday Life*. U California P, 2011.

Chaucer, Geoffrey. (1476) *Canterbury Tales*, edited, translated, introduction by Nevill Coghill. Rev. ed. Penguin Classics, 2003.

Debord, Guy-Ernest. 'Introduction to a critique of urban geography.' *Les Lèvres Nues*, 1955, translated by Ken Knabb, reprinted in *Situationist International Online*. www.cddc.vt.edu/sionline/presitu/geography.html. Accessed 12 Jan. 2018.

Harley, John Brian. 'Silences and secrecy: The hidden agenda of cartography in early modern Europe.' *Imago Mundi: The International Journal for the History of Cartography*, vol. 40, 1988, pp. 57–76. JSTOR www.jstor.org/stable/1151014. Accessed 12 Jan. 2018.

Hugo, Richard. *The Triggering Town*. W. W. Norton & Co., 2010.

Kempe, Margery. (circa early 15th century) *The Book of Margery Kempe*, translated and introduction by Barry Windeatt. Penguin Classics, 1986.

Lavery, Carl. 'Mourning Walk,' in *Walking, Writing, and Performance: Autobiographical Texts*, edited by Roberta Mock, pp. 25–56. Intellect Books, 2009.

Livingstone, Josephine, and Lovia Gyarkye. 'Death to the Flâneur.' *The New Republic Daily*, 27 March, 2017. newrepublic.com/article/141623/death-flaneur. Accessed 12 Jan. 2018.

Mackie, Chris. 'Guide to the classics: Homer's Odyssey.' *The Conversation*, 5 Sept. 2017. theconversation.com/guide-to-the-classsics-homers-odyssey-82911. Accessed 14 Jan. 2018.

Mastin, Luke. 'Other ancient civilisations—Epic of Gilamesh.' *Classical Literature*, 2009. www.ancient-literature.com/other_gilamesh.html. Accessed 14 Jan. 2018.

Mock, Roberta, editor. *Walking, Writing and Performance: Autobiographical Texts*, edited by Roberta Mock. Intellect Books, 2009.

———. 'Introduction: It's (not really) all about me, me, me,' in *Walking, Writing, and Performance: Autobiographical Texts*, edited by Roberta Mock, pp. 7–23. Intellect Books, 2009.

Moore, Dinty W. 'Mr. Plimpton's revenge.' *The Normal School*, Jan. 2010. www.google.com/maps/d/u/0/viewer?mid=1RiR5cfB3Jow PmbPRUWXob59yJGQ&hl=en_US&ll=40.08742355791788%2C-7 7.11176850000004&z=6. Accessed 14 Jan. 2018.

Smith, Phil. The 'Crab walks,' in *Walking, Writing, and Performance: Autobiographical Texts*, edited by Roberta Mock, pp. 57–140. Intellect Books, 2009.

Turchi, Peter. *Maps of the Imagination: The Writer as Cartographer.* U Trinity P, 2007.

Virilio, Paul. *The Paul Virilio Reader (European Perspectives: A Series in Social Thought and Cultural Criticism*, edited by Steve Redhead. U Columbia P, 2004.

7 SPATIAL EXPERIMENTS: AUTOBIOGRAPHICAL CARTOGRAPHY

Vanessa Berry

Cartography has recently undergone a renaissance as a creative form, with maps and mapping practices being used across the creative arts, as versatile and cross-disciplinary methods of making literary work: 'Every map tells a story, and writers yearning for new ways to tell stories are drawn to them' (Cep; Piatti, 'Mapping Literature'). Maps are used in creative, critical, and hybrid modes that combine artistic and literary genres and subgenres; for example, Rebecca Solnit's highly collaborative, colourful reinvention of the traditional atlas, *Infinite City* (2010) (which Michael Berger calls 'a labour of love between Solnit and a legion of historians, writers, artists and cartographers' (Berger)), and digital literary geography projects such as the ambitious *Literary Atlas of Europe* project (1 October 2006–), led by Barbara Piatti.

Creative and subversive forms of map-making are also being used in life-writing, informing and deepening the research and writing process. In works of autobiography such as the graphic memoir *Fun Home: A Family Tragicomic* (2006) by American cartoonist Alison Bechdel and the lyric mapping work *Body Geographic* (2013) by Barrie Jean Borich, maps are integrated into the text and used as a metaphor to structure and inform the narrative. Both these memoirs were produced with cartographic intent: as mappings of life stories, they relate to place, spatialising a personal network of locations, memories, and experiences across the text. *Body Geographic*, for instance, is structured around the notion of the body as a map that carries 'a geography of memory' (Borich 5). Peter Turchi says that 'Shakespeare, who left no metaphor unturned, claims, 'Thus is his cheek the map of days outworn,/When beauty lived and died as flowers do now,' and we are firmly placed—in a figure of speech, a sentiment, a voice, and a poetic tradition' (114). Turchi holds that 'Every piece of writing establishes its basis for assertion, its orientation, and must immediately begin to persuade readers of its authority, its ability to guide' (114). Casey N. Cep writes, 'Turchi argues … that all writers are mapmakers and all writing is like a map. For Turchi, the map is more than the metaphor: it is the organizing principle of narrative' (2014).

In this chapter, I chart the emergence of map-embedded and map-influenced life-writing. I examine how creative cartography can be used in the development of autobiographical writing and how it is a form for life-writing in itself, particularly in writing about and with place. A cartographical approach to life-writing is contrasted with place-focused mapping; in this, I draw on my work in *Mirror Sydney: an atlas of reflections* (2017), which mixes life-writing, cartography, and urban observation. In *Mirror Sydney*, I use creative cartography to represent the connections between locations, topography, the environment, and the self (9). In *Infinite City*, Solnit describes a map as 'a selection of relevant data that arises from relevant desires and questions' (9). In *Mirror Sydney*, one of these questions is how individual experiences in places intersect with their historical and cultural narratives, what Solnit calls in *Infinite City* the 'inexhaustible' quality of places (2) and their ability to support multiple interpretations. The aim of this chapter is to encourage experimentation of this kind: to consider working visually and spatially as well as textually in the development and construction of life-writing.

Introducing creative cartography

Maps are a pervasive form of visual communication, integrated into daily experiences of navigation. For many, these maps in everyday use are digital, embedded within devices. The GPS receivers in smartphones enable one's location to be easily pinpointed.

You are here: a pulsing blue dot.

> As I sit at my desk, in a house in suburban Sydney, I watch the blue dot on the screen of my phone. It is hovering in a grey space, between the square that represents the house and the white strip of the adjacent laneway. I look out my window to where the dot on the map is positioned, and see an oak tree, leaves glistening with raindrops, and a weathered wooden fence. This view is anything but grey, neutral space. (Berry)

This simple experience of comparison calls to mind the often-repeated cartographical aphorism by Alfred Korzybski, which he posits to as one of the three premises of general semantics: 'The map is not the territory' (205). Korzybski's statement acts as a reminder to avoid conflating the actual and its representation. The map is instead a 'distinct mode of visual representation' that operates under technical and cultural rules (Harley, 'Deconstructing' 3). The information represented by the map can only ever be a partial account. As Mark Monmonier suggests in *How to Lie With Maps* (1996), for maps' information to be understood, they must 'offer a selective, incomplete view of reality' (1). Korzybski's statement has been further interpreted by Peta Mitchell as the basis for the postmodern map metaphor, wherein 'the map becomes a key metaphor for the negotiation (physical and cognitive) required in order to derive meaning from our environment' (3).

In creative non-fiction, and particularly in life-writing, writers aim for 'the accurate portrayal of life,' representing as closely as possible the texture of real experience (Cheney, *Writing Creative Nonfiction* 34). Theodore A. Ress Cheney advises that the writer should 'simply paint' for the reader 'a realistic (though impressionistic) picture' rather than 'cluttering' the scene with 'with too many words,' because 'Our brains enjoy filling in details. … Our brains are made to solve problems, and they'll do it when given the least encouragement. … We can give that encouragement by providing a minimum of (carefully selected) information' (64). To create 'a comprehensive picture' of life the writer should also give the reader information, not by 'telling' the reader 'but by the inclusion of details from life' (Cheney, *Writing Creative Nonfiction* 65). Like the relationship between a territory and its map, however, this representation includes a process of selection and arrangement, a shaping of the real-life material into a textual form. This process of selection is shared across map-making and writing. In applying deconstructionist strategies from Michel Foucault and Jacques Derrida to the understanding of maps, John Brian Harley lists the steps involved in making a map: 'selection, omission, simplification, classification, the creation of hierarchies, and 'symbolization'' (Harley, 'Deconstructing' 10). Harley notes that these are 'all inherently rhetorical' and that 'maps are a cultural text' (10, 7). Although maps are not the territories they represent, they exert on them a powerful interpretive framework through this selective presentation of information (Harley, *The New Nature*; Harmon, The Map).

Subversive mappings

Harley was an influential figure in critical cartography, a field of geography that rose to prominence in the 1990s (Crampton and Krygier 17). Together with his co-editor David Woodward, in the founding series of the project *History of Cartography* (1987), Harley 'adopted a new definition of the map' to 'include examples of maps that did not fit with textbook cartography,' examining the relationships between maps, power, and knowledge (Crampton and Krygier 17). With their 1987 project, Harley and Woodward 'opened the door to many non-traditional and non-Western mapping traditions,' but their project 'almost certainly informed Harley's theoretical work, and not the other way around' (Crampton and Krygier 17). Jeremy Crampton and John Krygier say that

> If the theoretical critique cleared the conceptual space for alternative mappings it has fallen to a variety of practioners outside the academy to explore what this has meant in practice. Perhaps the most noteworthy has been map experimentation by the artistic community, especially with representation and the map's role in creating a sense of geographical meaning. (Crampton and Krygier 17)

Scholars in this area have also traced the long history of subversive or counter-mapping (Crampton and Krygier 17). Many of these subversive mappings have been produced in literary contexts: One example is the skull-like map of *Utopia* created by the 13th- and 14th-century artist Ambrosius Holbein to illustrate Thomas More's fictional work *Utopia* of 1516 (Bishop); another example is the allegorical map of *Le Pays de Tendre* (Figure 7.1) drawn up by 17th-century French novelist Madeleine de Scudéry as a 'social game' (Reitinger 109). De Scudéry also used the map as a part of her 1654 novel *Clélie* (109). More's maps and de Scudéry's maps use mapping conventions to produce fictional spaces that allow the reader to reflect on human experience, whether that be social structures and values or states of being such as love.

The map of *Le Pays de Tendre*—also referred to as *Carte du Tendre*—is a topographical representation of the qualities and experiences that comprise love, from respect and kindness to betrayal and cruelty. Giuliana Bruno describes how, with this map, 'the exterior world conveys an interior landscape' (2). By representing experience spatially, through topography, the map presents a narrative of emotion that the reader encounters as a 'narrative voyage': a 'moving topography' open to traversal as the eye

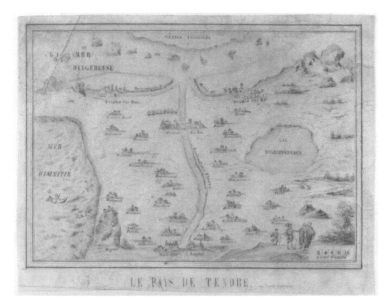

Figure 7.1 'Le Pays de Tendre,' by Madeleine de Scudéry. Courtesy of Cornell University - PJ Mode Collection Persuasive Cartography.

moves across the landforms, villages, and waterways that comprise the landscape of love and affection (2). The topographical features are a way of presenting affect: the rivers, for example, 'giv(e) expression to an ethos of fluidity and emotional drifting' (Reitinger 109).

The *Carte du Tendre* encourages multiple non-linear readings, in which 'the reading chosen (is) a performance of one among many possibilities' (McDonough 61). By allowing the reader to examine the experience of love by representing its embodied and emotional aspects, the *Carte du Tendre* performs what geographer Denis Wood argues is one of the key functions of maps: 'We are always mapping the invisible or the unattainable or the erasable, the future or the past, the whatever-is-not-here-present-to-our-senses-now and, through the gift of maps, transmuting it into everything it is not ... into the real, into the everyday' (15). By incorporating maps into literature, they can reveal 'the spatial dimension of texts,' whether this be the geographic territory on which the events of the narrative take place or the space the text signifies (Ryan 335–36).

Contemporary forms of experimental and unconventional cartography have been presented in anthologies (Harmon *You Are Here, The Map as Art: Contemporary Artists Explore Cartography*); published as creative reinterpretations of the atlas (Schalansky; Solnit; Solnit and Snedeker; Solnit and Jelly-Schapiro); and regularly exhibited in galleries worldwide (Watson 307). Contemporary uses of maps and mapping for creative, satirical, or subversive purposes draw on the 'power of maps' to express the unarticulated, ephemeral, or hidden (Wood 182). James Corner describes this as a creative practice of 'uncovering realities previously or imagined'; thus, 'mapping *unfolds* potential' (213). Rob Kitchin and Martin Dodge posit that 'maps are practices—they are always mappings; spatial practices enacted to solve relational problems' (335). In literary works, where map and text 'coexist and relate directly to each other,' this power to harness narrative potential and solve relational problems can be useful in storytelling (Bushell 154). Maps can be used, as in the *Carte du Tendre*, to reveal an interior landscape of memory and experience. They can also be used to present alternative narratives of places.

Memory maps

In the trilogy of atlases collaboratively authored by Solnit—San Francisco (2010), New Orleans (2013), and New York (2016)—maps are used to show the density of interpretations that coexist within urban environments in a way that, as Monica Manolescu says, 'translates the texture of place into cartographic discourse' (243). In *Infinite City*, Solnit writes about how each individual holds maps within them. Solnit posits that each of the city's 800,000 inhabitants 'possesses his or her own map of the place, a world of amities, amours, transit routes, resources and perils, radiating out from home'' (3). Solnit expands this definition to establish that citizens contain within themselves multiple maps that vary in temporal, spatial, and emotional scope.

In keeping with this idea, I included two memory maps as part of my creative non-fiction work *Mirror Sydney* (2017). *Mirror Sydney* pairs essays on Sydney's urban environment with hand-drawn maps that echo, expand, and re-present each essay in a visual form. The memory maps are 'Sydney at Age 8' (Figure 7.2)—which charts my memories of the city, presenting places and pathways important to me at that age—and 'Sydney Age 20'—which portrays the inner city, where I lived after moving from my family home. These maps are aesthetically similar, combining hand-drawn images and handwritten text, but they present a shift in places and details between the landscape of childhood and young adulthood. The process of making these maps was to imagine, in as much detail as possible, personal maps of the city at different ages, by anchoring memories to particular places and details. It was an exercise in externalising memories and representing them spatially, as networks of memories placed over the topography of the city and suburbs.

Such maps tell the city's stories differently, showing the intersection of individual narratives with broader social and historical elements. Solnit writes in *Infinite City* of how a map creates a link to actual territory and allows the reader to enter it, to 'alter it, add to it, plan with it' (8). How the reader does this varies depending on their connection to the space charted on the map. As Turchi says, 'the map doesn't include everything, and of course it can never be finished,' because 'its very inclusiveness ensures that it goes out date every time something is moved' or altered in the landscape (131).

Importantly, as Adam Gopnik points out, 'We chart our cities and we chart ourselves' (Gopnik; Turchi 131). My project, *Mirror Sydney*, involved exhibiting and presenting the Sydney maps included in the work. As the reviewers' remarks (Garrett, Lee, Nowra, and Patterson, to name just four) and readers' responses seemed to indicate, these hand-drawn maps connected with, and engaged, the viewer on a number of levels. Those who recognised the geography often compared my memories of place, as shown in *Mirror Sydney*, to their own memories of the same places. Others related to the era: the 1980s as it was experienced in the Australian suburbs. Interestingly, those viewers who said that they did not recognise the place or the era, or the network of houses or the mysterious sites and places of excitement and danger, used the maps to chart the experience of childhood from within the framework of their own childhood memories. Thus, the spatial connections between place and memory are sustained even when the time and place are not immediately recognisable. Because memory maps connect memories and places in a spatial representation, they are a form useful in the development of memoir and life-writing.

Importantly, memory maps need not be restricted to domestic space. They can equally be made for areas smaller or larger in scope, depending on the intentions of the writer. For example, 'Sydney at Age 8' (Figure 7.2), charts my memories of the city, presenting the places that were important to me at that young age. The map represents a suburban experience of the city through the eyes of the child who was, even though it is drawn by the adult who that once-child now is. Sydney has a wide suburban sprawl, and my childhood memories are a mixture of the micro level of home and its immediate environment and an understanding of

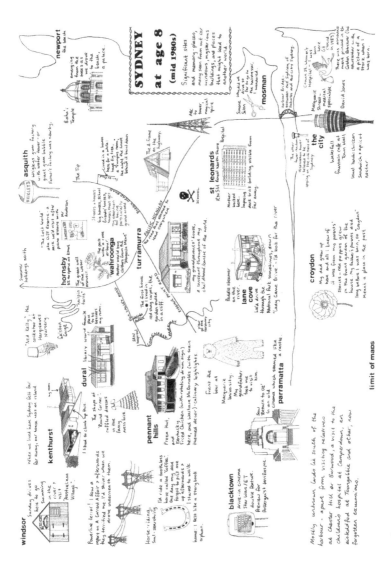

Figure 7.2 'Sydney Age 8,' by Vanessa Berry, from *Mirror Sydney: an atlas of reflections*, Giramondo Publishing, 2017.

the greater suburban network, often viewed through the car window on the long drives that were an everyday experience of my childhood. Its significant sites are both familiar (family homes, local shops, the library) and extraordinary (structures or details within the urban environment that stood out as unusual). The map includes hand-drawn images of these places and associated texts, arranged to reflect their prominence in my life at the time and their relative location.

Importantly, because memory maps connect memories and places in a spatial representation, they are a form useful in the development of memoir and life-writing; equally importantly, memory maps are useful as literary works per se. Robert McFarlane, in his book *The Wild Places* (2008), makes a distinction between two types of map: the grid map and the story map. The grid map is the map that 'reduces the world only to data,' whereas the story map is 'self-made, felt, sensuous,' with the potential to 'acknowledge the way memory and landscape layer and interleave' (MacFarlane 141). Thus, memory maps are a form of story map that connects memories and places. It is through specific experiences in a place—whether a journey or a memory—that stories emerge (see Van Noy).

Mapping life

The practice of mapping—organising details or elements in a spatial relationship—can inform life-writing in numerous ways. Maps and a cartographic approach have been used by non-fiction writers for structural, symbolic, and thematic purposes (Zhang et al.). Bechdel uses maps in the text and a cartographic approach to life-writing as an overarching structure for her graphic narrative *Fun Home: A Family Tragicomic*. At a PEN/Faulkner Foundation Award (PEN standing for poets, editors, and novelists)—an independent charitable arts foundation that supports the art of writing and encourages readers of all ages—reading at the time of *Fun Home*'s publication in 2007, Bechdel described *Fun Home* as a 'fairly accurate map of my life' (PEN/Faulkner). Elaborating on the similarities between cartoons and maps, Bechdel notes how both 'distil the chaotic three-dimensional world into a layer of pictures and a layer of words' (qtd. in Warhol 1). As a graphic memoir, the narrative is propelled by the interplay among these layers, a process described by Hilary Chute as 'present(ing) life narratives with doubled narration that visually and verbally represents the self' (5). The voices are split between that of the narrator, which overlays the images, those of the characters in the images, and those from the details of the images themselves. The whole relates back to, and indeed both stems from and is intrinsic to, Bechdel's 'memories of place,' the family home that was.

The philosopher Edward S. Casey identifies 'place memory' as a 'powerful but often neglected form of memory,' its power residing in its ability to keep or contain memories within it (213). In making memory maps, the physicality of place acts as an anchor for the ephemerality of memory (203–7). Even when that place no longer exists, or is no longer physically accessible as such to the writer, its details are a way of structuring, and prompting, memories (204–7). The ability of places to keep or contain memories has been used in the construction of mnemonics, such as the 'memory theatre' or 'memory palace' (205). Here, information is embedded in a physical environment, usually a house or architectural structure, and can be retrieved by mentally visiting the different rooms and elements of the structure (Yates 3). Rather than placing elements within a physical structure, however, memory mapping looks in that structure for memory anchors; places act as nodes for triggering, deepening, or enhancing memories (Yates 2–4). The simplest form of memory map is similar to the 'location sketch' described in Exercise 5 at the end of in this chapter; however, rather than being focused on one particular narrative, the aim of the memory map is to trigger and expand a wealth of memories contained within a place. A good way to experiment with memory mapping is to make a sketch map of a particularly resonant memory site, such as a childhood home or childhood landscape. Gaston Bachelard describes the childhood home as 'the entity that is most firmly fixed in our memories' (30). In the space of first or early homes, the child learns how to inhabit domestic space, a process which Bachelard describes as engraving: 'the house we were born in has engraved within us the hierarchy of the various functions of inhabiting' (15).

Bechdel's graphic memoir *Fun Home* is an example of a memoir that uses a visual representation of a childhood home as a major element in the narrative. In this work, the family home is central to the plot and acts symbolically to represent family dynamics. Bechdel uses the house, represented in detailed illustrations in the visual component of the narrative, to show to the reader aspects of her relationship with her father, her memories of whom she seeks to understand and reconcile with: 'He used his skillful artifice not to make things, but to make things appear to be what they were not' (16), and 'his bursts of kindness were as incandescent as his tantrums were dark' (21).

Bechdel begins *Fun Home* with the story of her father's obsessive renovation and decorating of the family home, a mid-19th-century house in a small town in Pennsylvania, a shell of its former glory, which the family bought in 1962 (8). In the space of the house, which her father had restored in meticulous detail, she notes there was 'something vital' missing (18). The house has an uneasy, brittle presence in the text, as the young Bechdel sees herself at odds with its fussy Victorian aesthetic. 'I was Spartan to my father's Athenian'; 'Modern to his Victorian'; 'I developed a contempt for useless ornament. What function was served by' these? (15–16). 'If anything, they obscured function. They were embellishments in the worst sense' (15–16). In carving out her own identity within the family, Bechdel shows the reader the house's corners, passageways, and hiding places as she evokes her childhood experiences within it (10–12). In a similar manner, Bechdel ties her father's identity to her memories of the house her father so loves (33): 'if my father was Icarus, he was also Daedalus' (7). In her graphic memoir Bechdel implicitly and explicitly likens the mythical Daedalus to his cave system and likens the terrible Minotaur to her father's unfathomable moods and sudden tempers (21) and to his 'monomaniacal restoration' and love of the labyrinth of their great old house: 'Indeed,' her father 'hid the Minotaur … and from which, as stray youths and maidens discovered to their peril … escape was impossible' (11–12).

Cartographic memoir

As Bechdel's 'map of my life' description suggests, *Fun Home* can be considered cartographically in that it connects a series of locations in a spatial relationship. In this aspect, it can be seen as an example of cartographic memoir. In discussing the performative function of maps in literary texts, Christina Ljungberg describes this process of interconnection and its relationship to identity: 'maps make meaning by relating one place, that is, point on the map, to another, which is what permits us to locate ourselves as subjects in the world' (290). *Fun Home* is structured around the places that shape Bechdel's life and her understandings of her identity: the Bechdel home in Beech Creek and surrounding landscape (8, 12); the funeral parlour in the front of the family home, which is the family business (33); the rooms of their old house where she stood not approving of her father's taste but nevertheless admiring the cleverness of her father (6–7); the trips to New York; and the college where she lived after moving out of home (27–29). These places are articulated in the highly specific, detailed illustrations that comprise the visual component of the graphic narrative. Like a map, the memoir makes visible and connects a series of places and the information—in this case remembered events—embedded within them.

Fun Home also includes maps, which are drawn into the image panels as part of the narrative. In chapter 5, Bechdel draws a section of a topographical map of the area to show its landscape of ridges and valleys and suggests the town's topographical enclosure has resulted in her family's insularity (126). The claustrophobia that the reader senses from Bechdel's descriptions of her family home is compounded by this 'peculiar topography' (126). Another set of maps in Bechdel's *Fun Home*, where the map from Kenneth Graeme's *The Wind in the Willows* is compared to the map of Beech Creek for its topographical similarities (146), has more of a transformative effect on the narrative. Bechdel loves the detail of *The Wind in the Willows* map, 'a chart, but also a vivid, almost animated picture' (147). Within this map are illustrations of the Kenneth Grahame characters: Toad in a car, speeding down one of the map's roads, for example. This chart provides a befitting analogy for *Fun Home*, which, through a cartographic approach to memoir, allows the reader to look into the map of Bechdel's life and see its animating details.

Body Geographic, by Borich, is a further example of cartographic memoir. The book is described in promotional material posted online in 2013 by the publishers, as a memoir that 'turns personal history into an inspired reflection on the points where place and person intersect, where running away meets running forward, and where dislocation means finding oneself' (Borich). In *Body Geographic*, under the subheading 'The Geography,' Borich describes having the maps of her life—the areas, places, and cities she has inhabited or does inhabit—tattooed onto her back: 'The actual woman's body in the middle of her life is neither map nor archetype, is both settlement and frontier. I choose, now, at age fifty, to treat the surface of my back as a cartographer's canvas. I stretch out on the tattooing table.... I came here to pull all my maps to the surface ... a marking more permanent. Of course it hurts when he maps in my history' (8).

Similarly to Bechdel in *Fun Home*, by engaging a cartographically structural approach and incorporating maps within the narrative, Borich uses cartographic principles to map out life and memory. Borich defines this approach as 'autogeography'; 'a self-portrait in the form of a panoramic map of memory, history, lyric intuition, awareness of sensory space, research and any other object or relic we pick up along the way that offers further evidence of does or did or will happen here' ('Autogeography' 99). *Body Geographic* takes the form of seven chapters, which Borich defines and titles as maps. These are textual maps which comprise vignettes that draw on personal, family, community, and historical memories. Borich uses the language and form of mapping to structure her texts; 'insets' in each chapter, for example, present diversions and deepening of detail in each map. Interspersed in the text are archival maps and images which provide a counterpoint to the textual narrative.

In contrast to Bechdel's description of maps distilling the three-dimensional world, Borich writes that 'maps obscure more than they reveal because their flatness is contrary to the layered experience of living' (*Body* 7). The way to address this is through the layering of multiple maps. For Borich, 'maps contain other maps,' and so she considers her body 'a stacked atlas of memory' (7). In contrast to city-based literary atlases like those of Solnit, Borich turns the concept of the atlas onto the self and the body, connecting the physical, embodied experience of life with place and memory, through her textual mapping. In this way, Borich's textual maps in a 'stacked atlas' are reminiscent of the rhizomatic cartographic form proposed by Gilles Deleuze and Félix Guattari, who describe a map as 'open and connectable in all of its dimensions' (12).

Yet a third example of a cartographic memoir is one that takes mapping and cartography as its subject. *In The Memory of the Map: a cartographic memoir* (2012), by Christopher Norment, is structured around the author's lifelong relationships to maps. In the work, Norment says that 'Memoir is the matrix in which I embed an exploration of how maps function in our lives' (3). Throughout his life, Norment has had an intimate relationship with maps. Many were topographical or street maps, but these are, nevertheless, 'conduits to, and expressions of, memory'(4). These expressions of childhood love of, and engagement with, maps are echoed in other creative non-fiction works on cartography by authors such as Katharine Harmon (2004), Judith Schalansky (2010), and Ken Jennings (2011). All these writers present stories of personal connections to maps as part of the introductory narratives to their projects. In the introduction to *You Are Here: personal geographies and other maps of the imagination* (2004), a work that is one of the first contemporary collections of creative cartography, Harmon writes of staring up at 'the imagined countries in the water-stained plaster' of her childhood bed-room ceiling (10). Schalanksy begins her ongoing project, *Atlas of Remote Islands: Fifty Islands I Have Never Set Foot on and Never Will* (2008), with a memory of travelling via the pages of an atlas during her childhood in East Germany (8–9). In *Maphead: Charting the Wide, Weird World of Geography Wonks* (2011), Jennings describes how, as a child, he relished the 'sense of depth, of comprehensiveness' he found in the world atlas (2). In the state road maps that Norment collected and pored over as a child, he is 'seduced by distance and the unknown' (20). Maps enabled him, he writes, to imagine the world beyond the immediacy and constraints of his home and life: 'a route and passage into the wide and wonderful world' (20). It is this power to open up spaces elsewhere, and to trigger memory and imagination, that makes maps and mapping so resonant and useful in life-writing, in their many flexible forms.

Conclusion

For writers, the representational and metaphoric potential of maps and mapping practices is an invitation to experiment. Questions arise: Is there a different way in which one could map this space? What stories could one show? What stories are hiding or elusive? How can the concept of mapping be used to shape the text? Such questions take up the proposal put forward by Sebastian Caquard and William Cartwright in their discussion of the narrative power of maps: 'the potential of maps to both decipher and tell stories is virtually unlimited' (101).

 ACTIVITY

Exercises for practice

Exercise 1: Where are you?

Using a map, either on a GPS-enabled phone or on a physical map, locate your current position. Reflect on this by writing one or two paragraphs, considering what the representation of the space you are in shows on the map and what it hides, and compare that to your embodied experience of the place.

Exercise 2: Emotional territory

Using the *Carte du Tendre* as inspiration, create a map that converts a state of being (e.g., love, distraction, anxiety) into a landscape, with features that represent different emotions, elements, or experiences of that state.

Exercise 3: Three-stage memory mapping

First draw a sketch map of a city/town/region in which you lived for a period. This could be childhood, adolescence, early adulthood, or now. Then, choose a section of this map to expand—this could be your home, room, or some other place of significance. Draw a detailed map of this area. Then, take one detail from this map and write a short piece of one or two paragraphs based on it. Once you have finished these three stages, consider how the act of remembering in space affected the type and intensity of memories that you have sketched out.

Exercise 4: One-page experimental exercise

For this exercise, you will need to have in mind a life story of some kind, such as a memory or an experience or a story about a community or a place. Using only one sheet of paper, experiment with sketching out the story spatially, so that all of the information of plot, mood, atmosphere, and character is presented on one page.

Exercise 5: Location sketch

With the same life story or a different one, select a location from the narrative. This can be of any scale: a domestic space, a town or city, a country, or a continent. Using a map of the physical environment—either self-drawn or copied from a street map or atlas (or digital equivalent)—as a guide, sketch out the elements of the life story onto the map, with key events connected with the specific place in which they occur.

Recommended Reading

Barry, Lynda. *What It Is*. Random House, 2009.

Borich, Barrie Jean. *Body Geographic*. U of Nebraska P, 2013.

Cooper, Becky. *Mapping Manhattan: A Love (and Sometimes Hate) Story in Maps by 75 New Yorkers*. Harry N. Abrams, 2013.

Harmon, Katharine. *You Are Here: Personal Geographies and Other Maps of the Imagination*. Princeton Architectural Press, 2003.

Harmon, Katherine. *The Map as Art: Contemporary Artists Explore Cartography*. Princeton Architectural Press, 2009.

Norment, Christopher. *In the Memory of the Map: a Cartographic Memoir*. U of Iowa P, 2012.

Solnit, Rebecca. *Infinite City: A San Francisco Atlas*. U of California P, 2010.

Stead, Naomi, *Mapping Sydney: Experimental Cartography and the Imagined City*. Local Consumption Publications, 2009.

Wood, Denis. *Everything Sings: Maps for a Narrative Atlas*. Siglio Press, 2008.

 ## Works Cited

Bachelard, Gaston. *The Poetics of Space*, translated by Maria Jolas. Beacon Press, 1994.

Bechdel, Alison. *Fun Home: A Family Tragicomic*. Houghton Mifflin, 2007.

———. 'PEN/Faulkner Event with Lynda Barry and Chris Ware.' Uploaded by Daniel Raeburn. Washington, DC, 9 Nov. 2007. archive.org/details/PenFaulkner071109BarryBechdelWare. Accessed 15 Dec. 2017.

Berger, Michael. 'Rebecca Solnit's Infinite City.' *The Rumpus*, 18 Nov. 2010. therumpus.net/therumpus.net/author/michael-berger/www.smh.com.au/. Accessed 8 June 2018.

Berry, Vanessa. *Mirror Sydney: An Atlas of Reflections*. Giramondo Publishing, 2017.

Bishop, Malcolm. 'Ambrosius Holbein's memento mori map for Sir Thomas More's Utopia. The meanings of a masterpiece of early sixteenth century graphic art.' *British Dental Journal,* vol. 199, 2005, pp. 107–12.

Borich, Barrie Jean. 'Autogeography,' in *Bending Genre*, edited by Margot Singer and Nicole Walker, pp. 97–102. Bloomsbury, 2013a.

———. *Body Geographic*. U Nebraska P, 2013b.

Bruno, Giuliana. *Atlas of Emotion: Journeys in Art, Architecture and Film*. Verso, 2002.

Bushell, Sally. The slipperiness of literary maps: Critical cartography and literary cartography. *Cartographica,* vol. 47, no. 3, 2012, pp. 149–60.

Caquard, Sebastien, and William Cartwright. 'Narrative cartography: From mapping stories to the narrative of maps and mapping.' *The Cartographic Journal,* vol. 51, no. 2, 2014, pp. 101–6.

Casey, Edward S. *Remembering: A Phenomenological Study.* U Indiana P, 2009.

Cep, Casey N. 'The Allure of the Map.' *The New Yorker.* 22 Jan. 2014. www.newyorker.com/contributors/casey-n-cep www.newyorker.com/. Accessed 4 March 2018.

Cheney, Theodore A. Rees. *Writing Creative Nonfiction: How to Use Fiction Techniques to Make Your Nonfiction More Interesting, Dramatic, and Vivid.* Ten Speed Press, 1991.

Chute, Hillary. *Graphic Women.* U Columbia P, 2010.

Corner, James. 'The agency of mapping: Speculation, critique and invention,' in *Mappings,* edited by Denis Cosgrove, pp. 213–52. Reaktion, 1999.

Crampton, Jeremy, and John Krygier. 'An introduction to critical cartography.' *ACME: an International E-Journal for Critical Geographies,* Special Issue—Critical Cartographies, vol. 4, no. 1, 2005, pp. 11–33. www.acme-journal.org/index.php/acme/article/view/723. Accessed 15 Dec. 2017.

Deleuze, Gilles, and Félix Guattari. *A Thousand Plateaus: Capitalism and Schizophrenia,* translated by Brian Massumi. Athlone Press, 1988.

Garrett, Bradley. 'Mirror sydney review: Vanessa Berry pictures another side of the city.' *The Sydney Morning Herald,* 27 Oct. 2017.

Gopnik, Adam. 'Street Furniture.' *The New Yorker,* 6 Nov. 2000. www.newyorker.com/contibutors/adam-gopnik. Accessed 4 June 2018.

Harley, John Brian. 'Deconstructing the map.' *Cartographica: The International Journal for Geographic Information and Geovisualization,* vol. 26, no. 2, Spring 1989, pp. 1–20. doi: 10.3138/E653-7827-1757-9T53. Accessed 15 Dec. 2017.

———. *The New Nature of Maps: Essays in the History of Cartography,* edited by Paul Laxton and J. H. Andrews. U Johns Hopkins P, 2001.

Harmon, Katharine. *You Are Here: Personal Geographies and Other Maps of the Imagination.* Princeton Architectural Press, 2004.

———. *The Map as Art: Contemporary Artists Explore Cartography.* Princeton Architectural Press, 2009.

Jennings, Ken. *Maphead: Charting the Wide, Weird World of Geography Wonks*. Simon and Schuster, 2011.

Kitchin, Rob, and Martin Dodge. 'Rethinking maps.' *Progress in Human Geography,* vol. 31, no. 3, June 2007, pp. 331–44. doi. org/10.1177/0309132507077082. Accessed 5 March 2018.

Korzybski, Alfred. *Alfred Korzybski: Collected Writings, 1920–1950*. Institute of General Semantics, 1990.

Lee, Tom. 'Eccentric Guides: Vanessa Berry's *Mirror Sydney*.' *Sydney Review of Books*. 16 February 2018. www.sydneyreviewofbooks.com/contributors/ tom-lee sydneyreviewofbooks.com/. Accessed 17 February 2018.

Ljungberg, Christina. *Creative Dynamics: Diagrammatic strategies in narrative*. John Benjamins Publishing Company, 2012.

Manolescu, Monica. 'Cartography and renewal in Rebecca Solnit's infinite city: A San Francisco Atlas.' *Canadian Review of American Studies,* vol. 44, no. 2, 2014, pp. 240–59. doi.org/10.3138/cras.2014.S04. Accessed 2 June 2018.

McDonough, Thomas F. 'Situationist Space.' *October,* vol. 67, Winter 1994, pp. 59–77.

McFarlane, Robert. *The Wild Places*. Granta Books, 2008.

Mitchell, Peta. *Cartographic Strategies of Postmodernity: The Figure of the Map in Contemporary Theory and Fiction*. Routledge, 2008.

Monmonier, Mark. *How to Lie with Maps*, 2nd ed. U of Chicago P, 1996.

More, Thomas (1516–51). *Utopia: Concerning the Highest State of the Republic and the New Island Utopia*, edited, introduction, and translated into English by Paul Turner. Penguin Books, 1965.

Norment, Christopher. *In the Memory of the Map: A Cartographic Memoir*. U Iowa P, 2012.

Nowra, Louis. 'Mirror Sydney by Vanessa Berry: Proustian view of city a must-read.' *The Australian*, 18 Nov. 2017. www.theaustralian.com.au/ Accessed 5 March 2018.

Patterson, Tom. 'Vanessa Berry mirror Sydney. Reviewed by Tom Patterson.' *The Newtown Review of Books*, 19 Oct. 2017. newtownreviewofbooks. com.au/tag/australian-non-fiction/.Accessed 20 Oct. 2017.

Piatti, Barbara, et al. *A Literary Atlas of Europe*. 1 Oct. 2006–present. www. literaturatlas.eu/en/. Accessed 8 June 2018.

———. "Mapping literature: The prototype of 'A literary map of Europe.'" Posted 2 April 2015. www.researchgate.net/publication/268361950. Accessed 8 June 2018.

Reitinger, Franz. 'Mapping relationships: Allegory, gender and the cartographical image in the eighteenth century France and England.' *Imago Mundi, The International Journal for the History of Cartography,* vol. 51, no. 1, 1999, pp. 106–30. doi.org/10.1080/03085699908592905. Accessed 18 Feb. 2018.

Ryan, Marie-Laure. 'Narrative cartography: Toward a visual narratology,' in *What Is Narratology? Questions and Answers Regarding the Status of a Theory*, edited by Tom Kindt and Hans-Harald Müller. De Gruyter, 2003.

Schalansky, Judith. *Atlas of Remote Islands: Fifty Islands I Have Never Set Foot on and Never Will*. Penguin Books, 2010.

Scudéry, Madeleine de. *Le Pays de Tendre*. Persuasive Maps: PJ mode collection. U Cornell P. 1800. digital.library.cornell.edu/catalog/ss:3293716. Accessed 2 March 2018.

Solnit, Rebecca. *Infinite City: A San Francisco Atlas*. U Los Angeles P, 2010.

Solnit, Rebecca, and Rebecca Snedeker. *Unfathomable City: A New Orleans Atlas*. U California P, 2013.

Solnit, Rebecca, and Joshua Jelly-Schapiro. *Nonstop Metropolis: A New York City Atlas*. U California P, 2016.

Turchi, Peter. *Maps of the Imagination: The Writer as Cartographer*. U Trinity P, 2004.

Van Noy, Rick. *Surveying the Interior: Literary Cartographers and the Sense of Place*. U Nevada P, 2003.

Warhol, Robyn. 'The space between: A narrative approach to Alison Bechdel's fun home.' *College Literature,* vol. 38, no. 3, 2011, pp. 1–20.

Watson, Ruth. 'Mapping and contemporary art.' *The Cartographic Journal,* Art and Cartography Special Issue, vol. 46, no. 4, 2009, pp. 293–307. doi.10.1179/000870409X125499973897079. Accessed 2 March 2018.

Wood, Denis. *Rethinking the Power of Maps*, 1st ed. Guilford Press, 2010.

Yates, Frances Amelia. *The Art of Memory*. Routledge, 1999.

Zhang, Liping, et al. 'Design and implementation of decision-making support system for thematic map cartography.' *The International Archives of the Photogrammetry, Remote Sensing and Spatial Information Sciences,* vol. XXXVII, part B2, Beijing, 2008. citex.ist.psu.edu/viewdoc/download?doi=10.1.1.640.3520&rep=rep1&type=pdf. Accessed 4 June 2018.

8 BRIEF ENCOUNTERS: CURATING GIFS, MEMES, AND SOCIAL MEDIA FOR SHORT STORY LIFE-WRITING

Emma Newport

From Samuel Johnson's comprehensive work *The lives of the most eminent English poets, with critical observations on their works/by Samuel Johnson* (1781)—which I refer to here as his 'Little Lives' of eminent poets, to the academic tools of the *Oxford Dictionary of National Biography*—brevity and life-writing have enjoyed and endured a long association (Einhaus 1–11; Stewart 80). In this age of the Internet, the documenting of everyday lives has migrated from the page to the digital space, hence allowing learner writers and others more freedom to easily access and actively participate in some form of life-writing practice as a part of ordinary life. Increasingly, life-writing has become instantaneous and fragmented yet inextricably connected to others' experiences. Brevity, instantaneity, and replication are the watchwords of social media, and with them come an association with the ephemeral.

I suggest that by increasing their abilities to collect, curate, and reflect on these forms of social media communications, new and developing writers, and others, can ask new questions about the limits of language, the fragmentary experience, and the performative element of social media. In doing so, I offer some practical strategies for encouraging the aspiring writer to write beyond the emotive first-person, self-reflective practice familiar in YouTube videos, vlogs, and Facebook posts. Often this mode of documenting experience is the first and perhaps only method of new life-writers. Such familiarity can be a trap for the new writer: the danger lies in repeating these forms as the primary strategy for life-writing rather than learning how to confront, and embrace, the challenge of communicating lives in an age of digital expression by adopting a more critical and creative use of social media source material. Encouraged by Nicholas Royle's experiments with, and ideas for, writing lives in a way that can be lively and perceptive while maintaining the sensitivity and vulnerability necessary to such texts, I propose that when developing writers think critically about brevity and life-writing, they are more able to focus their work in a way that results in a new edge and clarity to their writing.

Methodology

Susanna Egan argues in *Patterns of Experience in Autobiography* (2011) that despite the uniqueness of individual life, autobiographies collectively reveal recursive 'patterns of experience': to my mind, these factors suggest the need to propose investigative processes for examining patterns of experience that bridge the traditional anthologised biographical collection and the new forms that are scattered across cyberspace. In *The Selfish Gene* (1976), Richard Dawkins likened the gene to the meme: a unit of human cultural transmission, the meme acts as a mutating replicator within human cultural evolution. While this is a familiar discourse in the digital humanities, I offer a reconsideration of mimetic theory in life-writing through the process of tracing memes and social media posts; in doing so, I redefine recursiveness in life-writing and the relationship between collective and individual identities in digital spaces.

Royle posits a theory of literature centred on 'veering,' which considers writing and reading as an act centred on change, vacillation, and turning, and it thus provides a new way of thinking about the instabilities of biography and identity (Royle, *Veering* viii). Further to Royle's findings, it could be suggested that 'veering' provides a theoretical basis for considering the use of blinking, oscillating GIFs (graphics interchange format) in life-writing and for establishing a critical framework for analysing the fragmented, shifting life-writing practices that occur in the digital space. GIFs are suitable only for short animations; the sequential framing invites juxtapositions and humorous contrasts or exaggerations. By reflecting on how performed identities are built through the digital space, the learner writer builds on their skills. For example, Dennis Cooper's use of the GIF to write an experimental novel models an entirely new form of digital life-writing and serves to show how, by curating a GIF biography, the aspiring writer can experiment with the limits and interactions of language, image, and movement in writing lives and in so doing gain the opportunity to explore an entirely new way of thinking about digital life-writing.

Evelyn Hinz points in her 1992 essay 'Mimesis: The Dramatic Lineage of Auto/Biography' to the problem of mimesis in life-writing and the continual question of the relationship between subjective experience and narrative. Hinz argues that 'auto/biography' is teleological in nature and so 'accords with Aristotle's definition of a good plot as one wherein the end arises inevitably out of the beginning' (202). Taking this into account leads one to suspect that experimenting with memes and GIFs could encourage the developing writer to consider a number of facets— for instance, where narrative and meaning begins and how writers and readers transition from one to the next. Questions arise: Is life-writing inherently teleological, or can learner writers act as digital prospectors, unearthing the fragment they need from cyberspace in an almost archae-ological process and so help to redefine the practice of life-writing? If life-writing narratives 'unfold' as Hinz posits and the author of the life-writing utters the would-be or potential self and so in the process discovers the latent self, how can searching for GIFs and memes become a part of this discovery? Can learner writers find methods of reimagining the spaces that are both literal and suggestive in the gap between individual GIFs and memes? How is latency articulated in the blink of a GIF?

In this chapter, I advocate for a critical re-examination of the life-writing practices that emerge in digital spaces, a re-examination that encourages learner writers to play with this assumed ephemerality to produce a text that concretises a narrative in GIF and meme form but that at the same time links the narrative to a chain of replication of use that connects to several other stories. The looser connection between form, word, and meaning suggested by the GIF and the meme also opens the developing writer to the possibility of rethinking the gaps, fissures, and instabilities between what is said, what is unsaid, and what is understood between life-writer and reader.

Samuel Johnson's gifts to the future

When lexicographer, biographer, author, and journalist Samuel Johnson first anthologised fifty-one minibiographies of poets esteemed in the 18th century in his multivolume work collectively titled *The lives of the most eminent English poets, with critical observations on their works/by Samuel Johnson*, he called the act of miniature life-writing a 'minute kind of history' (i; Hamilton 85): According to Johnson's friend and biographer James Boswell, the author once wrote to him to say that he was engaged in writing 'little lives, and little Prefaces, to a little edition' (Boswell 149), an enterprise that had been 'set in motion by a consortium of London booksellers' (Pritchard 25). The tradition of brief life-writing can in fact be traced back to early medieval hagiography; however, Johnson is usually considered to be the philosopher-father of modern literary biography, because he broke new ground in the field of life-writing. Although best-known for producing the first English dictionary, as a life-writer, Johnson insisted that should an author '[profess] to write A Life, he must represent it really as it was,' thus moving away from idealised, hagiographical description of patrons and the patrons' preferred subjects (i–ii). In the advertisement accompanying the anthology, Johnson suggests a practice of life-writing that is spontaneous and fragmented and one that is centred on writing quickly and instinctively. Short biographical writing was an 'undertaking [that] was occasional and unforeseen,' and as an author, Johnson

> must be supposed to have engaged in it with less provision of materials than might have been accumulated by longer premeditation. Of the later writers at least I might, by attention and inquiry, have gleaned many particulars, which would have diversified and enlivened my biography. These omissions [are] now useless to lament. (i–ii)

The intensity of smallness offers its own particular challenges to the life-writer in the negotiation between selection and omission. Johnson approached the task with the misapprehension that it was neither 'very extensive [nor] difficult' to produce this 'minute kind of history,' although he then confesses his error on both counts (ii). In the 21st century, brevity and instantaneity have only intensified in life-writing practices. However, this suggestion of transience is countered by the significant life-writing practices that emerge online that memorialise and commemorate lost and past lives. Facebook pages and Twitter feeds become sites of active memorialisation, which not only record the passing of moments but also moments of passing—even the point of dying. Even so, in the present day, the digital sphere, and social media in particular, also offers new short forms, new spaces, and new resources for the experimental life-writer.

The point of brevity in life-writing

Most writers now actively participate in some form of life-writing prac-tice on a daily—even hourly—basis via Tweets and posts, which can contain the visual, the textual, or both. Facebook posts, Tweets, posts on Reddit, Tinder and Grindr profiles, YouTube comments and confes-sionals, digital diary apps, and personal websites turn life-writing into a frequently instantaneous, viral, and fragmented act yet one that is also wound into others' experiences across multiple platforms (Papacharissi). Skeins of commenters knot together across cyber space as people share the same few square inches of screen while divided by continents: physical strangers are compelled into a facsimile of digital intimacy as bloggers, posters, and commenters redefine relationality as an unstable, active, and proliferating process. This brief, undefined, and relational selfhood is iterated in the writing and posting practices that take place in cyberspace.

If brevity and life-writing have had a long and intimate association, following on from this, a more recent investigation of the use of brevity in creative writing can be seen in Royle's experiments with 'quick fic-tions': Royle's ideas, that quickness can be lively, vigorous, agile, and per-ceptive, serve to demonstrate that brevity in life-writing can also promote and enhance the sensitivity and vulnerability of the 'quick flesh' of 'quick fictions' and the sharp, refined, delicate, yet almost surgical precision of the act of writing (Royle, 'Quick Fiction' 23). Brevity is concise and terse but also signals brief lapses of time, in the sense of a small passage of time—a few frames—and the speed of brief writing. Thus, brevity is the watchword for much of digital acts of life-writing, because the documenting of everyday lives has migrated from the page to the digital spaces of social media platforms.

The post, the meme, the graphics interchange format

The post, the meme, and, in particular, the GIF are visual-textual inter-faces and modes of self-representation. GIFs are short animated video clips that are shared online: a bitmap image format with a limited colour pal-ette of 256 colours, which can be animated through constructing several sequential frames. Due to the use of a limited palette and pixilation, GIFs tend to display sharp graphics but low-resolution videos and photo images. The videos are usually clips from television shows, documentaries, films, or popular or unusual YouTube videos: GIFs are brief, just a few frames, and the clip is looped so that the GIF endlessly replays a small section of video. Typically, GIFs are used as avatars in forums—thus acting as a substitute or alternative identity or self—or are sent in messenger services or are posted on comments in online forums and on social media to communicate reactions or emotions. For example, Facebook God, a left-of-centre atheist, shares his views with a congregation of nearly four million digital subscribers as he comments on global politics. His posts on topics such as socialised healthcare, terrorism, and gun atrocities frequently attract GIF reactions among his followers. By collecting, curating, and reflecting on such forms of social media communications—that is, forms that relay and invite reactions and emotions to and in the viewer/reader—as GIFs, life-writers can ask questions about the limits of language, fragmentary experience, and the complexity of writing the self in the era of the digital human. In placing digital practice in conversation with the tradition of the art of short life-writing, life-writers can investigate smallness and instantaneity in new ways and can develop innovative methods that explore the fluidity and indeterminacy of the 21st-century self.

The rise of technology asks questions about whether the human factor in artificial intelligence remains a predominant, definite unit: computer languages, cybernetics, the rise in robotics, and the emergence of cyborg technology contribute to the advent of the posthuman moment (Hayles; Braidotti). Cyberspace is a digital landscape of memory and experience, inviting fresh thinking on the relationship between memory, life-writing, and selfhood, while the dependence of humans on material things and technological innovation have not only underpinned but also altered the evolution of humankind from its earliest development (Wolfe xxiv–xxvi; MacCormack). The technological advances in cybernetics and robotics are catalysing this dependence into ever-closer symbiosis. The materiality of digital visual media has led to new forms of storytelling and new formations of subjectivity, articulated through the concept of automediality: a term used by Sidonie Smith and Julie Watson to describe new developments in autobiography in the works of Jorg Dunne, Christian Moser, and other European scholars of life-writing (Smith and Watson 168). Automediality describes the way in which subjectivity is constructed online through combinations of visual and textual media. Historically, autobiography has tended to be understood as a process by which the human mind and memory act as a repository for the self, which itself is a discrete entity; autobiography also proposes, even supposes, the primacy of human culture (Gusdorf). However, influenced by poststructuralism, new methodologies such as automediality, auto/biography, and postmodern life-writing practices are able to interrogate and contest these imagined certainties of discrete selfhood, resulting in a methodology that is discursive in principle and practice (Baena). In doing so, the humanist conviction of the existence of a discrete self collapses into an abstracted, undefined, and unstable morass of fallible subconsciousness: nature, culture, mind, memory, language, and perception co-produce an awareness of existence in relation to others rather than a concrete and coherent individual self.

Processes of life-writing that Smith and Watson discuss include the autographic or graphic memoir, which offers 'at once an effect of amplification and simplification' (169); performance or visual art, in which a memory museum exhibits 'material artefacts [that] attest to authentic citation of her past' (174); autobiographical film and video or autodocumentary, which can be 'a highly personal, fragmentary form of collage' (181); and an online life, which suggests a shared identity and experience, with a view of the self as 'flexible, responsive and dynamic' and as under surveillance, subject to self-surveillance and exposed to voyeurism (184). The automediality in the production of GIFs, memes, and posts lies in these media's use in transmitting the feelings, reactions, and responses of the individual poster. Such responsiveness and dynamism define transmission in and across these media, which suggests the vigour and virality of a selfhood and identity beyond the merely human. With it arrive associations of movement and mutation, since the cyber human is both mutant and mutation: a fragmenting and fragmented self moving across multiple platforms and between GIF, video, comments section, blog, post, and meme. The self is an exploded collage scattered across various substrata of cyberspace. The posthuman moment documents the nexus between technology and humanity as it becomes ever-more intimate: if the life-writer is supposed to discover, or uncover, the latent self and is tasked to articulate the inchoate voice, then the practice must evolve and mutate in symbiosis with the transformations in documenting and transmitting the self, experience, and identity. The term *latency* is peculiarly transhuman: the state of existing but not yet being manifest, the cornerstone of Freudian psychotherapy, also refers to the digital delay before a transfer of data begins following an instruction for its transfer. Thus, the ongoing cyborgisation of humans as they digitally upload and transmit aspects of themselves and their identity generates a kind of 'digital immortality' (Sandberg and Bostrom 5). Consequently, a strange comorbidity exists between digital dynamism and a cybernetic ossification: the self is preserved and memorialised in perpetuity in a digital footprint yet also fragments and proliferates uncontrollably through likes, retweets, and reposts across multiple digital platforms. The telos of this posthuman moment could even extend to the transfer of the brain's mind pattern onto a different substrate: a process called uploading, which could allow individuals not only to transfer their existence to a more durable substrate but also to roam cyberspace without any clearly defined physical boundaries (Paul and Cox; Hauskeller 'My brain,' *Better Humans?*; O'Connell; Gutkind).

Although some suggest that the transhuman is an intermediary state before reaching the posthuman (Pepperell; Kaplan), I suggest that transhumanity can be understood as distinct from posthumanity. The transhuman is the continually changing or mutating human and human condition or existence, with concomitant suggestions of hybridity and cyborgisation, whereas the posthuman suggests a state beyond the human. The transhuman does not necessarily manifest or mutate to a state of posthumanity. This collision between motion, mutation, and their contrary—stasis—is captured in the unit of a blinking, oscillating GIF.

The graphics interchange format and the gap

Only suitable for short animations, the GIF is limited to mere seconds of animation or to low-resolution film clips, which are brief lapses of time: a few frames of film. Perpetual motion is contradictorily framed narrowly and statically as these looped videos veer and repeat, visualising latency in the blink of a GIF. Cooper's experimental GIF novel models an entirely new and literary way of thinking about these units of communication. His work shows how writers, including life-writers, can experiment with the limits of and interactions between language, image, and movement. These factors would seem to imply that GIFs can be metaphors and tools for the fragmented, shifting life-writing practices that can occur in any form but particularly in digital space. The GIF offers a narrow frame of meaning, bounded by the clearly defined edges of the video rhomboid, the spatial borders as distinct as precisely measured time frames. However, the GIF itself has neither end nor beginning: it is a super-short video that exists in perpetual loop. Hinz may suggest that 'auto/biography' is teleological in nature and that 'the end arises inevitably out of the beginning,' but life-writing that uses GIFs literally and figuratively automates biography into perpetual motion. The GIF veers disconcertingly, disorientingly: the eye may encounter the GIF mid-loop as the video fragment

swerves and lurches at a speed set by the GIF's creator, perhaps deceler-
ating movement until the actors are jerky marionettes or quickening it
to a flickering blur. The GIF veers: it is off-centre, veering away from
anthropocentric, logo-centric, egocentric or subject-centred motifs, a
process that is disruptive and dangerous as 'the sense of the haphazard,
or unpredictable, non-teleological de-centring … [that] haunts this little
word [veer]' (Royle, *Veering* 69). In experimenting with GIFs, writers distil and de-still their writing practice. For the life-writer, what life-writing
is comes under scrutiny: life-writing, one assumes, must be anthropocentric or egocentric; reveal some latent logos of existence; or share the subject
of a life; however, the viral GIF innervates a rete of replication through
cyberspace, creating an *unbodiment*: an infected tissue of tissuelessness
that nonetheless transmits—and mutates—human experience, reaction,
and emotion.

As a tool to uncover new arenas in which to explore posthuman existence and experience by participating in the quotidian life-writing practices of the average social media user, the search engine Giphy.com is
uniquely transhuman in its use as a tool for discovering and curating GIF
life-writing. The search engine's design origins germinated from a discussion that Giphy.com's founder Alex Chung had with his co-founder,
Jace Cooke, about the future of language and analytic philosophy and
how humans communicate with and beyond words (Chung; Crook).
Chung and Cooke's use of the term *humanist search engine* implies a
believer in or agent of humanism: the algorithm is gaining humaneness
at the same time as human agency, and the search engine also gains or
has sympathetic concern with and for human needs, interests, and wel-
fare. In theory, the humanist search engine places humans, or humanity
as a whole, at its centre and stresses the inherent value and potential
of human life, yet in the symbiosis between human and machine, or
human and algorithm, there is as much displacing and disembodying as
there is sympathetic conjoining. The GIF-specific search engine Giphy.
com is the one most commonly used in social media communication,
as it is linked via Facebook and WhatsApp. During the development
of Chung and Cooke's site, they began to regard GIFs as a language of
small vocabularies and idiomatic expressions, not least because GIFs take
major pieces of visual culture and turn them into a truncated lexicon of
emotion and reaction (Chung). In his vision for the future of cyberspace,
Chung shared his belief that the GIF would generate 'another level of
expression of humanity' as still images across the Internet will ultimately
be replaced by moving images (Chung). In particular, Chung declared

the Internet to be a 'sterile' place and declared that he regards the role of the GIF as desterilising, fertilising, and animating the Internet, transmitting units of emotion and cultural exchange that will not just supplement but revolutionise human communication: Chung, prophet of cyborgisation, determines that 'We all know that this world is coming' (Chung). For example, Giphy.com live giffed the Oscars for the first time in 2016 (Chung). Giphy.com's moment-by-moment productions resulted in a GIF that became one of the most shared media images of that year: a little unit of cultural and emotional transmission captured an interaction between the singer Lady Gaga and actor Leonardo di Caprio, who was recorded shifting from amusement to guilty annoyance.

This supposed revolution in communication and in the relationship between human and cyberspace invites further scrutiny. Chung and Cooke built their search engine with the goal of creating the first 'humanist' search engine in order to challenge the predominance of Google's method of creating algorithm-only search engines (Chung; Crook). At Giphy.com, they maintain a staff who curate a digital library of GIFs (Depp). The search engine represents the intersection between mathematical algorithm and human response as the company uses human and machine together in the mammoth task of relating images via tags and in the laborious process of eliminating tag spam. It is this practice of tag spam that allows spam generators to try to spread advertising or malicious content through popular tags which are not related to the content that the spam generators are sharing. The humanist search engine blurs the distinction between automated generation and the curated, cultivated acquisition and management practices of a traditional librarian. The physical library and the embodied librarian have been displaced— and disembodied—by the humanist search engine. However, to create a 'humanist,' or perhaps more accurately *posthumanist* or *transhumanist*, approach to constructing and managing a vast library of GIFs, Giphy. com has built its own custom 'web crawler.'

All Internet search engines, from Google to Giphy, depend on a web crawler, a sinister gothic monstrosity of an automated programme or script that methodically scans or 'crawls,' insectoid and devouring, through web pages to harvest an index of the data that it has been tasked to look for, a process also known as web crawling or spidering. Here, posthumanist mutation is monstrous. Giphy.com uses its own custom and trademarked crawler code of many thousands of lines, which the company continues to develop and refine; by comparison, the following example of a mere twelve lines of code creates a basic Python crawler that searches for URLs (uniform resource locator, a reference to or address for a resource on the Internet). Crawlers are also known by equally sinister science fiction terms as ants, automatic indexers, bots, web spiders, web robots, or web scutters and are provided under programme names such as Heritrix, Pavuk, Arachnode.net, or pycreep. It is this kind of didactic script writing that underpins the writer's search for GIFs when using the Giphy.com search engine, a tool that is ubiquitous and quotidian in its worldwide use in messenger services and social media, yet the fabric of the crawler, or even knowledge of the crawler's existence, is largely unknown to the majority of users:

```
import re, urllib
textfile = file('depth_1.txt','wt')
print 'Usage - "phocks.org/stumble/creepy/"
myurl = input("@> ")
for  i  in  re.findall('"href=["'](.["']+)["']"',  urllib.urlopen(myurl).
    read(), re.I):
    print i
    for  ee  in  re.findall('"href=["'](.["']+)["']"',  urllib.urlopen(i).read(),
        re.I):
        print ee
        textfile.write(ee+'\n')
textfile.close()
```

The crawler script is an unreadable and alien reading experience for the uninitiated. The robotisation of our daily lives is a hidden, half-known neo-language, which is written into the software of the devices that sit in our pockets and is written into our cars, our computers, and even our kettles. The inclusion of speech marks indicates a revolution in language and communication that has been intensifying for the past forty years as human instruction becomes digital action. The crawler makes strange familiar words (text, file, import, print, find all, open, read, write, file, close, my) through chopped spacing and spliced words and in their alien collocations with symbols, including parentheses, arrowheads, and at signs. Gaps and fissures break open, and words are grafted together, becoming newly animated in their splicing. Consequently, for the life-writer, the GIF and GIF search engine are tools and agents of transhumanism. The looser connection between form, word, and meaning suggested by the GIF also opens the life-writer to the possibility of rethinking the gaps and instabilities between what is said, what is unsaid, and what is understood, particularly in the relationship between life-writer and reader.

Aided by an invisible crawler, as the writer seeks GIFs, memes, or social media posts, they act as digital prospectors, unearthing fragments of human existence and experience across cyberspace in a digitised equivalent of an archaeological process. When someone acts as a digital prospector for GIFs by using the search engine Giphy.com, each search term produces tessellated scrolls of looped video fragments: a kind of animated graphic novel of nonsense that had been curated and constructed by using a web crawler. The images that are curated through this web crawler are supposedly congruous, yet the life-writer may excavate surprising meanings and representations of meanings. For example, in the search for just two words, *life + writing*, the visual representation of *life* as a GIF typically, and antonymically, is of *despair* and *death*: GIFs of pretended suicide (hands turned into guns and pointed at the head, or ironic hanging); office workers spinning listlessly in their chairs; animated images of collapsing on the floor or jumping out of windows overlaid with the text 'I'm done.' The GIF life is a brief yet endless parade of failure and suffering that is mediated or punctured by the humour of the GIF form and the often comic origins of the clips. Popular sources of GIFs include television sitcom shows such as *How I Met Your Mother* and *The Office* and viral animal videos. For example, a clip of a dog mowing down a child has been turned into a GIF and tagged as a visualisation of 'Me' being mown down by 'Life.'[1]

The irreverent bathos of these human failures detracts from the fundamental scepticism at the heart of these GIFs. The advent of the posthuman moment is not leading to an inexorably good revolution in the sensibility of cyberspace or to its fertilisation and gestation into something more humanlike in the manner Chung suggests. The GIF is not a facilitator of optimum posthuman communication, nor does it transcend language. Rather the GIF articulates what is being lost in the pre-cyborg human experience. The price of transference to the digital is to become increasingly cabined and confined, trapped in recursive interactions with machines. Already, the archivist of the 21st century must confront the fact that human experience and its history is now recorded in digital and not analogue forms. So the GIF iterates the plugged-in experience of the modern human, whose gaze is locked to the few square inches of slick glass and plastic in their hands and the happy sedation swiping its surface brings. The latency of the blink of the GIF suggests humanity on the threshold of becoming an automaton as much as it is automating: so the seemingly spontaneous motion of the GIF automates biographical writing.

A search via Giphy.com for *life + writing* reveals a GIF that depicts a squiggled black line, subtitled 'MY LIFE.'[2] Without pen or hand, the scribbled line expands and contracts, and the inscription 'MY LIFE' quivers with a suggestion of appearing and disappearing that is never fully realised. The automated GIF is an automaton: an automatic disordering of scribbles that perhaps were once produced organically but were more likely created by a computer script that wrote the GIF to produce a facsimile of handwriting. As humans are cyborgised, so the digital can be humanised, or at least coded to look human. In contrast to the appearance of activity suggested in the scribbled line, there is an odd passivity integral to the production of this metaphor. The life is being written, but by whom and for what reason and to what end is unknown. The metaphor thus generates the strange and melancholic reality of the experience of disorder and of life out of control: chaos and disorder seemingly spontaneous, their point of origin indiscernible.

The blink of the GIF disturbs and disorientates as it jerks and loops in mechanical dance, the speed set by the human hand of the GIF maker, who has sent the GIF out into the ether of cyberspace to veer and repeat endlessly and alone until another initiates the web crawler that collates and curates a series of related GIFs in the individual's search for the apt or the surprising. The GIF self-writes and self-produces meaning; it writes the process into the self. The GIF is not just a potential source for the autographic process: it is an autographic. Autography is concerned not necessarily with the 'project of unfolding life events but rather with consciously writing the self into each life process itself' (Baena, 33). What is being brought into being is mediated not through language but through a unit of culture. Automediation combines the self with self-producing and with the uncertainty of origin implied by the prefix *auto*, and the root verb *to mediate* suggests bringing about, conveyance, and intervention.[3] When the GIF is unearthed by the life-writer, the GIF becomes newly animated, oscillating with narrative and biographical potential.

In summation, the GIF is a unit of culture and a unit of meaning, and the life-writer can tessellate these units into a digital collage of the self. The GIF collages and automediates all the pieces that might be self in this moment into a transhuman experience of cyber-reality. It self-produces but also brings about intervention and disruption. It is mutable and mutating. There is no connective tissue between the elements of the collage, except the meaning that the viewer derives from watching in an uneasy and dislocating experience of endless movement and strange compression of time and space as images circle, appear, and disappear and as meaning becomes ever-more slippery and as narrative collapses. For the life-writer, the automediality of creating short GIF lives and the automediation of experience that occurs in the process of uncovering and curating a GIF life articulates the threshold, the latency of about to be, between the organic and artificial, between human and machine, between the narrated and the curated, and between auto and biography.

 ACTIVITY

Writing tasks for practice

1. Begin with a critical examination of traditional 'short' biographies from Samuel Johnson's *Lives of the Most Eminent English Poets*. Other examples you may wish to use include obituaries and the *Oxford Dictionary of National Biography*.

   How does Johnson begin each life? How does he use the authors' bibliographies?

   How do writers of obituaries and other short biographies employ anecdote and digression?

2. Write micro- and quick-fiction autobiographies of fifty to three hundred words, with a reflection on what and how a life is narrated in such small spaces. What aspects of narrative are included, and which are omitted? What factors shape the decision-making process?

3. Explore your archive of old social media posts and tweets. What do you learn about spontaneous and/or deliberate acts of life-writing? Do any surprising narratives emerge?

4. Look at the preface of Dennis Cooper's *Zac's Haunted House GIF Novel*. 2015. (www.kiddiepunk.com/zacshauntedhouse/index. html). The preface is the author's introduction to a literary work, which usually addresses the origin of the story or concept and perhaps how that idea developed during the writing of the work. Two GIFs feature in the preface: an automaton and a flickering image of a pair of blood-red eyes opening. What meaning does the reader derive from these images? How does the animation of the GIFs affect the reading experience?

5. Using a search engine such as Giphy.com, curate a GIF or meme biography or autobiography in which a life is told through 'found' social media posts, GIFS, or memes. Do not write posts or make GIFs or memes to suit your own purposes.

Recommended Reading

Baena, Rosalia. *Transculturing Auto/Biography: Forms of Life Writing.* Routledge, 2013.

Braidotti, Rosi. *The Posthuman.* John Wiley & Sons, 2013.

Cooper, Dennis. *Zac's Haunted House GIF Novel* (2015) www.kiddiepunk.com/zacshauntedhouse/index.html.

Einhaus, Ann-Marie, editor. *The Cambridge Companion to the English Short Story*, edited by Ann-Marie Einhaus. U Cambridge P, 2016.

Gusdorf, Georges. 'Conditions and limits of autobiography,' in *Autobiography: Essays Theoretical and Critical*, edited by James Olney, pp. 28–48. U Princeton P, circa 1980.

Gutkind, Lee. *Almost Human: Making Robots Think.* W. W. Norton & Company, 2010.

Hayles, N. Katherine. *How We Became Posthuman: Virtual Bodies in Cybernetics, Literature, and Informatics.* U Chicago P, 2008.

Hinz, Evelyn J. 'Mimesis: The dramatic lineage of auto-biography,' in *Essays on Life Writing: From Genre to Critical Practice*, edited by Marlene Kadar, pp. 195–212. U Toronto P, 1992.

Kadar, Marlene, editor. *Essays on Life Writing: From Genre to Critical Practice*, edited by Marlene Kadar. U Toronto P, 1992.

Olney, James, editor. *Autobiography: Essays Theoretical and Critical*, edited by James Olney. U Princeton P, 1980.

Pepperell, Robert. 'Posthuman and Extended Experience.' *Journal of Evolution and Technology,* vol. 14, April 2005. jetpress.org/volume14/pepperell.html.

Royle, Nicholas, editor. *Veering: A Theory of Literature.* Edinburgh UP, 2011.

 Works Cited

Baena, Rosalia. *Transculturing Auto/Biography: Forms of Life Writing.* Routledge, 2013.

Boswell, James. *The Life of Samuel Johnson, by James Boswell*, edited and abridged with an introduction and notes by Christopher Hibbert. New York: Penguin Classics, 1986. (Original title: *The Life of Samuel Johnson, LL.D. by James Boswell, Esq.* London: Printed by Henry Baldwin for Charles Dilly, 10 Apr. 1791.)

Braidotti, Rosi. *The Posthuman.* John Wiley & Sons, 2013.

Chung, Alex. 'In Conversation with Jemima Kiss.' Jemima Kiss and Alex Chung—Centre Stage Collision 2016. *Collision Conference*. New Orleans, April 2016. Uploaded by Collision Conference on May 2016. videos. websummit.net/speakers/Alex_Chung_Jemima_Kiss.html. Accessed 8 Nov. 2017.

Collision Conference. 'Ten thousand words-Alex Chung of Giphy & Jemima Kiss of the Guardian.' *YouTube*. Uploaded by Collision Conference on 5 May 2016. www.youtube.com/watch?v=1H3-_qFbp0M www.youtube.com/channel/UC6MiQVyK_WaFLU5vlT2b8A. Accessed 8 Nov. 2017.

Cooper, Dennis. *Zac's Haunted House GIF Novel*. 2015. www.kiddiepunk.com/zacshauntedhouse/index.html. Accessed 10 Oct. 2017.

Crook, Jordan. 'Jace Cooke: Giphy Gif Search Engine Rolls Out Private Artist Profiles to Help Organize, Monetize The Gif Community.' Oath Tech Network, 2013–2018. Tech Crunch, 23 May 2013. techcrunch.com/tagjacecooke/. Accessed 8 Nov. 2017.

Dawkins, Richard. *The Selfish Gene*. U Oxford P, 1976.

Depp, Michael, editor. "Giphy's Chung wants to build 'The first humanist search engine.'" *NetNewsCheck*, 28 Apr. 2016. www.netnewscheck.com/article/50056/giphys-chung-wants-to-build-the-first-humanist-search-engine www.netnewscheck.com/tag/alex-chung www.netnewscheck.com/tag/collision-2016. Accessed 8 Nov. 2017.

Egan, Susanna. *Patterns of Experience in Autobiography*. 1984. New ed. U North Carolina P, 2011.

Einhaus, Ann-Marie. editor. 'Introduction,' in *The Cambridge Companion to the English Short Story*, edited by Anne-Marie Einhaus, pp. 1–11. U Cambridge P, 2016.

Gusdorf, Georges. 'Conditions and limits of autobiography,' in *Autobiography: Essays Theoretical and Critical*, edited by James Olney, pp. 28–48. U Princeton P, circa 1980.

Gutkind, Lee. *Almost Human: Making Robots Think*. W. W. Norton & Company, 2010.

Hamilton, Nigel. *Biography: A Brief History*. U Harvard P, 2009.

Hauskeller, Michael. 'My brain, my mind, and I: Some philosophical assumptions of mind-uploading.' *Journal of Machine Consciousness*, vol. 4, no. 1, 2012, pp. 187–200.

———. *Better Humans?: Understanding the Enhancement Project*. Routledge, 2014.

Hayles, N. Katherine. *How We Became Posthuman: Virtual Bodies in Cybernetics, Literature, and Informatics*. U Chicago P, 2008.

Hinz, Evelyn J. 'Mimesis: The dramatic lineage of auto-biography,' in *Essays on Life Writing: From Genre to Critical Practice*, edited by Marlene Kadar, pp. 195–212 . U Toronto P, 1992.

Johnson, Samuel. *The lives of the most eminent English poets, with critical observations on their works/by Samuel Johnson*. First separate English ed. London: Printed for C. Bathurst et al., 1781. (Originally published as the first ten volumes of *The works of the English poets*. London: Printed for C. Bathurst et al., 1779.)

———— (1779–81). *Lives of the Most Eminent English Poets: in One Volume*. Wolf Den Books, 2006.

Kaplan, David. *Readings in the Philosophy of Technology*. Rowman & Littlefield, 2009.

MacCormack, Patricia. *Posthuman Ethics: Embodiment and Cultural Theory*. Ashgate, 2012.

O'Connell, Mark. *To Be a Machine: Adventures among Cyborgs, Utopians, Hackers, and the Futurists Solving the Modest Problem of Death*. Granta Books, 2017.

Oxford Dictionary of National Biography. 1st ed. Reprint, edited by Colin Matthew and Brian Harrison. U Oxford P, 2007.

Papacharissi, Zizi, editor. *A Networked Self: Identity, Community, and Culture on Social Network Sites*. Routledge, 2010.

Paul, G. S., and E. D. Cox. *Beyond Humanity: Cyber Evolution and Future Minds*. Charles River Media, 1996.

Pepperell, Robert. 'Posthuman and Extended Experience.' *Journal of Evolution and Technology*, vol. 14, April 2005. jetpress.org/volume14/pepperell.html. Accessed 3 May 2018.

Pritchard, William H. "Johnson's 'lives.'" *The Hudson Review*, vol. 60, no. 1, Spring 2007, pp. 25–35. *JSTOR* www.jstor.org/stable/2046460. Accessed 3 May 2018.

Royle, Nicholas. 'Quick fiction: Some remarks on writing today.' *Mosaic*, vol. 47, no. 1, 2014, pp. 23–29.

———— editor. *Veering: A Theory of Literature*. U Edinburgh P, 2011.

Smith, Sidonie, and Julia Watson. 'The visual-verbal-virtual contexts of life narrative,' in *Reading Autobiography: A Guide for Interpreting Life Narratives*, edited by Louis Castner, 2nd ed., pp. 167–92. U Minnesota P, 2010.

Stewart, David. 'Romantic short fiction,' in *The Cambridge Companion to the English Short Story*, edited by Anne-Marie Einhaus, pp. 73–86. U Cambridge P, 2016.

Wolfe, Carey. *What Is Posthumanism?* U Minnesota P, 2010.

Notes

1. See media.giphy.com/media/17XAjPucc8Qda/giphy-downsized.gif [Accessed 10 October 2017]
2. See giphy.com/gifs/life-photography-scared-DvIaQ0DZcgV7a [Accessed 10 October 2017]
3. Greek αὐτο, meaning self, one's own, by oneself, independently; and αὐτός, meaning self, of uncertain origin.

9 BIOGRAPHICAL LYRIC: WRITING LIVES IN POEMS

Page Richards

One of the most beautiful and new shapes for writing lives comes from the oldest genre in English writing: lyric poetry. The landscape of lyric is always changing and so too are the materials for life-writing. Before the 18th century, idealised hagiographical descriptions of the exemplary or infamous life had long been the original benchmarks for meriting a life story. Lexicographer, journalist, and biographer Samuel Johnson extended the perimeters of biography to include interest in the history of nearly any life. In 1750 he famously wrote, 'I have often thought there has rarely passed a life of which a judicious and faithful narrative would not be useful' (S. Johnson, *The Rambler* LX): traditionally, modern English biographical writing is associated with prose and, in particular, with narrative. Modern-day biography, Hermione Lee explains, 'is a form of narrative,' carrying with it deep associations of journalism, detective stories, and even gossip (5). She adds, 'The telling of life-stories is the dominant narrative mode of our times' (17). Catherine N. Parke notes that 'the origins of biography and the novel are substantially allied'; there exists an expected and ongoing 'dispute' of near relations, whether of technique or interwoven elements (19). Ann Thwaite describes the kinship differently: biographers, she says, are not 'primarily fact-gatherers' but essentially storytellers, like fiction writers of plots (17). Eric Homberger and John Charmley put it plainly: 'Biographers share with novelists … a love affair with narrative' (xiii).

New forms

Writer, scholar, and teacher of life-writing Charles Johnson muses about how any culture or community overcomes an abiding inertia to find ways to tell new stories of their selves, and he asks, 'just what *is* a story?' (C. Johnson, 'The End' 33). Focusing on histories and biographies of black lives, which have become, he says, visibly outworn in our times, he wonders how we may find ways to update them ('The End' 42). In particular, he considers that the problem for the outworn story may lie as much in an era's outworn instruments as in anything else (Davis 807–19). He harbours mistrust of our accepted storytelling habits: 'One of the things that has happened with my practice is I have a suspicion of language and stories, a suspicion about the danger we can fall into with the stories we tell ourselves about ourselves' (Wilhelm): 'we must continuously' find ways to update our histories and tell new stories *of* ourselves *to* ourselves (Davis 807–19). To tell updated stories, he says, we often need new grammars or new vocabularies, new apparatus (C. Johnson, 'The End' 42), what he calls 'new forms of art' (C. Johnson, *Taming* 12). New instruments, he reasons, often open the way to begin reshaping our points of entry into history-making and to telling our stories afresh (Davis 807).

Recently in history, an important evolution of life-writing has been taking hold: 'biographical lyric.' Evidence of this new variation of species can be heard as subgenre pooling in the titles of major works such as Marilyn Nelson's *Carver: A Life in Poems* (2001) and Ruth Padel's *Darwin: A Life in Poems* (2009). These books of lyric poetry follow the publication in 1986 of the poet, novelist, and dramatist Rita Dove's *Thomas and Beulah*, which tells the lives of her maternal grandparents in what is sometimes called even a 'double biography,' a groundbreaking work in the field of life-writing.

Dove's book marks and changes the field of biography and lyric poetry. Her new experimental approach demonstrates contemporary elements of life-writing never before seen and offers a way to update time-worn approaches that we use for the telling of our stories. Speaking about the backstory for composing *Thomas and Beulah*, Dove discusses these new, and specifically lyric, possibilities for updating her life story. She 'felt [she] was moving,' she says, 'into a territory' that she was not 'quite sure of' but found 'immensely exciting'; and she grew to 'realize' that what she was 'trying to tell,' was 'not a narrative as we know narratives but actually the moments that matter most in our lives' (qtd. in Cavalieri 138; Dalley 11–15).

Exponential expansion in life-writing increasingly includes new and exciting primary and secondary work on intersections of poetry and biography. Emma Johnson writes in her 2017 review of *Truth and Beauty: Verse Biography in Canada, Australia and New Zealand* (2016) that 'the emerging cultural practice of verse biography sits on the cusp of becoming something in particular': 'The range of possibilities before the institution of a canon or genre settles, and the freedom this entails, is exciting to consider' (E. Johnson). Robert McGill remarks that this early collection of essays on the subject 'has only scratched the surface,' focusing as it does mainly on the 'long poem' and single-author studies (McGill). On such large shifting and still-undulating terrain, my focus here is on introducing intersections of biography with lyric poetry rather than, say, the 'long poem' or narrative poetry.

(Re)directing focus

The unexpected practices of biographical lyric are beginning to appear internationally, updating and acknowledging how lyric offers power to elicit and invent perspectives for 'telling' in constructing lives in this interdependent age of social media and geopolitical connections. Postcolonial reconstructions are remapping worldwide the economic, social, and discursive lines of power. Scholars and critics are widely and urgently (re) conceiving how a life, lives, or voices in the 'spaces between' are historically marginalised, or left out of (economic, cultural, political) representations. Forms such as the biographical lyric emerge as one of the many new paths for promulgating updated understandings of historical and cultural methodologies in relation to 'intersubjectivity.' Jessica Benjamin explains that 'The intersubjective view maintains that the individual grows in and through the relationship to other subjects' (19–20).

Dove's experiments forge from lyric poetry an instrument commonly resistant to not only narrative but individual representation, a new instrument for the biographical. Dove writes, 'I realize that we don't actually think of lives in very cohesive strands, but we remember as beads on a necklace: moments that matter to us come in flashes, and the connections are submerged .... So you have moments, and poems, which are complements of each other' (qtd. in Cavalieri 138).

Dove's emphasis on building a life story from a series of non-linear 'flashes' links, in her view, to an idea of memory as 'beads': beads of memory *like* poems themselves—a series of fragments or 'flashes,' potentially interchangeable (or at the least highly flexible) on a thread of time. Yet as historian of lyric and cultural historiographer Seth Lerer shows (129–141), lyric poems have no special stronghold on 'flashes,' non-linear sequencing, or 'submerged' connections, especially in the modern and postmodern eras of fiction, nonfiction, and life-writing. Narrative often plays out, and plays on, such temporal 'flashing' as well (Puckett). Dove's remark on lyric's essential non-linearity, however, touches on some-thing temporal even more clearly, closely, and historically linked to lyric poetry's patterns of practice, action, and identity—namely, temporal self-resistance.

Narrative biography, historically, has made the material of memory one of its many 'raw materials' towards the detective work of building a biographical case (Puckett). Following Dove's lead, one could recognise that contemporary understandings of memory point towards its unreli-ability and, in particular, its deceptive linear delivery; the neuroscientist Steven Rose asserts that contemporary findings of the brain ratify what we see explored across many disciplines: 'Historical 'reality' and biolog-ical 'reality' are not one and the same' (380). Further, he highlights that 'memories are highly dynamic and unstable records. Each time you seem to be 'remembering' an event, you are actually not re-membering the event itself but the last time you re-membered it' (380). This dynamism is pinned to discoveries that 'memory is not confined to a small set of neurons at all, but has to be understood as a property of the entire brain, even the entire organism' (383). This would suggest a biological and sys-temic understanding of 'subjectivity' and 'objectivity' forever tumultuous if conjoined (389).

On the huge spectrum of poetry, the lyric form is the least narrative and therefore, to a certain degree, the least expected for the biographical encounter. Mapping out important differences in major works of bio-graphical lyric (emerging as they do from a range of periods and social and cultural histories) plays an equal part in the process. Yet lyric poetry has never been considered an eligible instrument for telling either history or the lives of individual ordinary people.

Lyric poetry, on a broad stroke of instrument, looks canonically to the symbolic, the anonymous, and often the universal. The lyric has founda-tions in the traditional song and chorus, together with the longstanding complexities of witness, dancer, and singer. With few exceptions, the lyric poem has rarely been found to make rich intersections with the telling of history. Retaining a legacy going back to the classical era, lyric poetry in English is a renowned short and symbolic form; like epic poetry, long as it is, early lyric poetry relied on the formulaic, the universal, or the collective voice to fashion its stamp on history (Reece 48).

Speaking about crafting in *Thomas and Beulah*, Dove said she 'was consciously trying to put a narrative into short lyric poems—stringing the lyric moments one after the other like beads on a necklace'; she added, 'I was working the lyric moment against the narrative impulse, so that they would counterpoint each other' (Thomas). Dove notes that in the United States, 'there has been an unfortunate division between narrative poetry and lyric poetry': 'A good poem usually has both. A lyric may not have a traditional narrative line, but it all depends what you define as story' (Thomas).

The lyric

Lyric poetry references the classical melodic thread (*melos*) and the trope of immanent 'madness' in the works of canonical lyric poets of the era. As Alessandro Barchiesi states, 'The poetic genre' of lyric, from the classical period and onwards, 'is deeply involved' in the discourse, among others, of madness and illness (64). This thread is later evidenced in Renaissance mythography. For example, Theseus's lines in William Shakespeare's play *A Midsummer Night's Dream* underscore the inherited chasm located between lyric poetry and a human history of reason:

> Lovers and madmen have such seething brains,
> Such shaping fantasies, that apprehend
> More than cool reason ever comprehends.
> The lunatic, the lover, and the poet
> Are of imagination all compact:
> One sees more devils than vast hell can hold,
> ... the madman: the lover, all as frantic. (5.1.4–10)

This proverbial link, between poetry and madness, persistently configures the gesture of the iconic lyric poet, disengaged from argument, which many commonly associate with history in narrative. In such historical contexts for the 'telling' of lives, and especially an individual life, lyric poetry carries a legacy of being disqualified, so to speak, from making history. The lyric poem already carries forwards generic features (invocation of the atemporal, the allegorical, and the choral) that seem at odds with historical methodology. In the modern era, the telling of cause-and-effect relations in history, including life-writing (under history's large wing) has been dominated by prose. Without even a clear or historical association of agency (sometimes named a 'lyric voice,' 'speaker,' or 'subject'), lyric poetry, in contrast, has rarely been in the running for telling or making biography (Greene).

Thus, biographical lyric poetry breaks with auto/biography corridor text conventions and fundamentally breaks the conventions of bedding biography with narrative. It also breaks, in the modern age, what is considered as equally 'standard': lyric's tenuous associations with (if ever lyric was linked to life-writing, that is) the autobiographical. Lyric poems in the modern period increasingly establish a pattern of featuring the speaking subject 'I,' a first-person 'voice' often considered to stage a coherent consciousness and personhood, but nevertheless a projection of a first-person lyrical 'life' rather than a history of a 'life' or a history in narrative which associates with third-person biography. As Tim Dolin notes, 'The tension between aesthetic value and the value of authentic self-expression … is central to the Romantic and post-Romantic poets', and stirrings in poems by the Romantics—William Wordsworth, for example—are often ascribed to 'self-expression' or what is modernly ascribed as a cogent 'lyric subject,' the speaking 'I' (2).

In the earliest periods of English literature, secular lyric poetry features no such construction of an 'individual,' not to mention 'authorship.' Lerer describes lyric's roots as 'depersonalized forms that seek not the recovery of individuated voices but the verities of social statement and the ventriloquizings of the bardic' (130). Lerer says clearly that 'Few modern readers would find in the corpus of Old English the expected personal identity we seek in lyric poetry' (129). Reassessing secular lyric in the context of 'historical conditions' rather than modern lyric theory, however, Lerer reveals complex lyric roots in the contexts of communities that are neither individuated (on 'privacy of the domestic') nor 'anonymous,' as still often identified in modern readings of medieval poems (130, 132). In his surveys of post-Norman Conquest poems, he observes that poems are largely 'beset by the loss of language, landscape, and national institutions' (131). Lerer discovers lyric assemblies of voicing in post–Norman Conquest and early medieval poems: not 'just the outpourings of a lyric voice but an assessment of the idea of lyricality itself' (133). Importantly, he finds assemblies not simply of the elegiac, as often remarked of early lyric stance, but also of the 'metanostalgic,' already 'conscious of the pastness of its history' (141).

Meshing the autobiographical 'I'

'Subjectivity' and poetry have a long history. From Greek lyric poet Archilochus through to Robert Creeley's 2014 statement that, but for the dance of 'moving from A to B,' poetry 'has no purpose,' debates surrounding 'lyric subjectivity' remain historically connected to questions pertaining to lyric voice and lyric voicing, raising basic questions: In a poem, who is speaking? Who is listening? The philosopher Thomas Nagel is not alone in posing the question of 'subjectivity,' where 'point of view' transmogrifies to a 'point of viewing,' and the human 'subject,' considering the world as a 'whole,' may speak 'as if from nowhere' (Nagel 61). The intersubjective is opened out in Timothy Morton's encompassing eco-philosophy; 'all entities whatsoever are interconnected in an interobjective system that elsewhere I call *the mesh*' (83). Morton outlines an interconnectedness of being and objects in states of ever-becoming:

> Meshes are potent metaphors for the strange interconnectedness of things, an interconnectedness that does not allow for perfect, lossless transmission of information, but is instead full of gaps and absences. When an object is born it is instantly enmeshed into a relationship with other objects in the mesh. (83)

Poet Mark Strand puts this revision of 'master' narratives of connectedness and gaps, intersubjectivity and interobjectivity, more simply: in the first stanza of *Keeping Things Whole*, the speaker notes the personal 'I' as 'the absence/ ... of field' in a 'field.' In the second stanza, a public and more present body of 'I' begins to displace 'the air' as it 'moves'; then as the body steps forwards, the 'air' immediately closes ('moves in') to fill 'the spaces' where his body has 'been.' In the third stanza, after noting that everyone has a particular reason for moving, the speaker inextricably links the whole of 'I' to the hole of 'I,' ever mutually and perpetually interacting and productive:

> I move
> to keep things whole. (3.3–4)

Thus, one can look back to a poet like Dove, having a hunch, that there is an 'updated' instrument in lyric to be had not just for biography but for perceiving what we take to be (interconnected) 'lives' worth telling. Commenting on her poems, Dove says that dwelling in lyric 'to talk about the everyday, the ordinary lives of people who happen to be black was really something that hadn't been done, and I felt that this *was* important' (qtd. in Bourne).

Building a life story

The lyric poem structurally pulls comparatively backwards, as much as it drives forwards. The poet James Longenbach explains clearly that lyric poetry, including what we understand to be early oral poems, is identified by the following lines: 'The earliest surviving poetry in the Western tradition is organized in lines' (18). The 'line is what distinguishes our experience of poetry as poetry' (xi): 'We need at least two lines to begin to hear how the line is functioning' (28). Taking Donald Justice's poem 'Nostalgia and Complaint of the Grandparents,' Longenbach argues sonic undertow, the backwards sonic pull of any lyric action in English, while moving forwards on syntax:

> At the end of the penultimate line of the first stanza we emphasize the word 'dead' not only because of the enjamb-ment but because the syllable rhymes with 'spread' in the line preceding. The syntax urges us forward but the allure of sim-ilar sounds pulls us back. (20)

The implied family albums, the photos all 'outspread' to view, under-score the poet's refrain, which is at once his final point:

> *The dead*
> *Don't get around much anymore.* ('Nostalgia,' refrain)

This 'tension' of poetic lines produces a simultaneous and sonic 'disrup-tion,' again pulling backwards in sound on the very act of forging ahead syntactically. Thus, it can be suggested that lyric poems have long and formal structural associations with acts of self-resistance. This particular pattern carries on to working paradigms associated in history with poems (Booth). As Amittai F. Aviram notes a 'structure of paradox' makes up the 'core' of experience in lyric (2004). These types of elements that one hears in the lyric poem, suggest Kristin Hanson and Paul Kiparsky, occur on the very act of 'tightening' looseness, in a 'world beyond the control of the speaker it invokes' (40). Foundational self-resistance in lyric is argua-bly most recognisable in the lyric poem's inextricable ties with the topos of the ineffable, where language comments on the very act of its own irruption as immediate failure. This discursive action of self-resistance is key to lyric history. The trope that originates, in practice and spirit, with the failure of words to express adequately, has a history going back to the English lyric's earliest appearance (Curtius 159–62).

In the genre's earliest specimens, lyric historians found that very early fragments of lyric poetry from the post–Norman Conquest period, writ-ten at the time when England was in the process of rebuilding homes and structures that had been razed during the conquests, establish a pattern: a register of self-contradictory experience for being an exile-in-place, or at once 'not-at-home at home' (Lerer 135). Lyric lines of self-resistance reg-ister this displacement-in-place and begin to irrupt into a once-familiar and at the same time now-alien landscape (135):

Now your hall shall be built with the spade,
And you, wretch, shall be brought inside it;
Now all your garments shall be sought out,
Your house be swept and all the sweepings thrown out.[1]

In these utterances of dis-location, on location, a pattern of lyric stance in post–Norman Conquest verse emerges (Lerer 143): a state of temporal self-alienation happening-in-place, drawn from within the familiar 'hall,' the bodily 'house' (143). Lerer explains that this on-the-spot displacement of familiar building materials includes the materials of language itself: this interrupts old patterns of alliteration and reveals, in this early post–Norman Conquest lyric, the 'occasional bursts of personal feeling' (143). Lyricality comes into existence, then, through an immediacy of self-*re-view*, on the very instance of moving forwards, a perspective that Lerer underscores as a performance of *exile-in-place* (129–43).

As demonstrated in the poem above, lyric's prosodic hallmark of inner 'tension,' its simultaneous forwards and backwards motion, is already framed by, at least, two overlapping time frames, two overlapping bodies (Lerer 143). It is from this historical perspective of development that lyric distributes the experience of self-resistance and self-multiplication among competing experiences of time on a limited space (Lerer), so much so that one hears Longenbach's words: in lyric poetry, 'the notion of a speaker may or may not be useful'; the very material of a poem might feel more like a 'concatenation of various linguistic strands than like the utterance of a single person' (14). In major biographical lyric such as that pioneered by Dove in *Thomas and Beulah* (1986), one can see the emerging historical and prosodic perspectives on a potentially 'speaker-less' genre that offer an important key. A potentially 'speaker-less' genre, Longenbach suggests (14), provides unexpected invitations to 'telling' a life. To put it another way, on overlapping temporal frames of voices exiled-in-place, the new biographical lyric is at work, and the nature of that work is life-writing.

Rita Dove's *Thomas and Beulah*

In Thomas's story, 'The Event' (Dove 11), one immediately notices the details of 'self-resistance,' and 'exile-in-place,' when each of the two historical figures, Thomas and Lem, appear together in a biographical lyric in third-person:

Ever since they'd left the Tennessee ridge
with nothing to boast of. (1–2)

That is, all Thomas and Lem seemingly had at this stage were their 'good looks' and a 'mandolin' (3). As the poem opens, so too does Thomas's voice; not exactly *as* his voice, but displaced onto the note of silver 'falsetto' (7), backed by his friend Lem 'plucking' at his mandolin (6). The introduction of Thomas's body also opens not exactly as his own body but as deeply intertwined on a non-individuated prominent plural personal pronoun voice, 'they' (1): an inseparable presence from the other 'Negro,' Lem. Thomas's biographical lyric 'birth' strikes two time frames instantly, a before and an after experienced. The riverboat carrying Thomas moves forwards, while an immediate alienation from his friend's accident uproots him from his web of identity of the Tennessee ridge, from which he will never emerge as 'him-self.' His biographical lyric entrance identifies an act of self-alienation. In this opening, he is at once at home, inseparable, connected to Lem, where the 'falsett*o*' (emphasis added) strikes an auditory chord on the long *o* of mandolin, harking back to his song of home in Tennessee and part of Lem's world. Yet the falsetto simultaneously marks a Thomas exiled from his inseparability with his friend Lem, who 'stripped' (17), suddenly 'dove' overboard to swim (18), and drowned, leaving at Thomas's 'feet' (24) nothing more than Lem's clothes, 'a stinking circle of rags,' and the 'half-shell mandolin' where the boat's paddlewheel 'turned the water' (25–27) 'gently' (28). While the long *o* pulls back in sonic continuity, the syntax immediately carries forwards, towards the now 'half-shell' of the mandolin: now too the alienated, or exiled-in-place, 'half-shell' of Thomas.

In this passage, what I call lyric 'born retrospection' (where the time frames of before and after stage immediate self-alienation) intersects the biographical in two ways. It identifies this biographical lyrical subject, Thomas, and like subjects in biographical lyric, as figuring of 'thin skin.' Thomas is not Thomas. Where in the history of narrative biography we often consider individuated figures, this Thomas from the start in third-person biographical lyric is *not-Thomas*. In this, one hears an echo from perspectives of craft: poet Myung Mi Kim writes, 'Poetry is a site of *un*naming': 'Poetry produces new ways of participating in perception, thinking, historical being and becoming' (Keller 355).

Upon presentation, Thomas is joined on a thin skin of non-separabilities: in brief, he is inseparable from his friend Lem—he is one Negro among others, 'leaning' on the riverboat's rail, one singer of a communal song (4–7). The moment of his separation, a seeming moment of individuation, is the very same moment as his self-alienation. When Thomas is separated from his friend, his fellow Negro, and his instrument of song (all at the very moment of his entrance onto a scene of his inseparability from his many points of 'home'), he is no longer at home at home. He is a *second* version of a *not-Thomas*, one alienated from the first *not-Thomas*, who was once inseparable but whom he now no longer has the potential to experience. Thomas watches his separations enacted as Lem slips under the paddlewheel, 'dissolved' (21–23).

The alienation-in-place directs one to a *subject* Thomas—or, more accurately, the subject *not-Thomas*—as already potential 'material' for making biographical lyric in the first place. The figure of Thomas is theoretically and perpetually open to be chosen for the subject of narrative or lyric biography, or any form of life-writing.

Dove's grandmother's (Beulah's) childhood story, 'Taking in Wash' (Dove 47), is a third-person biographical lyric told from Beulah's perspective in retrospect. Dove's use of third-person technique in biographical lyric allows one to discern in Beulah's poem a simultaneous forwards-present/backwards-past movement and a pastness in the present and vice versa, a poetic double frame; two overlapping time frames, two overlapping bodies, a pattern of lyric as identified by Lerer in his analysis of Old English lyric (143), within Beulah's biographical lyric; and hence an element of Beulah's biographical history. Beulah's entrance/presence in, and the gateway into, her biographical lyric, is at once intertwined with and inseparable from that her father, 'Papa,' who nicknamed her 'Pearl' (1), when he came home 'swaying' in his drunkenness (2):

> Papa called her Pearl when he came home
> [drunk] (1)

Beulah/ 'Pearl's' 'Mama' names her 'Pearl,' as her 'Papa's girl' (6, 11). In Beulah/'Pearl's' biographical lyric, this separateness-cum-inseparability is made implicit and explicit: 'Papa' *came* home, and Beulah was *already* there, *at* home (1–2). These techniques act by defining clearly each of the figures in the work—Beulah, Beulah's mother ('Mama'), Beulah's father ('Papa'), and the 'ornery' family dog ('Sheba')—giving each their own distinctive characters, hence creating reader awareness of which of the figures is 'talking' at any one time, albeit through Beulah's perspective in a third-person biographical lyric.

Metaphorically—as well as 'literally' and historically, since Beulah is 'Papa's' daughter by birth—her mother ('Mama') ties the father and daughter together: one figure dependent on the other for voice, entrance, and presence in the biographical lyric. They are a family unit yet at the same time, in the poem and in actuality, separate beings. In her biographical lyric, Beulah, as a child, and her father's pride in being inseparable is obvious: she, Beulah, was 'Papa's' girl (11), his 'Pearl' from the opening of her biographical lyric (1). 'Tonight' (16), in the kitchen/ laundry room, she 'waits,' standing there 'until he turns' (19–21), and shows his fondness of her in 'his smile sliding all over' (21).

Similarly to Beulah, Dove's great-grandfather ('Pearl's' 'Papa') is introduced as inseparable. Beulah/'Pearl' is framed by 'Papa' in his nickname for her, and one immediately 'hears' this *thin skin* of inseparability ratified: 'She was Papa's girl' (11). Dove's great-grandfather, Beulah's 'Papa,' can identify himself as individuated only under the illusion of a drunken stupor: 'as if the wind touched only him' (2). His Cherokee blood equally belies any mystifications of individuation; it offers no impediment of inseparability with his daughter's oneness in being 'black as she was' (11). Thus, born retrospection begins for Beulah the moment of her entrance, and presence, into this very night, 'Tonight.' The linear tension and structural tension of born retrospection, which begins on a dream of herself screaming as a beast (12–16), pulls backwards in time on the word 'Once' and towards the linking verb 'was,' which on one hand connotes 'isness' on her being black (11) and on the other hand acts as a past/ present linking verb which propels her simultaneously into the current self-alienation of family. The word 'Once' sticks out on the parallel limb of a stanza with 'Tonight,' both balanced on two time frames at the same time. Thus, it can be said that all the time frames are present, whether or not all are *in* the present, thereby carving out biographical lyric experience. It is through this lens of the biographical that history-making is reformulated.

Conclusion

Biographical lyric is still developing; yet the genre holds one's attention. Longenbach notes, 'Some poems have a prominent argument; some poems don't. But all poems live or die on their capacity to lure us from their beginnings' (120). In my investigations I found clear indications that there are new possibilities for how we tell our life stories: biographical lyric powerfully offers essential, if unexpected, momentum for *not* removing ourselves from newly appreciated personal and global disappearances.

ACTIVITY

Practice exercises for writing biographical lyric

Part I: Choose a biographical subject (in person, photographs, or similar):

1. Study your biographical subject closely, for ten minutes, then stop looking.

   Immediately write down at least five of these observations, using the third person:

   For example, 'the fingers on her left hand are longer than the fingers on her right hand,' or 'his brown leather shoes seem to be a mix of mud and buckles.'

2. Study your subject again, and make further observations: is it at a special event for your subject, a moment of transition, or a particular time of day?

   Keeping these observations in mind, choose five comparisons, using similes.

   For example—around the period of a divorce—'Her tall black bag she carries looks like a small building in Chestnut Hill, next to the parking lot.'

Write five comparisons, using metaphors.

   For example, 'Her tall black bag is a small building with three floors and dozens of windows to search.'

   Write five comparisons, using a well-known saying.

   For example, 'Her tall black bag, full of messages from her ex-husband, makes the scales fall from her eyes.'

3. Return to your subject, and create a specific set of indirect questions to use in an imagined initial interview. Look for self-resistances and contradictions in your work.

   For example, 'I've noticed that you like to have a lot of choices when you shop for clothes, but you can't decide on any once you're there,' and 'I've noticed that you like to eat, but you slow down at your dinner and never finish your food.'

Part II: structure and scaffolding

1. As a frame, choose one of your observed self-resistances.

   For example, She likes a lot of choices when she shops for bathing suits. But she drags them into the dressing room and slams the curtain.

2. Separate the two parts, and begin with the first observation:

   She likes to a lot of choices when she shops for bathing suits.

   Now come up with three similes for this person's 'shopping' for bathing suits.

   For example, She shops for bathing suits like my little brother who

   ... piles up green and yellow legos.

   ... like a bird who has found the leftovers at a café table.

   ... like the wind picking up leaves on a windy October night.

3. Write three metaphors and then three proverbs for the same observed act of 'shopping':

   For the metaphor, She shops for bathing suits, a goose circling the waves of air for recent crumbs.

   For the proverb, She shops for bathing suits, hands full, carpe diem.

4. Choose your favourite line in each category, beginning with the opening observation: 'she shops for bathing suits.' Then, choose from among your lines to build the first scaffolding for your poem:

   For example: She shops for bathing suits

   like the wind picking up leaves on a windy night,

   circling the waves of air,

   hands full, carpe diem.

   But she drags them into the dressing room,

   and slams the curtain.

Make a list of things you know about this woman: her habits, her patterns, her emotions, her changes, her range as a biographical figure in her time and place.

Part III: the initial music for your poem

She shops for bathing suits
like the wind picking up leaves on a windy night,
circling the waves of air,
hands full, carpe diem.
But she drags them into the dressing room
and slams the curtain.

Try the poem above in several metres and stanzaic patterns.

Couplets: She shops for bathing suits

like the wind picking up leaves on a windy night,

circling the waves of air,

hands full, carpe diem.

But she drags them into the dressing room

and slams the curtain.

Tercets: She shops for bathing suits

like the wind picking up leaves on a windy night,

circling the waves of air,

hands full, carpe diem.

But she drags them into the dressing room

and slams the curtain.

Quatrains: She shops for bathing suits

like the wind picking up leaves on a windy night,

circling the waves of air,

hands full, carpe diem.

But she drags them into the dressing room

and slams the curtain.

Which music best makes sense of the story you are starting to tell? Quatrains historically signal the ballad and a narrative shape. Tercets signal a spiral of achievement and rest or backtracking, two steps forwards, one step back. The couplet signals deep comparisons.

Try a provisional title!

At Bloomingdale's

tall black bag she carries
looks like a small building
in Chestnut Hill, next to a parking lot.

She stops for bathing suits
like the wind picking up leaves on a windy night,
circling the waves of air,

hands full, carpe diem.
She drags them into the dressing room
and slams the curtain. Her tall black bag

full of messages
from her ex-husband
makes the scales fall from her eyes.

 Recommended Reading

Dickie, Margaret. *Lyric Contingencies: Emily Dickenson and Wallace Stevens*, U Pennsylvania P, 1991.

Dove, Rita. *The poet's world*. Library of Congress, 1995.

_____. *Thomas and Beulah*. Carnegie-Mellon UP, 1986.

Justice, Donald. 'Nostalgia and Complaint of the Grandparents.' www.poetryfoundation.org/poems/47907/nostalgia-and-complaint-of-the-grandparents.

Longenbach, James. *The Art of the Poetic Line*. Graywolf Press, 2008.

Nelson, Marilyn. *Carver: A Life in Poems*. 1st ed. Coretta Scott King Author Honor Books. Front Street, 2001.

Regalado, Nancy Freeman. 'Who Tells the Stories of Poetry? Villon and his Readers' in *Telling the Story in the Middle Ages*, edited by Kathryn A. Duys, Elizabeth Emery, and Laurie Postlewate, pp. 61–74. D. S. Brewer, 2015.

Tucker, Herbert. 'Dramatic Monologue and the Overhearing of Lyric,' in *Lyric Poetry: Beyond New Criticism*, edited by Chaviva Hosek and Patricia Parker, pp. 226–43. U Cornell P, 1985.

 ## Works Cited

Aviram, Amittai F. 'Lyric poetry and subjectivity.' Prose. Literature and Philosophy. PHP, 2004. www.amittai.com. Accessed 5 Dec. 2017.

Barchiesi, Alessandro. 'Palingenre: Death, Rebirth and Horatian Iambos,' in *Horace and Greek Lyric Poetry*, edited by MichaelPaschalis. Vol. 1, pp.47–69 . Rethymnon, 2002.

Benjamin, Jessica. *Beyond Doer and Done To: Recognition Theory, Intersubjectivity, and the Third*. Routledge, 2017.

Booth, Stephen. *Precious Nonsense: The Gettysburg Address, Ben Jonson's Epitaphs on His Children and Twelfth Night*. U California P, 1998.

Bourne, Daniel. *Artful Dodge*. Original Interviews. 'Changing the whole neighborhood: A conversation with Rita Dove.' 2 Oct. 2010. www.artfuldodge.sites.wooster.edu/contents/rita-dove. Accessed 5 Dec. 2017.

Cavalieri, Grace. 'Brushed by an Angel's Wings,' in *Conversations with Rita Dove*, edited by Earl G. Ingersoll, pp.136–47 . The U of Mississippi P, 2003.

Creeley, Robert. *The Mouth and 'The Language.'* Modern Literature Collection: The First 50 Years. Washington U Libraries. Nov. 2014. omeka.wustl.edu/omeka/items/show/12192. Accessed 5 Dec. 2017.

Curtius, Ernst Robert. *European Literature and the Latin Middle Ages*, translated by Willard R. Trask. Routledge & Kegan Paul, 1953.

Dalley, Hamish. 'Rita Dove: An interview.' *American Poetry Review,* vol. 24, no. 2, Mar./Apr. 1995, pp. 11–15. *JSTOR* www.jstor.org/stable/277817366. Accessed 7 Dec. 2017.

Davis, Geoffrey. "'The threads that connect us': An interview with Charles Johnson." *Callaloo,* vol. 33, no. 3, Summer 2010, pp. 807–19. www.10.1353/cal.2010.0018. Accessed 7 Dec. 2017.

Dolin, Tim. 'Life-lyrics: Autobiography, poetic form, and personal loss in Hardy's moments of vision.' *Victorian Poetry,* vol. 50, no. 1, Spring 2012, pp. 1–19.

Dove, Rita. *Thomas and Beulah*. U Carnegie Mellon P, 1986.

Dronke, Peter. *The Medieval Lyric*, 2nd. ed. Hutchinson, 1978.

Greene, Roland. 'Sir Philip Sidney's Psalms, the Sixteenth-Century Psalter, and the nature of lyric.' *Studies in English Literature, 1500–1900,* vol. 30, no.1, The English Renaissance, Winter 1990, pp. 19–40.

Hanson, Kristin, and Paul Kiparsky. 'The nature of verse and its consequences for the mixed form,' in *Prosimetrum: Crosscultural Perspectives on Narrative in Prose and Verse*, edited by Joseph Harris, Karl Reichl. D. S. Brewer, 1997.

Homberger, Eric, and John Charmley.editors. 'Introduction,' in *The Troubled Face of Biography*, edited by Eric Homberger and John Charmley, pp. ix–xv. Macmillan, 1998.

Johnson, Charles. 'The End of the Black American Narrative: A New Century Calls for New Stories Grounded in the Present, Leaving behind the Painful History of Slavery and its Consequences,' in *The American Scholar*, edited by Robert Wilson, vol. 77, no. 3, Summer 2008, pp. 32–42. *JSTOR*, www.jstor.org/stable/41221894. Accessed 15 Nov. 2017.

———. *Taming the Ox: Buddhist Stories and Reflections on Politics, Race, Culture, and Spiritual Practice*. Shambhala, 2014.

Johnson, Emma. 'Book review: Truth and beauty: Verse biography in Canada, Australia and New Zealand,' in *The Reader: The Booksellers New Zealand Blog Web*, edited by Anna Jackson et al. 23 Feb. 2017. booksellersnz.wordpress.com/. Accessed 15 Nov. 2017.

Johnson, Samuel (1709–1784). 'Dignity and usefulness of biography.' *The Rambler*. No. 60. 13 Oct. 1750. (Early American Imprints. 2nd series; no. 4458) Philadelphia: Printed by Robert Carr for Samuel F. Bradford and John Conrad, 1803. [electronic resource] www.johnsonessays.com/the-rambler/dignity-usefulness-biography/. Accessed 7 Dec. 2017.

Justice, Donald. 'Nostalgia and Complaint of the Grandparents.' www.poetryfoundation.org/poems/47907/nostalgia-and-complaint-of-the-grandparents. Accessed 15 Nov. 2017.

Keller, Lynn. 'An interview with Myung Mi Kim.' *Contemporary Literature,* vol. 49, no.3, Fall 2008, pp. 335–56.

Lee, Hermione. *Biography: A Very Short Introduction*. Oxford UP, 2009.

Lerer, Seth. 'The genre of the grave and origins of the middle English lyric.' *MLQ,* vol. 58, no. 2, 1997, pp. 127–61.

Longenbach, James. *The Art of the Poetic Line*. Graywolf Press, 2008.

McGill, Robert. 'Review of Truth and Beauty: Verse Biography in Canada, Australia and New Zealand: Verse Biography and the Loneliness of the Single-Author Study.' 4 Oct. 2017. www.robert-mcgill.com/notebook/review-verse-biography-and-lonliness-single-autho/. Accessed 5 Dec. 2017.

Morton, Timothy. *Hyperobjects: Philosophy and Ecology after the End of the World*. U Minnesota P, 2013.

Nagel, Thomas. *The View from Nowhere*. U Oxford P, 1986.

Nelson, Marilyn. *Carver: A Life in Poems*, 1st ed. Coretta Scott King Author Honor Books. Front Street, 2001.

Padel, Ruth. *Darwin: A Life in Poems*. Alfred A. Knopf, 2012.

Parke, Catherine N. *Biography: Writing Lives*. Routledge, 2002.

Puckett, Kent. *Narrative Theory: A Critical Introduction*. U Cambridge P, 2016.

Reece, Steve. 'Orality and Literacy: Ancient Greek Literature as Oral Literature,' in *A Companion to Greek Literature*, edited by Martin Hose and David Schenker, pp. 45–57. John Wiley and Sons, Inc., 2015.

Rose, Steven. *The Making of Memory: From Molecules to Mind*. New ed. Vintage, 2003.

Shakespeare, William. *A Midsummer Night's Dream*, in *The Riverside Shakespeare*, edited by G. Blakemore Evans, pp. 251–84, 276. 2nd ed. Houghton Mifflin Company, 1974.

Strand, Mark. *New Selected Poems*. Alfred A. Knopf, 2007.

Thomas, M. Wynn. 'An Interview with Rita Dove by M. W. Thomas,' *Modern American Poetry*. 12 Aug. 1995. www.english.illinois.edu/maps/poets/a_f/dove/mwthomas.htm. Accessed 15 Nov. 2017.

Thwaite, Ann. 'Writing Lives,' in *The Troubled Face of Biography*, edited by Eric Homberger and John Charmley, pp. 17–32. Macmillan, 1998.

Wilhelm, Steve. 'The Way of the Writer: Charles Johnson about Art, Dharma, Race and Political Action.' *Northwest Dharma News,* vol. 30, no. 1, Spring 2017. northwestdharma.org/../the-way-of-the-writer-charles-johnson-about-art-. Accessed 5 Dec. 2017.

Wordsworth, William. 'Lines Composed a Few Miles above Tintern Abbey on Revisiting the Banks of the Wye during a Tour. 13 July 1798,' in *The Norton Anthology of Poetry: Shorter, Fifth Edition*, edited by Margaret Ferguson et al., pp. 458–61. W. W. Norton & Company, 2005.

Notes

1. The text and translations by Lerer are based on that of Peter Dronke's 1978 modifications of the following text: *English Lyrics of the Thirteenth Century.* Clarendon, 1932. Dronke's book appeared as *The Medieval Lyric*, 2nd ed. Hutchinson, 1978.

10 WRITING LINES, WRITING LIVES: THE ART OF POETIC BIOGRAPHY

Jessica L. Wilkinson

In the last several decades, the biographical long poem—or 'poetic biography'—has enjoyed a period of quiet prosperity. Including more formal works such as James Mcauley's *Captain Quiros* (1964); the feminist experiments of Susan Howe in *The Liberties* (1980); the humorous games in Dennis Cooley's *Bloody Jack* (2002); and the speculative biographical work in Campbell McGrath's *Shannon: A Poem of the Lewis and Clark Expedition* (2009), this 'genre' demonstrates a breadth of play that has the potential to expand our understandings of how biography can be written and framed.

Biography scholars in recent years have discussed developments and shifts in how writers are approaching lives. Sidonie Smith and Julia Watson argue in *Reading Autobiography: A Guide for Interpreting Life Narratives* (2010) that '*New biography* … signals many kinds of practices that exploit the boundaries drawn between biography and fiction at particular moments and seeks innovative modes adequate to the complexity of narrating a life at various moments of paradigm shift' (9). Smith and Watson's research draws attention to the tensions between 'real' and 'fiction' and between knowing and not knowing, which are increasingly emphasised by contemporary biographers. The Personal Narratives Group contributes similar insights when they argue for 'the *truths* of our experiences' rather than for a single truth or revelation of 'as it actually was' (261; emphasis mine). This scholarship seems to encourage biography writers to explore more nuanced or experimental modes of writing a life; but there has been little attention paid to the potential offered by the poetic form when it comes to expanding the biographical field.

David McCooey suggests that biographical poetry 'is commonly revisionary … because of the figurative nature of such poetry and its lack of the usual burdens of proof' (109), a sentiment that seems to be reflected by some of the poets engaging with this genre. Cole Swensen elaborates on the slipperiness of poetry, suggesting that 'poetry—amid all its ambiguity and ornamentation—is not only perfectly capable of conveying truth; it can also attain a unique relationship to truth because it implicitly acknowledges and interrogates the limitations of language' (58). It is not surprising, given poetry's provocative capabilities, that poets have considered this mode to offer promising attributes for new biographical enquiries, especially when attempting to portray the lives and experiences of marginal, misrepresented, or forgotten historical figures. In the context of women's histories, for example, poetic representations have the potential to 'enlarge our perspective of the [historical] record,' as Sarah Alpern et al. demand of feminist biographers. Further, poetic biography may prove to be an appropriate form to convey the life and experiences of any historical characters, including those whose lives have been widely documented and written about. Line, metaphor, rhythm and musicality, play, gesture, and frisson can all be enlisted to engage with information and fact to produce a multidimensional biographical narrative that 'meets' the individual subject in a manner that befits their character and that is formally attentive when it comes to cultural, social, and political sensitivities.

This chapter explores the under-analysed field of poetic biography through the works of four poets: Edward Sanders's *Chekhov*, Ruth Padel's *Darwin: A Life in Poems*, Emily Ballou's *The Darwin Poems*, and Dennis Cooley's *Bloody Jack*. Each demonstrates a different approach to the form; they are united, however, in their dedication to extensive research on their respective subjects, and each book clearly demonstrates the author's decisions regarding how to represent each subject through poetic lines and play. Analysing these works affords one the opportunity to propose reasons why 'poetry + biography' presents an exciting challenge to the boundaries of non-fiction writing and also to contemplate how this experimental form might help us to reconceive what constitutes biography writing, in enabling us to push beyond the traditions of the biographical canon.

A Beat poet writes Anton Chekhov

Edward Sanders has dedicated numerous books to documentary or 'investigative' poetry (his term), including one on the great Russian playwright and short story writer Anton Pavlovich Chekhov. In his long and radical essay *Investigative Poetry*, Sanders states that for poetry 'to go forward … [it] has to begin a voyage into the description of *historical reality*' (7). Drawing on the work of Charles Olson (particularly his 'Projective Verse' manifesto) and also that of Allen Ginsberg (Poetry Archive), Sanders argues that the poetic form can open itself to 'data clusters' to present a new kind of history writing, which he calls 'history-poesy' or 'investigative poetry.'

Of the texts discussed in this chapter, *Chekhov* (1995) seems to be the most conventionally biographical in the way that it conveys details from the subject's birth to death; these details are conveyed through fluent writing that is not particularly demanding of one's ability to decipher complex poetic metaphors or to 'connect the dots' between juxtaposed factual content to reveal hidden gestures about the subject's life. *Chekhov* is a book of over two hundred pages that contains between one and ten individually titled poems. The order is more or less chronological. Reading the text, we speed through at a galloping pace due to mostly short laconic lines drifting across the white space of the page. The most unusual inclusions are perhaps the hand-drawn glyphs or diagrams, such as maps, that appear occasionally throughout the book.

In the notes section, Sanders informs us of the genesis of his book: as a young Beat writer, he saw *Ivanov* when he came to New York City in the 1950s. From there unfolded a fascination with the playwright and author, and he read all the translations of his work he could find. In a letter to Bunin Suvorin (27 October 1888), Chekhov states, 'You are right in demanding that an artist should take an intelligent attitude to his work, but you confuse two things: solving a problem and stating a problem correctly. It is only the second that is obligatory for the artist' (Chekhov). The first poem in Sanders's study of Chekhov ('The Phantom from Taganrog' 13–14) raises questions about the subject, a fitting beginning, perhaps, for the life of a man who is known for his statement that artists are to raise questions, not necessarily answer them: 'Who was this man/ called Chekhov' (l.1–2), Sanders asks, this man who was a 'very energetic guy' (l.4). As the poem snakes down the page (a characteristic trait of Sanders's poetry), the poet notes that we can grasp Chekhov's life and character through his artistic works, abundant extant correspondence, and the recorded words of others (writers, family members). However, he notes that these provide mere 'glimpse[s]' (l.7) of his 'genius' (l.14).

This poem implicitly acknowledges the frustrations of any biographer in suggesting the impossibility of representing the subject (or, by extension, any historical character). Despite the abundance of materials, the past is irrecoverable—we might be 'looking at sand' (l.16) and 'phantom[s]' (l.31) in the historical past or 'time-mist' (l.3). Sanders also uses the word 'swerve' (l.15), which could be used to describe both the visual appearance of his poems (snaking down the page), but it more profoundly gestures towards his own practice in investigative poetry, swerving from the norm in the way that it incorporates and communicates historical facts. However, this 'swerve' might also recognise that biographers (of all kinds) are in the same boat, 'calling out' but not necessarily hearing a clear response from our subjects, confirming the accuracy of our approach.

The opening poem, then, sets up those to follow—this will be *Sanders's* Chekhov—and also sets the tone and style for the book as a whole. As a poet who draws influence from the Beat poets, his language exhibits eccentricities that are also evident in his other publications. Sanders is fond of hyphenation: the 'TB doom-drum' begins its ominous beat that will take Chekhov's life. Flicking through the book, one can locate almost one hyphenation on every page—later in the book, for instance, 'morphine shoot-ups' are administered to Chekhov, who is suffering 'brain-vim' as a result of the advancing TB (222). Sanders also employs elisions ('quick'ning'), which create similar rhythmic effects as the hyphenation, and contemporary slang—for example, 'a right wing nut' tried to stab Gorky (219)—throughout his biographical account. This playful use of language brings Sanders, as biographer, to the fore, revealing the fact that all biographies are contingent on their authors' decisions when it comes to shaping, framing, and conveying their subjects.

Sanders proceeds to set a rather sweeping historical backdrop and context to the tale of Chekhov's life, regarding social and political trouble in not only 19th-century Russia but also going back further and wider (including a brief history of serfdom—Chekhov's father was a serf). Against this backdrop, the poems then cover the setbacks and successes in his writing and personal life, including family financial troubles, his twin careers as journalist and physician, the major milestones for his writing (play performances, publications), his unusual marriage, and his gradual decline towards death from tuberculosis.

Sanders says that '[e]ach point in history can be debated. There's a fact blizzard … trillions of factional units one can choose,' and he adds that 'your own taste and your own abilities, your own historical outlook, your own politics, your own ethics … everything comes into play as you choose to pluck the heart of your verse with all those possible notes' (Steve 125). In *Chekhov*, Sanders blends selected quotations from

Chekhov's letters and other historical sources (listed at the back of the book) with his own characteristic turn of phrase. Although Sanders's text has been interpreted by some critics as simplistic and silly, for readers or writers unfamiliar with the extent of poetry's capabilities, *Chekhov* provides a subtle introduction to how factual details of a subject's life can be played with through poetic biography.

Discovery and invention

Ruth Padel's *Darwin: A Life in Poems* and Emily Ballou's *The Darwin Poems* were published in 2009, the bicentenary of Charles Darwin's birth. Whereas Ballou's interest in writing of Darwin was sparked by a sign she encountered on a regular walk she would take while living in the Blue Mountains, Australia (the sign read 'Charles Darwin passed this way'), Padel was commissioned to write some Darwin poems for the Bristol Festival of Ideas and the Natural History Museum, London, and the book developed from there. Both writers approached research in different ways: Padel, a descendant of Darwin, had the benefit of conversations with her grandmother, Nora (Darwin's granddaughter, who edited several of his books), and she lists key books consulted in her 'Author's Note' (*Darwin: A Life* xiii). She also refers to some site-based trips that aided her writing of the poems, including trips to Galapagos and Brazil (which Darwin visited during his voyage on the *Beagle* as a young man). Ballou appears to have engaged in much more extensive archival research, as detailed in her 'Some Notes on the Text'; she consulted 'Darwin's correspondence, writings, personal journals and notebooks' in several library archives and at Down House (*The Darwin Poems* 193).

Given that both poets are writing about the life of Charles Darwin, one expects some crossover in details, and there are some poems that address particular aspects of Darwin's life. Both include poems about Darwin's visits to the Fitzwilliam Museum to see Titian's *Venus*. Interestingly, Ballou and Padel each suggest that Darwin was viewing different paintings; Ballou, in her notes, says that it is *Venus Crowned by Cupid with a Lute Player* by Titian, while Padel, in the margins of her book says that it is 'probably *Sleeping Venus* by Padovanino, now labelled 'After Titian'' (*Darwin: A Life* 20). Both poets also utilise Darwin's 'For' and 'Against' list in his 'Memorandum on Marriage ' (Darwin, 'This is the Question Marry Not Marry' 1–2). Further, both incorporate Darwin's terms and expressions and showcase the detailed nature of his scientific eye and mind. Aside from these similarities, the two books are vastly dissimilar as each poet approaches their subject differently, exhibiting unique motivations, styles, and creative decisions. These points of difference, which generate different reading experiences, show how diverse and rich poetic biography can be.

The back cover of Padel's book classifies it as 'poetry/biography', although Padel insists, 'I didn't mean to write a biography and I never would, because I respect scholarship too much and you'd really have to do the full scholarship' (qtd. in MacKenzie 4). I would contest this interesting claim as adhering too strongly to the limitations and traditions of biography writing. There is a sense, too, in Padel's poems in *Darwin: A Life in Poems* that she dare not abuse the materials on which she draws facts—in her 'Author's Note', she says: 'Many feelings, … which the poems attribute to him, or imply, are of course interpretation' (xviii). The poems themselves are interrupted by marginal annotations that provide clear biographical facts and sources. This structural format does perhaps suggest an anxiety that poetry is unable to communicate biographical subject matter or an adherence to traditional biographical knowledge making—Padel says that the structure 'gave me a scaffold, so the poems could be as fluid as they liked inside' (White 'An Interview'). Nevertheless, the competing font sizes in her actual copy of *Darwin: A Life in Poems*, and the fact that the biographical details are pushed to the margins, giving precedence to the poetic lines, could be considered a triumph for poetic biography.

Padel's book is split into five 'chapters' as might be imitating a traditional biography, each with separately titled poems which, aside from a handful of exceptions, have a uniform format: every second line is slightly indented. In chapter one, 'Boy (1809–1831),' the first eleven poems in the book are grouped under the heading 'Finding the Name in the Flower.' The first four of these short poems are, in the order presented, 'The Chapel'; 'The Year My Mother Died'; 'Stealing the Attention of Dogs'; and 'The Miser.' Padel demonstrates attentiveness to the aesthetics of the poems, using poetic devices, including enjambment, juxtaposition, consonance, alliteration, metaphor, rhyme, and part-rhyme. In the poem 'The Year My Mother Died,' for instance, 'No embrace' (l.3) falls between a quote from Darwin remembering his father crying at this loss and one telling of his sisters' grief-stricken silence: they 'did not' at any time 'speak her name' (l.5). The effect is to conjure a sense of Darwin as a 'timid' boy feeling dreadfully alone in this mourning household, the alliterative *s* enhancing the weight of 'silence.'

This short poem (the second in the book) showcases the extensive quotation that is prominent throughout Padel's work, most often taken from Darwin's correspondence, diaries, notebooks, or *Autobiography*. Padel notes, 'I have had to tinker with some of [these quotations] as they became poems. But I have not changed their sense. Nor, I hope, what I most wanted to give: [Darwin's] voice' (*Darwin: A Life* xviii). The poem has Darwin remembering—or attempting to remember—his mother, whose death, when he was eight, had a profound effect on him. Quotations are punctuated with sparse words from Padel: 'No embrace', 'Her memory,' 'silence,' and 'No memento of her' visage (1.3). These final lines, addressing the silence that surrounded his mother's death, perhaps foreshadow Darwin's own silence following the death of his favourite daughter, Annie. There is certainly a tendency for Padel to draw connections between disparate aspects or events, perhaps as her way to psychoanalytically examine and explain Darwin's actions and decisions in life. As she notes, her cousin Randal's book *Annie's Box* helped her to understand 'the feelings that Darwin would have had growing up and how this would come to bear on his later life'; this also had an impact on how she crafted the book, in having aspects noted in earlier poems 'answered' in later poems (Padel, *Darwin: A Life* xvii). Indeed, the final line in 'The Year My Mother Died' resonates happily in the penultimate poem of *Darwin: A Life in Poems*, when 'a miniature' of a 'a pretty face,' one that had been hidden and 'kept secret' since his mother's death years before, is discovered amongst his brother's effects—it is confirmed by his sisters to be 'a good likeness' of their mother (139; Padel, 'An interview' 2009b).

That final line in 'The Year My Mother Died'—'no memento of her' looks—also leaves us questioning the impetus behind Charles's mania for collecting. As revealed in 'The Miser,' the fourth poem of the group 'Finding the Name In the Flower' and the poem overleaf from 'The Year My Mother Died,' 'Collecting' is to 'assert control'; to 'gather' then list diverse objects and things is to 'summon in one place' and 'recall to order'; to 'recall to order' is to 'collect' oneself and 'smother what you feel'; 'making, like Orpheus, a system against loss' (1.16). Darwin's collecting resonates through Padel's construction of this verse biography, itself a collection and arrangement of quotes, of fragments, of thoughts (indeed, readers will also note the 'facts,' in a small font, that accompany each poem, in the margins). Formally, then, one might see *Darwin* as an homage to the poet's ancestor not only in showcasing his scientific and personal thoughts but also formally in the collision of fact and hypothesis and through the fact of the book's collage of quotes and anecdotes.

Ballou's *The Darwin Poems* addresses events and occurrences in Darwin's life in chronological order. They are mostly written in third person, and yet each more or less stays 'close' to either Darwin's perspective or that of someone close to him. Remarkably, Ballou's poems tap into these subjective perspectives in convincing ways: her language choices meet the myriad personas in Darwin's life. This is achieved partly through thorough research in Darwin archives, enabling the poet to incorporate direct or paraphrased quotations from various voices into the weave of her poems. Ballou takes poetic licence in seamlessly working quotations into the poetic lines, although she thoroughly acknowledges these sources at the rear of the book.

Vicky MacKenzie suggests that Ballou's 'imaginative responses' to the research material, and her 'inhabitation' of Darwin in *The Darwin Poems* 'means her collection is further from traditional biography than Padel's' (7). Yet perhaps this same fact draws Ballou's text more fully into the realm of 'poetic biography' in taking advantage of what poetry can offer to the writing of a life. Ballou, I argue, loosens her hold on the fact reliance of traditional biography writing and brings the strengths of the poetry medium to the fore. She states in an article on her Darwin project that poetry, with its myriad devices and forms, is an ideal medium through which to examine and convey the man 'without closing him in' ('Darwin as Metaphor' 2). The poet aimed for 'emotional proximity' and to 'capture the tone' and 'temperatures of a life' rather than to set out purely factual, chronological aspects (Ballou, 'Darwin as Metaphor' 2). These sentiments are raised by Swensen in her discussion of documentary poetry:

> the fully complex version [of truth] must incite the imagination of the reader, must get the reader beyond simply absorbing facts and into a responsive engagement with them because that engagement is a crucial part of truth. It's the emotional part, which can't be told; it must be felt, which can be achieved through imagination, but not through idea. (58–59)

Swensen, like Ballou, suggests that through the 'interstices opened up by figurative language, ambiguity, juxtaposition, sound relationships, and rhythmic patterns, room can be made for those aspects of truth that can't be articulated' (59). Yet Ballou also acknowledges the significance of poetry to Darwin himself, not only his expressed love for reading poetry as a younger man—an activity that he regrets not continuing into his later life—but also for the poetic nature of Darwin's own writing, which Ballou describes as taking on 'the power of free-verse: associative, rhythmic, leaping' ('Darwin as Metaphor' 6). To quote Ballou, 'Darwin also used metaphors (and similes) as figures of speech and rhetorical strategies within his notebooks and scientific writings to orient and clarify for himself and his readers, to move ideas forward, to splice two disparate concepts, or smash them together in a new way' (3).

In the poem 'December 27, 1839' (*The Darwin Poems* 96–97), Ballou participates in this kind of associative, rhythmic leaping and splices two disparate aspects together: Darwin's observations of a spur-dog, a type of dogfish shark, caught during his *Beagle* voyage, and observations of his first-born child, William.

Drawing from two different resources—Darwin's 'red notebook' diary of observations during the *Beagle* voyage (specifically an entry dated 28 August 1832) and his 'Notebook of Observations on the Darwin children (1839–1856)' (*The Darwin Poems* 200–6)—Ballou collides the imagery of both dogfish and child (without the poet's notes, we might mistake the details on the former for those on the latter) and in so doing accentuates, through juxtaposition, the connections between these two important aspects of Darwin's life: his family and his scientific work. Additional flourishes enhance this connective frisson, including the use of homophonic '*squalus*' (dogfish) and 'squalled' (the baby's cry). In keeping with Darwin's loving humour, Ballou inserts her own joke via Darwin's voice, a suggestion for William's name: '*Squalus Darwinii!*' (*The Darwin Poems* 96). As we discover in the poet's notes, the poems that feature italics without quote marks indicate Ballou's own 'notebook jottings' while researching in the Darwin archives. This particular poem, then, draws on *three* notebooks, as Ballou interweaves her own note-taking with that of her subject. Ballou also reveals her intentions to showcase the 'coralline' qualities of Darwin's mind and work, bringing to mind his evolutionary tree diagram of his theory of life:

> it's not just Darwin's connection to the natural world as observer which he shares with many poets .... it is the *coralline* quality of Darwin's mind and work, the proliferation and variety of his thought ... his use of simile and metaphor, and the minutiae of his vision ... his long perspective ... that makes poetry such a fertile form with which to represent him. ('Darwin as Metaphor' 2)

While in either poetry or biography circles, two books on Darwin may appear to be 'competing' texts, Ballou's statement implicitly makes room for divergent texts that may be spawned from different motivations, filtered through myriad poets' pens. Padel's collecting and collage could be said to frame Darwin's work in a manner that calls to mind his own careful collecting, arrangement, and observations of artefacts. Ballou's research set her on a different pathway, to produce an imaginative rendering, harmonising Darwin's personal and scientific thoughts with her own inhabitation of his thinking.

Unruly Bloody Jack

The 'subject' of Dennis Cooley's *Bloody Jack*, Manitoban outlaw John 'Bloody Jack' Krafchenko, was hanged for shooting dead (possibly by accident) a bank manager in Plum Coulee, Manitoba. I place 'subject' in inverted commas because we do not finish Cooley's book with a solid grasp of this character, other than that he seems to have been a lady's man with an unpredictable temper and a petty criminal with a talent for boxing. Rather, it seems to be Cooley's intention to avoid capturing slippery 'Kraf' and instead to let him run loose across his text. There is a sense that Cooley is conveying the 'unknowability' of Krafchenko, perhaps because despite accessing police files and archival documents, there is much that he could not find out about parts of his life. Cooley does not seem interested in 'locking down' those missing facts. Perhaps the best we can hope for are glimpses of this life, as suggested in the poem 'strobic flies' (45), where white space, metaphor (stuttering, strobic, flick, parted, flaking), symbols (/), and puns (flies, which could be a wilful typo for 'files') produce a rich and layered text that creates a sense of Krafchenko's mystery. By scattering only a few words across the page (seven of which are the word 'flick'), Cooley generates a frustrating sense that we might grasp only flickers and flakes of this character.

Bloody Jack is a wild, irreducible text that not only subverts biography writing but pushes the limits of 'poetry' as well. Alongside free verse poems, the text includes play script, visual poems, sound poems, newspaper reports, court transcripts, a handwritten letter, and a brief musical score with lyrics. There is a letter to Cooley's editor complaining about the poet's text ('Dear Editor, I for one am not in the least amused by Dennis Cooley's writings. And I know from talking to others that they have had it up to here with all this filthy language' [89]), a book review that censures the text ('In this book Cooley is toying with us, if he is not, in fact, merely playing with himself' [142]), and numerous fleeting lines in which

Cooley provides self-critique ('One poet, crazed evidently by the bandit, went so far as to write an entire book' [58]). The first edition of Cooley's *Bloody Jack* was published in 1984. When the second edition was released, in 2002, several new poems were added, including a crossword puzzle, clues for which refer not only to events in Krafchenko's life but to some in Cooley's as well.

Cooley's reluctance to provide narrative—even a discernible poetic narrative—reveals a deeper significance to *Bloody Jack* as a book that explores and challenges power and authority: not merely the authority wielded by legal and criminal justice systems but the authority of biographers over their subjects and for how readers receive information that has been framed by the biographer. Cooley distances himself from this kind of authorial control; the crossword in the book's second edition, explicitly invites the reader to participate in 'solving' the text, but there is no authorised 'solution.' Further, the pun in the title 'they have cross words' has us thinking not only of puzzles and arguments but also about the crossing of lives within the space of this text as a whole. That is, in many poems, we are unsure where Krafchenko ends and Cooley begins, or where Cooley ends and Krafchenko begins, and whether we are reading biographical or autobiographical details. Cooley presents *his* Krafchenko, but, more so than the previous texts discussed in this chapter, *Bloody Jack* exposes and explodes the seams of traditional biography writing and has us consider the many different ways that we might 'know' or imagine a historical subject, without reducing that character to a set of dry facts 'captured' in a book. Cooley swerves from fact and towards experiment and play. The irregular text that is *Bloody Jack* emphasises the poet's repeated attempts at 'trying' to give voice to an authentic Krafchenko; the 'failure' to achieve coherence and clarity (as might be the goal with a more traditional biographical text) becomes a strength of this work, as Cooley locates the spirit of his subject in the wildness of a roving format, in the ambiguity of puns, the layering of metaphor, and the inconclusiveness of a revised/revisable text.

Conclusion

The four texts discussed in this chapter demonstrate different approaches to writing about historical subjects. They do not simply present poems about their subjects; each book extends from serious and thoughtful research (of different kinds), and each harnesses aspects of the poetic form in its attempts to reimagine its subject in new ways. As readers, we are encouraged to be more attentive to the poet's language gestures; we are led to 'read between the lines,' to make connections and inferences, and to perceive metaphor or implication, and there is a sense in each of the above works that the respective poets take advantage of poetry's devices and dimensions in this regard. In doing so, each work challenges the boundaries of non-fiction—specifically, biography—writing, by testing our adherence to sanctioned modes of receiving factual information. I recall Cole Swensen's comments: 'the fully complex version [of truth] … must get the reader beyond simply absorbing facts and into a responsive engagement with them because that engagement is a crucial part of truth' (58–59). What becomes particularly apparent, through analysing key texts undertaking this kind of experimentation, is how each poet's unique perspective and style generates the frame through which we view their character: their representation is one of many possible representations, including Sanders's Beat style, Padel's selective quotation, Ballou's imaginative inhabitation, and Cooley's playful blurring of fact, fiction, self, and subject. Poetic biography tests the boundaries of more conventional modes of life-writing by challenging our relationship to facts; the poetic form and its myriad devices has the potential to lead us beyond mere attentiveness to factual information and towards a more layered experience of felt 'truths' incited by the poets' imaginative frameworks.

 ACTIVITY

Exercises for practice

These exercises could assist you in writing at least four poems for a biographical poem suite:

Step 1:

Choose a historical figure of personal interest to you—perhaps a film star, a musician, a prime minister or president, an outlaw. It is best to focus on someone well known, to make research easier.

Step 2:

Jot down some initial thoughts that you have on this person. What springs to mind when you think about them? Are there any historical details of note? What do you wish you knew? Can you think of any moments when you felt connected to this character?

Step 3:

Get to know your subject more intimately by reading, watching, and comparing the information about them that you have gathered together. Make a timeline of events in the subject's life. Is there anything you come across that is not widely known about the character?

Writing tasks for practice

Poem 1: A free verse ekphrastic poem, based on a portrait or photograph

Ekphrasis is the verbal representation of visual representation. For this exercise, study a portrait or photograph of your subject, then jot down one line for each of the following aspects:

a) The subject's physical attributes; their attire; their demeanour; their stance; and their most distinguishing feature.

b) For the final line, make a suggestion about what the subject is thinking at the moment in time depicted in the image.

Poem 2: A poem inhabiting the voice of your subject

Think about an important event that happened during the life of your subject. Turn to your research notes, and gather together any information on this event—if possible, supplement this with newspaper reports, reviews, photographs, and so on.

Now write a ten-line poem, split into two stanzas of five lines each, and adopt the 'I' perspective of your subject. Use the past tense.

In the first stanza, your subject will set the scene and describe the event. Use poetic devices such as alliteration, assonance, and consonance to help enliven the telling.

In the second stanza, your subject will reflect on that event with hindsight. Use inference to explore your subject's feelings about the experience.

Poem 3: A found poem/collage poem

Select three textual artefacts relating to your subject—for instance, a newspaper article, diary entry, autopsy report. Photocopy these texts. Now cut out the most interesting words and lines. Are there any interesting juxtapositions that you can create by colliding these different sources? Paste your fragments onto an A4 piece of paper and photocopy the final product to disguise the 'cuts'.

Poem 4: A poem that places you within the frame

Revisit Step 2, and compose a poem that reflects on the process of writing on your subject. What information have you struggled to access? Use the field of the page to playfully exorcise these frustrations and interruptions; you might use repetition, visual play or different fonts.

 ## Recommended Reading

Albiston, Jordie. *The Hanging of Jean Lee*. Black Pepper, 1998.

Alpern, Sarah et al., editors. *The Challenge of Feminist Biography: Writing the Lives of Modern American Women*. U of Illinois P, 1992.

Ballou, Emily. *The Darwin Poems*. UWA Publishing, 2009.

Bowering, Marilyn. *Human Bodies: New and Collected Poems 1987–1999*. Porcepic Books, 1999.

Chevalier, Julie. *Darger: His Girls*. Puncher & Wattman, 2012.

Cooley, Dennis. *Bloody Jack*. Turnstone Press, 1984.

_____. *Bloody Jack*. U of Alberta P, 2002.

Dove, Rita. *Thomas and Beulah*. U Carnegie-Mellon P, 1986.

_____. *Sonata Mulattica*. W. W. Norton & Company, 2009.

Hejinian, Lyn. *Gesualdo*. Tuumba Press, 1978.

Hemphill, Stephanie. *Your Own, Sylvia*. Alfred A. Knopf, 2007.

Lo, Miriam Wei Wei. *Against Certain Capture*. Five Islands Press, 2004.

McCooey, David. 'Lives of the Poets.' *Meanjin*, vol. 61, no. 1, 2002, pp. 104–113.

Ondaatje, Michael. *The Collected Works of Billy the Kid*. Vintage, 2008.

Rodriguez, Judith. *The Hanging of Minnie Thwaites*. Arcade Publications, 2012.

Scobie, Stephen. *McAlmon's Chinese Opera*. Quadrant Editions, 1980.

_____. *And Forget My Name: A Speculative Biography of Bob Dylan*. Ekstasis, 1999.

Swenson, Cole. *Noise That Stays Noise: Essays*. U of Michigan P, 2011.

Wilkinson, Jessica. "'Out of bounds of the bound margin': Susan Howe meets Mangan in Melville's Marginalia." *Criticism: A Quarterly for Literature and the Arts,* vol. 53, no. 2, 2011, pp. 265–94.

 ## Works Cited

Alpern, Sarah, et al., editors. *The Challenge of Feminist Biography: Writing the Lives of Modern American Women*. U Illinois P, 1992.

Ballou, Emily. *The Darwin Poems*. U Washington P, 2009.

_____. 'Darwin as Metaphor.' *Interdisciplinary Studies in the Long Nineteenth Century,* vol. 11, 2010. pp. 1–17. www.19.bbk.ac.uk/articles/10.16995/ntn.569. Accessed 4 Dec. 2017.

Chekhov, Anton. *Letters of Anton Chekhov to His Family and Friends*, translated by Constance Garnett. Project Gutenberg, 2004. www.gutenberg.org/files/6408/6408-h/6408-h.htm. Accessed 4 Dec. 2017.

Cooley, Dennis. *Bloody Jack*. Turnstone Press, 1984.

_____. *Bloody Jack*. U Alberta P, 2002.

Darwin, Charles. 'This the Question Marry Not Marry' [Memorandum on Marriage] (1838). *Darwin Online*, pp. 1–2. darwin-online.org.uk/. Accessed 18 Dec. 2008.

Howe, Susan. *The Liberties*. Loon Books, 1980.

MacKenzie, Vicky. 'A new species of biography: The darwin poetry of Ruth Padel and Emily Ballou.' *Postgraduate English*, vol. 24, 2012, pp. 1–19. www.community.dur.ac.uk/postgraduate.english/ojs/index.php/pg. Accessed 4 Dec. 2017.

McAuley, James. *Captain Quiros*. Angus and Robertson, 1964.

McCooey, David. 'Lives of the poets.' *Meanjin,* vol. 61, no. 1, 2002, pp. 104–13.

McGrath, Campbell. *Shannon: A Poem of the Lewis and Clark Expedition*. Ecco Press, 2009.

Padel, Ruth. *Darwin: A Life in Poems*. Vintage, 2009a.

_____. 'An interview with Ruth Padel.' Conducted by James Byrne for *The Wolf Magazine*, issue 20, Apr. 2009b. www.ruthpadel.com/interview-in-the-wolf-april-2009/. Accessed 4 Dec. 2017.

Personal Narratives Group. *Interpreting Women's Lives: Feminist Theory and Personal Narratives*. edited by Joy Webster Barbre et al. U Indiana P, 1989.

Poetry Archive. 'Allen Ginsberg—.' www.poetryarchive.org/allen-ginsberg. Accessed 4 Dec. 2017.

Sanders, Edward. *Investigative Poetry*. City Lights, 1976.

_____. *Chekhov*. Black Sparrow Press, 1995.

Smith, Sidonie, and Julia Watson, editors. *Reading Autobiography: A Guide for Interpreting Life Narratives*, 1st ed., edited by Therese Boyd. U Minnesota P, 2010.

Swensen, Cole. *Noise That Stays Noise*. U Michigan P, 2011.

Steve, Paul. 'An American History, Line by Line: An Interview with Edward Sanders.' Conducted by Paul Steve. *New Letters*, vol. 76, no. 1, Fall 2009, p. 123–26. www.newletters.org/magazine/volume-76-issue-1. Accessed 5 Dec. 2017.

White, Paul. 'Interview with Emily Ballou.' Conducted by Paul White for the *Darwin Correspondence Project*, 28 May 2009. Transcript and voice recording posted by U of Cambridge. www.darwinproject.ac.uk/yags/video www.darwinprojectac.uk/interview-with-emily-ballou. Accessed 4 Dec. 2017.

YOUNG LIVES: NEW GROWTH

11 GIVING VOICE: A DIFFERENT APPROACH TO LIFE-WRITING

Willa McDonald[1]

Inexperience and age are not barriers to good life-writing. While there is the temptation for some young people to write shallowly about their experiences—'Krazy Me at Kuta Beach'—most are capable of writing riveting tales that move beyond superficiality and convey insight, if not wisdom, if they put in the time and effort. While creative writing, even fact-based writing, is much harder to produce than a social media post or a diary entry, aspiring writers can craft stellar work once they accept that it takes planning, imagination, and a great deal of rewriting.

One tested method to help writers improve their work is the adoption of a four-pronged approach which breaks the writing task down into layers. By writing to their intellects, their emotions, their bodies, and their spirits, writers can connect more deeply with themselves, their stories, and their readers. The boundaries between these four layers are far from distinct, but by directing writers to at least consider each one separately—and to use the techniques associated with each layer—they can evaluate their work and rewrite it in useful ways. Rather than fostering formulaic responses, this method allows writers to take their own experiences seriously and to produce writing that is both reflective and engaging. Not only do better manuscripts result, but the writing process is more satisfying.

Writing memory

Many young writers are drawn to writing about their own lives because they think it is easy: 'What's so hard about writing about yourself? What's to research?' They are intrigued when they are asked to look inwards to find the heart of their story, to find that approach that is unique to themselves, and then outwards for the context and larger issue underpinning their idea. Assuming their story will come entirely from their memories, they are often surprised to discover how unreliable memory can be. Yet the capriciousness of memory is well known, particularly when the event was emotionally charged. Eye witnesses to accidents or crimes are notoriously unreliable about the details of what they saw. The research of the Innocence Project proves the point. This organisation, which has been in operation for twenty-five years, attempts to exonerate people in the United States wrongly convicted of crimes (Innocence Project. 'Eyewitness Misidentification'). It has found that in 70% of cases where DNA testing has led to the overturning of a wrongful conviction, the fault lay in eyewitness misidentification (Innocence Project. 'Eyewitness Misidentification').

Although our memories feel true, they are extremely vulnerable to suggestion, manipulation, and the needs of storytelling. Neurologist Oliver Sacks, in his memoir, *Uncle Tungsten: Memories of a Chemical Boyhood* (2016), vividly recalled bombing raids in the neighbourhood of his London home during the London Blitz:

> One night, a thousand-pound bomb fell into the garden next to ours, but fortunately it failed to explode. All of us, the entire street, it seemed, crept away ... walking as softly as we could (might vibration set the thing off?). The streets were pitch dark, for the blackout was in force, and we all carried electric torches dimmed with red crêpe paper. ... On another occasion, an incendiary bomb, a thermite bomb, fell behind our house and burned with a terrible, white-hot heat. (23)

A few months after the book was published, Sacks was told by one of his older brothers that it was not possible he could have remembered the bombings; he had been at school at the time. Instead, the memory came from a letter written to him by his elder brother, David. Sacks later said elsewhere, 'Clearly, I had not only been enthralled, but must have constructed the scene in my mind, from David's words, and then appropriated it, and taken it for a memory of my own' ('Speak, Memory' 1).

Sacks is not alone in 'recalling' a false memory. Psychologist Elizabeth Loftus has repeatedly demonstrated that memories can be manipulated and even planted. In one well-known experiment, she and her research assistant interviewed twenty-four people, asking them to remember various true events as well as a false one. The latter concerned the invented incident of having been lost in a shopping mall as a young child. After the interviews, one quarter of the participants remembered having had such an experience (Loftus and Pickrell). Later studies have shown that at least some kind of false memory can be implanted in up to 50% of experiment subjects (Wade et al.; Hyman and Pentland; Lindsay and Read).

These cases demonstrate that our memories do not work like video cameras or computers. Individual recollections are not simply retrieved; they are reconstructed by our minds, with the essential aim of preserving our sense of ourselves and our histories. We cannot write the past except through the present: the two are inextricably interwoven, each informing and creating the other (Renza; Lejeune; Couser; Smith and Watson). Even if the writer did have a perfect recollection of their past, they are no longer the same person who experienced the events being written about. The way an eight-year-old processes an experience in the present moment is different to the way they will look back on that event when they are fifteen or thirty-five or fifty-five. The writing of memoir is always a creative act, not only in the remembering but also in the way we selectively choose the memories to write about and then communicate them to the reader.

There has been much debate in recent decades about the nature of autobiographical writing. Philippe Lejeune triggered the debate in France with his proposal of an 'autobiographical pact' based on an understanding between the writer, the reader, and the publisher that the memoir must represent the author's world. The pact could be implicit rather than explicit and did not pin down a reader to one way of reading the text. Since then, other commentators have drawn a distinction between the verifiable facts, such as date of birth, and autobiographical truth that 'resides in the intersubjective exchange between narrator and reader aimed at producing a shared understanding of the meaning of a life' (Smith and Watson 16). In demonstrating the nebulous nature of 'truth' in life-writing, Sidonie Smith and Julia Watson ask,

> Are we expecting fidelity to the facts of their biographies, to lived experience, to self-understanding, to the historical moment, to social community, to prevailing beliefs about diverse identities, to the norms of autobiography as a literary genre itself? And truth to whom and for what? Other readers, a loved one, the narrating I, or for the coherent person we imagine ourselves to be? (16)

The debate has implications for life-writing. Life-writers want creative freedom, but at the same time, they do well to remember their reader's expectations. The memoirist Patti Miller says, 'A memoir must begin with and answer to the requirements of truthful exploration of an actual life' (12). Generally, readers anticipate life-writing to be based on real occurrences, real situations. There are many cases where life-writers have been found to have been fraudulent with their material—for example, Misha Defonseca's *Misha: A Memoir of the Holocaust Years* (1997), James Frey's *A Million Little Pieces* (2003), and Norma Khouri's *Forbidden Love* (2003). Although writers sometimes argue that changes to the facts helped them achieve emotional truthfulness (Kolhatkar), they should never set out to deceive their readers—not least because readers can be unforgiving when they feel duped. While there are many examples of texts that successfully blend fact and fiction, they work because of the pact the writer has forged with the reader, either directly through the title or a claim or disclaimer at the front of the book or indirectly through the choice of language, layout, and cover design. Winfried Georg Sebald, Bruce Chatwin, and Helen Garner are all writers whose work ventures into the borderline between fact and fiction, though in different ways.

Writing the intellect

One of the techniques used by writers to help resolve the ethical conundrums they inevitably face in life-writing is research. Family memorabilia, letters, diaries, and documents can all provide the writer with the opportunity to write their life from a new angle and with factual accuracy and integrity. So too can interviews, archival research, or field trips to revisit important places. Besides filling the gaps in memory and clarifying the facts of the story, research provides details that can make the work glow (Miller; Eisenhuth and McDonald; King; Lamott; Zinsser). Research can also provide a greater awareness of the personal background to a narrative, as well as its social, cultural, or political framework. The latter is important, even if only as a scaffold to the writing, potentially providing meaning and context.

New life-writers soon learn that to avoid the dreaded 'so what?' factor, there should be at least the shadow of something deeper resonating in their work, making it fresh and appealing to a wider audience than just their friends. The best life-writing always, even if only subtly, deals with 'big ideas.' David Sedaris's humorous pieces always dig at more serious themes, whether the silliness of our fashion pretensions or the tensions of family life; Alice Pung's lyrical writing speaks to the Asian migrant experience in Australia; and Indigenous life-writing around the world is playing a crucial role in presenting alternative histories to those written under colonialism. Sally Morgan's *My Place* (1987), for example, traces her search for her Aboriginal heritage and is credited with helping to open the way for the government enquiry into the Stolen Generations (Schaffer)—a practice which involved the forced removal of Indigenous children from their families under government policy in Australia over most of the 20th century.

People throughout history have used life-writing to further a political point, explain a movement, or protest against the actions of a particular regime. Testimonial life-writing is a response to cultural violence and is an important aspect of a literature of resistance. Used by civil rights activists, feminists, Indigenous groups, and survivors of persecution, it works to retrieve identity by claiming a voice, making a point, or establishing a community. It seeks redress for injustices and advocates the rights of marginalised communities by speaking out loud about the actual circumstances of a life or lives. Elie Weisel used it to witness the horrors of the Holocaust in his memoir *Night* (1960); Claude Brown used it in his remembrance of growing up black in Harlem, in *Manchild in the Promised Land* (1965); and Rachel Blau DuPlessis and Ann Snitow collected in *The Feminist Memoir Project* (1998), the life-writing of feminists who wrote as part of the Women's Liberation Movement in the United States from the 1960s onwards.

While most good life-writing tries to balance ideas and emotions, there is a branch of it where the intellect takes precedence: the personal essay. In 1580, Michel de Montaigne, known as the father of the personal essay, published his collection of *Essays*. The title comes from the French verb *essayer*: to attempt, to test, to weigh up. It involves the notion of the careful consideration of a topic. While St Augustine, Bishop of Hippo (*Confessions* of St Augustine), is said to have written the first Western autobiography in 397–400 CE, Michel de Montaigne (*Essays of Montaigne*) took his writing in a secular direction. He eschewed the theological ruminations that had become common among writers after Augustine. He blended intellectual knowledge with personal observation and insights, using his own perceptions as his starting point: '[I] myself am the matter of my book,' he once famously wrote ('Preface'). His digressions into personal anecdotes were originally seen as lacking in proper style, but his form has endured and is now widely used across modern media, including blogs, magazine columns, and books.

Usually inquisitive and confessional in tone rather than polemical, the personal essay is a flexible form. It can be used to comment on anything, such as travel, hobbies, politics, and memories of childhood. In this way, it is democratic. The writer's own expertise can't be questioned, even on issues that matter. While the focus on the personal could be dismissed as self-indulgent, in exploring the microcosm of the individual's world, the accomplished essayist always makes broader commentary—social, political, or philosophical. It is in this place where the public and private meet that essays are most successful. By exploring meaning for the individual writer, the essay inevitably speaks to the many (Eisenhuth and McDonald).

Writing to the emotions

To craft an absorbing manuscript, the aspiring writer must reach past the facts and context, the 'intellectual' nub of the story, to connect with the reader emotionally. As said earlier, a life story written without stirring the emotions would be a dry document indeed. As also said earlier, from the *Confessions* of Augustine to the *Essays* of Montaigne and the spectacular spate of life-writing published in recent decades, successful life-writing has demonstrated that the more honest writers are with themselves, the more strongly readers relate to the text; the more profoundly writers connect with themselves and their own humanity, the more original their stories become.

Yet it can take time for new writers to understand that merely describing their own emotions—no matter how passionate and justified they are—is insufficient to draw readers into the narrative. 'Mirroring' rarely works. To be fruitful, writers need to 'write to the emotions,' which involves the use of literary techniques. For example, the writer's careful cultivation of a persona is crucial. A 'what about me' voice will drive readers away. The persona can be the writer at a different age, humorous, slick, or poetic, but it must always have what Vivian Gornick calls a 'detached empathy' that can transform the text into something of value to the disinterested reader.

Dialogue is another useful method that allows readers to experience a scene as if they were there. It lets them learn quickly about character, emotion, and mood and is a useful tool in the writer's *show-do-not-tell* toolbox. For example, 'Diana, get back here now!' is far more telling than 'She yelled for her niece Diana to return.' Dialogue can show the relationships between people, reveal tensions, create atmosphere, and reveal underlying emotions. Evocative dialogue also can add to the rhythm of the storytelling, bringing energy and dynamism to the text.

One of the best ways of showing emotion is through the character's actions. If the writer can demonstrate how the emotions affect the person's behaviour, the reader is more likely to be engaged. Instead of writing 'Jan was afraid to check out the crashing noise in the kitchen,' try 'She lay in the dark, barely breathing, straining to hear footsteps, a whisper, or any other confirmation there were intruders.' By being placed in the mind of the character, the reader is no longer passively observing but rather drawn inside the story to experience the emotion directly.

Sometimes what a character does not say can be the most telling. Subtext, often demonstrated in the contrast between what a character is saying and how they are behaving, can signal emotion in sophisticated ways, presenting deeper layers of meaning. The actions of a tight-lipped mother obsessively tidying a coffee table when her daughter returns home with her boyfriend in tow have the potential to convey the atmosphere of a scene better than the dialogue alone. In this way, conflict can be added to increase the tension. "Why of course you can stay', she said, stabbing at the magazines with the duster' works better than 'She pretended she was happy for Dean to stay, even though she was furious with her daughter.'

It is important to be specific rather than vague when trying to convey emotion. Identify the feeling, then try to express it. If the feeling is awe, for example, then instead of writing 'I had never felt anything like it before in my entire life', try 'I gaped, overwhelmed by the mountain's grandeur.' The use of sensory language also helps convey the emotional tone of a piece. Metaphor, simile, and colourful language can be used to convey emotions without ever using a specific emotion word. For example,

> Warm air enveloped her the moment she stepped through the final gate into the sanctuary, a rainforest enclosed by vaulting ceilings of glass, a fairyland of a thousand beating wings. She stopped stock still, among the tropical plants, holding her breath—her shirt transformed into a multicoloured quilt of quivering triangles.

The writer may need to set up the story before the emotion can be correctly conveyed. A decision has to be made about the emotion that the writer wants to stir in the reader. Some scenes can be emotionally confusing if not handled well because they often contain different emotions for the people portrayed, as well as for the reader. An employer, for example, can be shown as a bully, his cruelty expressed by the pleasure he takes in his actions. But the people around him may take no pleasure in his behaviour; nor may the reader. There has to be enough of the narrative leading up to that moment to ensure the reader's sympathies lie where the writer wants them to—for example, with the person being bullied.

Life-writing requires not only honesty and a sense of authenticity but also restraint. Sentimentality is a trap for writers trying to convey their feelings. As Michael Ignatieff has described it, 'Sentimental art sacrifices nuance, ambivalence, and complexity in favour of strong emotion' (293). The stronger the emotions inherent in the scene, the less they need to be embellished in the writing. All of the techniques described here can be used by the life-writer to avoid sentimentality and emotionally connect with the reader.

Writing the body

Asking writers to 'write the body,' by using techniques such as subtext or the inclusion of body language, helps them to think about inventive ways to convey emotions to their readers. We experience the world through our bodies. Our bodies are our sources of knowledge and the containers of our memories. So many of the stories writers choose to write—including speed dating, coping with illness, and success or failure in sport—benefit when the writers slow down and take the time to describe their own actions and reactions. If we write acknowledging our bodily presence in the world, we are more likely as writers to show rather than tell.

Focusing on the body can suggest complete scenes or revelatory moments of detail. How much better is it when a tennis player describes her movements in the game than when she merely states she played? If we take time to notice body language—such as someone blushing, twirling their hair absent-mindedly, or smiling behind their hand—it can be far more telling than merely stating that a person is embarrassed, distracted, or flirtatious (Miller; Eisenhuth and McDonald; King; Lamott; Zinsser).

Most of the time, we are unaware of our bodies and the way they function. They are invisible to us. We breathe and digest and walk without thinking about those processes. Some skills we have learned—such as driving or playing a musical instrument—become so automatic that we do not think about them. Our bodies 'disappear' when we are successfully using them. We become aware of our bodies only when we are ill or in discomfort (Leder).

At the same time, our bodies—and body language—play a large role in our communications. There is a saying: 'body language is more truthful than the spoken word.' Albert Mehrabian's oft-quoted 1971 research asserted that communication comprises words, voice, tone of voice, and body language, but not in equal measure. In situations where the feeling is at odds with the communication, body language and tone can mean much more than the words used. Mehrabian's research showed that in such a situation, body language accounted for around 55% of the meaning (Belludi; Mehrabian; Thompson).

Our feelings, intentions, and emotions are processed through the limbic system, which reacts to the world in real time through our bodies (Navarro). Our bodies telegraph our intentions even if our words are absent, contradictory, or slow to follow. Joe Navarro notes that people are constantly throwing off signals that may be non-verbal, communicated through body movements (such as hand gestures and posture), facial expressions, tone, and volume. Sad news can make our eyes well up with tears and our bottom lips quiver; a boring lecture can make us yawn and shift in our seats; running late for work can make us grind our teeth and rub our necks. When we are with someone we love, *isopraxis* occurs, where we mirror our beloved's behaviour. According to Joe Navarro, body reactions such as these are hardwired and consistent across the globe: 'Children who are born blind, having never seen these behaviours will also perform them. A blind child will cover his eyes when he hears something he doesn't like in the same way my neighbour does whenever I ask him to help me move heavy objects.'

Life-writing that comes from a place of illness demonstrates that writers approach conveying their corporality in different ways. Some writers distance themselves from their bodies, whereas others fully inhabit them even during the harrowing days of sickness. For example, Christopher Hitchens, in 'Topic of Cancer' (2010), his moving piece about his diagnosis with oesophageal cancer, talks about his body as a separate, distinct entity:

> I have more than once in my time woken up feeling like death. But nothing prepared me for the early morning last June when I came to consciousness feeling as if I were actually shackled to my own corpse. The whole cave of my chest and thorax seemed to have been hollowed out and then refilled with slow-drying cement. I could faintly hear myself breathe but could not manage to inflate my lungs. My heart was either beating too much or too little.

Gillian Mears, on the other hand, fully inhabits her body in her account of a major illness:

> When I'm weighed in a basket I'm 39 kilograms. Naked I look like a concentration camp victim. My liver shutting down has lent my skin a dreadful, snakeskin-yellow hue. I feel stranded in a script penned by a horror writer devoid of skill. (13)

Gretel Ehrlich uses metaphor to describe the experience of being struck by lightning, not once but twice:

> Deep in an ocean. I am suspended motionless. The water is gray. That's all there is, and before that? My arms are held out straight, cruciate, my head and legs hang limp. Nothing moves. Brown kelp lies flat in mud and fish are buried in liquid clouds of dust. There are no shadows or sounds. Should there be? I don't know if I am alive, but if not, how do I know I am dead? ... A single heartbeat stirs the gray water. Blue trickles in, just a tiny stream. Then a long silence. Another heartbeat. (3–4)

Regardless of the approach taken, if a writer can connect with being a fleshy, bodily presence in the world, it will make their writing deeper and more interesting.

Writing to the spirit

Finally, writers are asked to 'write to the spirit.' The best life-writing does much more than merely retell events, even within a broader context. It is an inquiry into what it means to be human. As Miller writes, 'Experience needs to be filtered through the weathers of the self, remade by the processes of reflection, until it finds its richest form' (11).

There is no room for blame or bitterness in a life story. Writers must write with sufficient detachment for them to interrogate their own role in their tale (Gornick). By deliberating on who they were before and after the event detailed in the manuscript, and in what ways their relationships to themselves and others have changed, the writer uses the work as a means to self-knowledge. The writer and the reader are joined on an inward voyage of discovery that enriches the writing and makes it meaningful. As Annie Dillard so eloquently wrote in *The Writing Life*,

Why are we reading if not in hope that the writer will magnify and dramatize our days, will illuminate and inspire us with wisdom, courage, and the possibility of meaningfulness, and will press upon our minds the deepest mysteries, so we may feel again their majesty and power? (72–73)

As Elizabeth J. Andrew observes, once the writer has recorded the main scenes and events, it is then useful to review the draft manuscript with the following questions in mind: What changed? Why? How? When? What is the cause? What is the effect? Who was I before, during, and after this event? What was my relationship to these events, and what is it today? These questions matter and have the potential to enrich both the writer and the readers. By looking beyond the mere retelling of events or the relaying of interesting titbits, depth is added to the writing. This may involve the writer examining their own experiences in the search for an overarching coherence, shape, or meaning. That meaning may be religious—and relate to one's god—but not necessarily. It could just as easily be truth or nature or justice or some other value that requires the writer to reflect deeply on their words.

Life-writing is a unique and powerful tool. It allows the ordinary person to be heard; witnesses hidden histories; speaks back to those in positions of power; and allows the writer and the reader to learn more about themselves. Because it involves both enquiry and confession, in its best moments, it explores rather than asserts, containing both a searching and a willingness to be vulnerable. By allowing writers to explore their personal truths and express themselves on any topic, from travel to sexuality, it is flexible and democratic. When writers follow the four-pronged approach outlined in the second paragraph of this chapter, they are encouraged to redraft their stories, refining and revising them layer by layer as they connect with their intellects, their emotions, their bodies, and their spirits, giving their writing substance and readability.

 ACTIVITY

Exercises for practice

Exercise 1: Write a piece beginning with 'I remember.' This could comprise many small memories or one large memory. Do not censor any; let your mind flow.

Exercise 2: Describe a room. Without ever using 'feeling' words, describe the room as if you loathe it. Now describe the same room again but this time as if you love it.

Exercise 3: Work with a partner, and take it in turns to act out an emotion—for example, anger, embarrassment, shyness, or exhilaration—and observe the ways each of you expresses those emotions through your bodies.

Exercise 4: Recreate a remembered conversation. Be as accurate as possible. Now add to the scene any non-verbal language that you remember the participants using. Reflect on any changes to tone or tension when the body language is added.

Exercise 5: Write about one of the following topics:

- running
- the night sky
- the colour blue
- your favourite place
- how you learned about sex
- a teacher you had
- the angriest you've ever been

🔍 Recommended Reading

Dillard, Annie. *The Writing Life*. Harper Perennial, (1989) 2003.

Eisenhuth, Suzie, and Willa McDonald, editors. *The Writer's Reader: Understanding Journalism and Non-Fiction*. Cambridge UP, 2007.

Gornick, Vivian. *The Situation and the Story: The Art of Personal Narrative*. Farrar, Strauss & Giroux, 2001.

Ignatieff, Michael. 'The Stories We Tell: Television and Humanitarian Aid,' in *Hard Choices: Moral Dilemmas in Humanitarian Intervention*, edited by Jonathan Moore, pp. 287–302. Rowman and Littlefield, 1998.

King, Stephen. *On Writing: A Memoir of the Craft*. Hodder and Stoughton, 2000.

Lamott, Anne. Bird by Bird: Some Instructions on Writing and Life. Anchor/ Random House, 1994.

Miller, Patti. *The Memoir Book*. Allen & Unwin, 2007.

Strayed, Cheryl. *Cheryl Strayed*, #14. Longform Podcast. longform.org/posts/longform-podcast-144-cheryl-strayed. Accessed 8 Dec. 2017.

Zinsser, William. *On Writing Well*. Harper Collins, (1976) 1994.

 ## Works Cited

Andrew, Elizabeth Jarrett. 'Giving Your Story a Plot.' *Elizabeth Jarrett Andrew: Tending the Spiritual Lives of Writers and Readers*, 25 Mar. 2013. www.elizabethjarretandrew.com//2013/03/giving-your-story-a-plot/. Accessed 8 Dec. 2017.

Augustine, of Hippo, Saint. *The Confessions of St. Augustine* [397–400 CE], edited and translated by Thomas à Kempis et al. P. F. Collier & Son, 1909.

Belludi, Nagesh. *Albert Mehrabian's 7-38-55 Rule of Personal Communication*. Posted 4 Oct. 2008. www.psychologytoday.com/au/blog/beyond-words201109/is-nonverbal-communication-numbers. Accessed 18 Apr. 2019.

Blau DuPlessis, Rachel, and Snitow Ann, editors. *The Feminist Memoir Project*. Three Rivers Press, 1998.

Brown, Claude. *Manchild in a Promised Land*. Hill & Wang, 1965.

Couser, G. Thomas. 'Memoir's ethics', in *Memoir: An Introduction*, edited by Brendan O'Neill, pp. 79–107. U of Oxford P, 2012.

Defonseca, Misha. *Misha: A Memoir of the Holocaust Years*. Mt. Ivy Press, 1997.

Dillard, Annie. *The Writing Life*. Harper Perennial, 2013.

Ehrlich, Gretel. *A Match to the Heart: One Woman's Story of Being Struck by Lightning*. Penguin, 1995.

Eisenhuth, Susie, and Willa McDonald, editors. *The Writer's Reader: Understanding Journalism and Non-Fiction*. U Cambridge P, 2007.

Frey, James. *A Million Little Pieces*. N. A. Talese/Doubleday, 2003.

Gornick, Vivian. *The Situation and the Story: The Art of Personal Narrative*. Farrar, Strauss & Giroux, 2001.

Hitchens, Christopher. 'Topic of Cancer.' *Vanity Fair*, Aug. 2010. www.vanityfair.com/culture/features/2010/09/hitchens-201009. Accessed 8 Dec. 2017.

Hyman Jr, Ira E., and Joel Pentland. 'The Role of Mental Imagery in the Creation of False Childhood Memories.' *Journal of Memory and Language*, vol. 35, no. 2, Apr. 1996, pp. 101–17.

Ignatieff, Michael. 'The Stories We Tell: Television and Humanitarian Aid,' in *Hard Choices: Moral Dilemmas in Humanitarian Intervention*, edited by Jonathon Moore, pp. 287–302. Rowman and Littlefield, 1998.

Innocence Project. 'Eyewitness Misidentification.' *The Causes*. The Innocence Project. 2017. www.innocenceproject.org/causes/eyewitness-misidentification/. Accessed 8 Dec. 2018.

Khouri, Norma. *Forbidden Love*. Bantam Books, 2003.

King, Stephen. *On Writing: A Memoir of the Craft*. Hodder and Stoughton, 2000.

Kolhatkar, Sheelah. 'The awful untruth.' *The Observer*, 23 Jan. 2006. observer.com/2006/01/the-awful-truth-3. Accessed 8 Dec. 2017.

Lamott, Anne. *Bird by Bird: Some Instructions on Writing and Life*. Random House, 1994.

Leder, Drew. *The Absent Body*. U Chicago P, 1990.

Lejeune, Philippe. 'The Autobiographical Pact' and 'The Autobiographical Pact (bis),' in *On Autobiography*, edited and with a foreword by John Paul Eakin and Katherine Leary, pp. 3–30, 119–37. U Minnesota P, 1989.

Lindsay, D. Stephen, and J. Don Read. 'The Recovered Memories Controversy: Where Do We Go From Here?' in *Recovered Memories: Seeking the Middle Ground*, edited by G. M. Davies and T. Dalgleish, pp. 71–94. Wiley, 2001.

Loftus, Elizabeth F. 'The reality of repressed memories.' *American Psychologist,* vol. 48, 1993, pp. 518–37.

Loftus, Elizabeth F., and Jacqueline E. Pickrell. 'The formation of false memories.' *Psychiatric Annals,* vol. 25, no. 12, 1995, pp. 720–25.

Mears, Gillian. 'Alive in Ant and Bee', in *Best Australian Essays*, edited by Drusilla Modjeska, pp. 1–15. Black Inc., 2007.

Mehrabian, Albert. *Silent Messages*. Wadsworth Publishing Company, 1971.

Miller, Patti. *The Memoir Book*. Allen & Unwin, 2007.

Montaigne, Michel de. *The Essays of Montaigne (Complete), by Michel de Montaigne*, translated by Charles Cotton and William Carew Hazlitt. Reeves and Turner, 1877. Project Gutenberg. E-book. Produced by David Widger. Released 17 Sept. 2006, updated 5 Sept. 2012. www.gutenberg.org/files/3600/3600-h/3600-h.html. Accessed 8 Dec. 2017. (Originally *Essais*, published by Simon Millanges and Jean Richer Simon, March 1580.)

Morgan, Sally. *My Place*. Freemantle Arts Centre Press, 1987.

Navarro, Joe. 'Body Language Basics: The Honesty of Body Language.' *Psychology Today,* 21 Aug. 2011. www.psychologytoday.com/blog/spycatcher/201108/body-language-basics. Accessed 8 Dec. 2017.

Pung, Alice. *Unpolished Gem*. Black Inc., 2006.

Renza, Luis A. 'The veto of the imagination: A theory of autobiography.' *New Literary History*, vol. 9, no. 1, Self-Confrontation and Social Vision, Autumn 1977, pp. 1–26. Published online by John Hopkins UP. DOI: 10.2307/46834. *JSTOR*, www.jstor.org/stable/468434. Accessed 8 Dec. 2017.

Sacks, Oliver. 'Speak, Memory.' *New York Review of Books*, 21 Feb. 2013, pp. 1–7. www.nybooks.com/articles/2013/02/21/speak-memory/. Accessed 8 Dec. 2017.

——. *Uncle Tungsten: Memories of a Chemical Boyhood*. Picador, 2016.

Schaffer, Kay. 'Stolen generation narrative in local and global contexts.' *Antipodes*, vol. 16, no.1, June 2002, pp. 5–10.

Sedaris, David. *Me Talk Pretty One Day*. Little, Brown and Company, 2000.

Smith, Sidonie, and Julia Watson. *Reading Autobiography: A Guide for Interpreting Life Narratives*. 2nd ed. U Minnesota P, 2010.

Thompson, Jeff. *Is Nonverbal Communication a Numbers Game?* Posted 30 Sept. 2011. www.psychologytoday.com/au/blog/beyond-words201109/is-nonverbal-communication-numbers. Accessed 18 Apr. 2019.

Wade, Kimberley, et al. 'A picture is worth a thousand lies: Using false photographs to create false childhood memories.' *Psychonomic Bulletin & Review*, vol. 9, no. 3, 2002, pp. 597–603.

Weisel, Elie. *Night*. Hill & Wang, 1960.

Zinsser, William. *On Writing Well*. HarperCollins, 1994.

Notes

1. With thanks to Dr Kate Rossmanith for introducing me to the concept of 'writing the body' and Dr Bunty Avieson for her sage suggestions regarding the draft text of this article, including the suggestion of Exercise 3.

12 AUTOBIOGRAPHICAL WRITING FOR CHILDREN: AHN DO'S *THE LITTLE REFUGEE* AND MALALA YOUSAFZAI'S *MALALA'S MAGIC PENCIL*

Kate Douglas

Ahn Do is one of Australia's best-known and most highly regarded comedians, having success in stand-up, on television, in films, and in print. His comedy, across these forms, is infused with autobiographical storytelling. Do has also penned two award-winning autobiographical texts: the first of these is *The Happiest Refugee* (2010), which details his family's dangerous journey to Australia as refugees from Vietnam and his and his family's experiences settling into life in Australia. The second is (the written and illustrated) *The Little Refugee* (2011), which tells his migration story and is written for a child readership.

Do's is not the first memoir in recent times to be adapted for young readers. Malala Yousafzai's *I Am Malala: The Girl Who Stood Up for Education and Was Shot by the Taliban* was published in 2013 and adapted the following year (into a different text) for young readers. In 2017, Malala published another memoir—a picture book for readers aged four to eight—*Malala's Magic Pencil*, by Malala Yousafzai, illustrated by Kerascoët. There are many examples of memoirs adapted for children, including Daniel James Brown's *The Boys in the Boat* (2015), Robert Hodge's *Ugly* (2013), Sonia Nazario's *Enrique's Journey* (2007), and Charles Wilson and Eric Schlosser's *Chew On This: Everything You Don't*

Want to Know About Fast Food. (2006), a young adult version of their bestselling book *Fast Food Nation: The Dark Side of the All-American Meal* (2001). Authors potentially have much to gain from such adaptations, most obviously an increased readership, book sales, and the literary kudos associated with crossing literary genres. Further, there have been many examples of successful memoirs written explicitly for young readers or that have had significant crossover appeal for young readers—for instance, child soldier memoirs, such as Ishmael Beah's *A Long Way Gone* (2007), and the plethora of memoirs about adolescent drug or alcohol addiction, such as Koren Zailckas's *Smashed—Growing Up a Drunk Girl* (2005).

But considering the popularity of children's and young adult literature (Beckton), and despite the growth of non-fiction genres for child and young adult readers (Brien) and the importance of these genres in educational curricula (Abrahamson and Carter, Betty; Martens et al.; Sharp and Parkes; Carter, Betty, and Abrahamson), there is little scholarship in the field of life-writing on life-writing for children and young adults and almost no scholarship that explores crossover non-fictions and the remediation of adult memoirs for child and young adult readerships.

This chapter works at the intersection of young adult memoir, scholarship on young adult writing more generally (Beckton; Carter, Imogen), and life-writing for, by, and about children (Douglas and Poletti) to consider the practice and cultural work of life-writing for children. Drawing on the examples of Ahn Do's and Malala Yousafzai's memoirs written for children, I consider the transition that these autobiographical stories take as they move from being an autobiography written for an adult readership to an autobiography written for children. Do's *The Little Refugee* and Yousafzai's *Malala's Magic Pencil* reflect a desire to share life-writing with a child readership and a belief in children's ability to comprehend and understand this story as a life story worth reading. I am also conscious of the positioning of life narratives for children as modelling tools for writing a different kind of autobiography. The chapter also considers some important issues for both scholarly and creative life narrative practice: what issues arise when an author seeks to adapt their life narrative for a young readership? Collaboration seems central to ensuring an effective and meaningful transition between adult story/storyteller and child reader. What are the implications for scholars who seek to 'read' child-authored texts in academic contexts?

The Little Refugee

Do co-authored *The Little Refugee* with his wife, Suzanne Do, and the book is illustrated by award-winning author/illustrator Bruce Whatley.[1] Whatley has worked on more than eighty children's picture books, and although he is based in Australia, his work is also published internationally (BruceWhatley.com).[2] *The Little Refugee* is aimed at readers aged four to eight (Webb).[3]

The opening page plays on comic stereotypes of Vietnam that might be familiar to, and are thus coded for, adult readers. But children will likely find them interesting too. Do writes, 'I was born in a faraway country called Vietnam. It's a crazy place—strange food, snakes in bottles, five people squashed onto the back of one little motorbike.'[4] As a comedian, Do adheres to the idea that some of the best comedy comes from laughing at yourself. The reader is also invited to laugh, with Do's permission— and this works to remind young readers, simply, of the ethics associated with humour. The narrative is told by a knowing, retrospective narrator (they fill in the child's knowledge gaps retrospectively). But the voice, language, and tone are childish. This dialogic approach is common in autobiographical writing about childhood, as it allows authors a 'best of both worlds' approach where they are able to deploy the innocent child narrator for affect (in this instance, for both child and adult readers) but still include information that an adult would possess but that a child would not have had access to at the time (Douglas, *Contesting Childhood* 93).

The harsh realities of Do's experience as a refugee are embedded within the text, but the tone remains positive throughout the telling; for example, he explains that though his family was poor and his house was always overcrowded, his childhood was filled with love and others to play with (Do). This is the challenge that authors face throughout their life narrative: how to tell a life story, which is also a trauma story, to children in a way that is accessible to them. As Marlene Kadar argues, 'questions about appropriateness and suffering come into play when the reader is a child or a young adult' (43). Children's books attend to diverse levels of literacy, and thus pictures are an essential part of conveying a story.

The memoir's visual style is a mix of photorealist-style and comic-style drawings. The comic-style drawings are in a sepia tone; the photorealist drawings are in a blue-grey tone, reminiscent of black-and-white photographs, but the blue effect captures the effects of the sea journey (e.g., the ominous sky and sea). The contrast is effective in conveying Do's childhood experiences alongside the broader social and political contexts affecting his life. For instance, in the early pages of the memoir, we see

Do playing happily with his family and chickens. The children are smiling. On the following page we see soldiers in the Vietnam War: one,
probably injured, being carried by another. The unhappy face of the soldier at the rear offers a stark contrast to that of the innocent children in
the opposite picture. The narrator explains that as a child, he didn't know
much about the war or how many people were dying: soldiers, moth-
ers, fathers, and children (Do). Again, the juxtaposition is important:
the unknowing, innocent children and the retrospective adult narrator
explaining what he knows now (that many people, including children,
were dying at this very moment).

The narrator then proceeds to explain how he became a refugee. As I
have discussed elsewhere, representations of refugees and asylum seekers
pervade the Australian public sphere, and much of this reporting is negative, scaremongering rhetoric (Douglas, 'Silence Speaks' 546; Douglas
and Graham). So the representation of ethnic and cultural identities in
children's life-writing can be a highly political act (Davis 185). Autobiographical writing for children 'may also be engaged in a didactic project—
the reader accompanies the writer as his or her self-as-child learns about
heritage culture and experiences historical events' (185). Life narratives
attempt to locate individual lives within the wider social, cultural, and
political contexts affecting these lives (Smith and Watson; Couser); children's life narrative is no different. Kadar explains that 'In recent years,
the auto/biographical genres have been widely used in order to represent
intense traumatic events for a young adult readership, including the specific historical events of World War II, the rise of facism, and the Holocaust' (44). These stories leak 'into other lands, other generations, and
other communities through a young adult readership' (44). But as Kadar
argues, adult anxieties about children too often pervade the representations made for children within children's literature and our critical conversations about children's literatures (43). This is despite the plethora of
research that shows the value of children reading challenging texts about
the world around them. For example, Prisca Martens et al. suggest in
their research on the instrumental value of non-fictional picture books
that 'through experiences with global literature children develop richer
understandings of themselves as complex cultural beings and a perception of themselves as capable problem-solvers who identify issues and
take action to solve them' (609). Global literatures promote intercultural
understanding and encourage young readers to make sense of the world
they live in (Short). This is clearly a goal of Do's *The Little Refugee* and

Yousafzai's *Malala's Magic Pencil*, and it is important to consider how these authors go about this complex task.

In Do's *The Little Refugee*, the narrator is careful to explain two things: his father and uncles were fighting alongside Australian and American soldiers, and this made them vulnerable after the war, because they fought on the losing side. The narrator explains how they had little choice but to become boat people. The representation of the overcrowded, unsafe boat on the stormy seas is juxtaposed with an image of Do's mother holding him and his brother close and reassuring them that everything will be okay. This is perhaps the primary way that *The Little Refugee* represents the trauma experienced by Do and his family: by contrasting the traumatic experience with a representation of hope—the love of family, the value of optimism, resilience, and so forth. So, even when the story becomes frightening (pirates come aboard their boat, steal their valuables, and threaten to kill Do's little brother), the trauma is always contrasted with representations of optimism (the refugees stand defiantly against the pirates, and the boy Ahn Do asks the pirate to fill his water bottle). As Kadar muses, 'believing in the educative value of such stories, adults encourage younger people to read them. A dance ensues between the horror represented and the testimonial character of the stories' (47).

Do and his family are rescued shortly after this incident and arrive in Australia. The tone of the story then shifts to a representation of the family's transition into Australian life, including more hardship (language barriers, financial pressures) but also some humour, a consistent sense of optimism, and ultimately a triumphant ending: Do is appointed class captain. Do writes, that despite the 'dangers' and 'hardships,' his mum and dad always filled him with a sense of hope that everything would turn out okay. It may be easy to read this text cynically—as overly didactic and moralising about ideal migration outcomes. Do is an example of a refugee who has become successful in Australian society. As Heather Sharp and Vicki Parkes argue in their analysis of the use of World War I picture books in Australian schools, 'picture books … are a powerful pedagogical tool in the enculturation of values and ideas to the reader' (129). Thus, readers and writers have responsibilities here—to engage critically in their approach to writing about children and locating children in the world. For instance, though Do's and Yousafzai's books have happy endings, they are careful to convey their trauma—to show that their lives were dangerous and endangered. These representations are important for the visibility they bring to the issues and lives they represent.

Malala Yousafzai and *Malala's Magic Pencil*

Malala Yousafzai is a Nobel Prize–winning life narrative author and educational activist from Pakistan. After being shot in the head at close range by the Taliban in 2012, Malala's incredible recovery and resilience, and her ongoing commitment to activism, have provided inspiration for people (of all ages) all over the world.

Though Malala is perhaps best known as a political activist, her primary activist tool is her life-writing (Douglas, 'Malala Yousafzai' 297). Her life-writing began with the pseudonymous blog that she wrote for the BBC in 2009; she has since written two print memoirs: her co-authored (with Christine Lamb) memoir *I Am Malala* (2013), which was followed by the publication of a 'young readers' edition' co-authored by Patricia McCormick (2016). There have also been numerous biographical texts about her life. For instance, in 2009, Adam B. Ellick and Irfan Ashraf made the short documentary 'Class Dismissed: Malala's Story,' which profiled the experiences of Malala and her activist father Ziauddin at the coalface of the violent opposition to educational inequality in the Swat Valley in Pakistan. The documentary film *He Named Me Malala*, directed by Davis Guggenheim, was released in 2015 (*He Named Me Malala*; Douglas, 'Malala Yousafzai' 297).

As I argue elsewhere, 'collectively these texts represent a collaborative archive: a cumulative series of life narrative texts authored by Malala and others which have become authoritative narratives in circulating Malala's life story' (Douglas, 'Malala Yousafzai' 297). As Matt Petronzio (*Mashable.com*) reports, Malala explains her reasoning for writing this book:

> I have met many young children who want to know about what happened in my life and why I believe in education for all, so it was important for me to share my story with them
>
> ...
>
> For this age, a picture book felt like the best way—to use pictures and to simplify the events in a way that younger kids can understand. There are scary parts to my story or details that are complicated to explain, but I wanted to be able to share it with a younger audience as best as I could. (Petronzio)

The book stems from a desire for inclusivity in life-writing: an aspiration to reach as wide a readership as possible because of an investment in the cultural value of life-writing for child readers.

Malala's latest book, *Malala's Magic Pencil*, is a significant addition to Malala's collaborative life narrative archive. In this work, she collaborates with Kerascoët: the collective name for award-winning French illustrators Marie Pommepuy and Sébastien Cosset. The adage 'a picture is worth a thousand words' captures the challenge that faces Malala and her collaborators. The collaboration allows Malala to layer her life narrative on the graphics by Kerascoët and allows Kerascoët to offer a visual, complementary representation of Malala's life story. In the spirit of Malala's previous life narratives (in which she worked with co-authors and documentary makers), Malala collaborates to gain the skills needed to circulate an appropriate book for her target readership.

Those who are familiar with Malala, the life narrative texts that she has authored, and the news and documentaries about her are accustomed to reading a particular type of narrative: an adolescent Malala and Malala as an accomplished young woman. In *Malala's Magic Pencil*, we meet a different, younger Malala. This picture book is not simply an adaptation of her previous published works (perhaps less directly aligned to the memoir for adult reader as Ahn Do's picture book is). In *Malala's Magic Pencil*, Malala's concerns are, initially, different from those that readers have heard about in her previous life narratives: they are more childish and simple and are in accordance with the limits of childhood knowledge. The reader is aware that this is a narrative strategy: Malala is twenty years old as she adopts the first-person narrative voice of her childish self. As mentioned earlier, adopting a child's perspective and voice, of course, is not uncommon amongst adult writers of fiction and non-fiction and of picture books. What makes Malala's approach here new and unusual is that this book is one of multiple life narrative texts by Malala and that in writing for children, Malala shows how a life narrative story can be retold to reach diverse readerships. So, even though the plot and representations in *Malala's Magic Pencil* initially seem different from her previous memoirs, the representations are recognisably adjacent—meaningful to a child reader but coded for adult readers.

For example, the book opens with a double page, featuring soft colours—pastel blue shades and sketched drawings of the mountains and the city—the landscape of Malala's life, with golden hand-drawn, flowers and leaves and the sun drawn over the top of the landscape. As the *Publishers Weekly* review of the book notes, 'Kerascoët's bright, reportorial watercolors match the text's directness and sincerity, adding gold embellishments to give Malala's hopes and optimism a radiant physicality.' Cartoon Malala is in the bottom right-hand side of the pages, wearing soft-pink and white clothing, which contrasts beautifully with the blue pastel landscape and functions to highlight Malala on the page. Over the top of cartoon Malala is one simple sentence in a simple small black font: 'Do you believe in magic?' Malala holds a notebook and pen. It is not clear whether it is Malala asking the question or whether the question is being asked of Malala, so the effect is that it is both, and thus the book, in its opening page, aligns the child reader with Malala. In asking a question, the opening page invites engagement from the reader: an opportunity to think and reflect on the very notion of belief and what we know to be true. The first page also invites parallels to genres and stories common to children's literature: magical fairy tales, faraway lands, adventure, conflict, and overcoming adversity.

As Imogen Carter notes, it is a

> tricky business writing for young children about human rights: too heavy-handed and your work has an excessively moralising air, too heartfelt and it sounds schmaltzy. Having captured the world's attention as a schoolgirl blogger (Makai, Gul) under Taliban rule in Pakistan, Malala Yousafzai knows a thing or two about striking the right tone.

As the book progresses, it becomes more and more of a 'how to' narrative on representing traumatic lives and experiences for a child readership: it offers one approach for sharing a trauma life narrative, by being true to events and without patronising young readers. For example, the reader learns that Malala is inspired by a television programme she watched as a child, in which a boy solved problems with a magic pencil—by drawing items or people that could help. The reader then learns that Malala imagines what she would do if she had a magic pencil. Initially her concerns relate to her own immediate life (e.g., she imagines she would place a lock on her door so that her brothers could not bother her; she would stop time so that she could sleep in). The pictures depict Malala with her magic pencil, fixing her problems. She then imagines fixing her family's immediate problems: she would create the best buildings for her father to teach in; she would draw a ball so that her brothers could play. (*Malala's Magic Pencil* represents Malala's growing consciousness of the hardship children often experience in the world (Douglas *Contesting Childhood*; Douglas and Graham). In the book, after witnessing some children 'fishing for scraps' in a rubbish pile, Malala asks her father why these children are not in school. A frame depicts Malala and her gentle-faced father sitting together while her father explains the inequalities affecting children's, and more particularly girls' education. Malala explains 'School was my favourite place. But I had never considered myself lucky to be able to go.' In the next page, Malala is in the top right-hand corner, looking out of a window, her head in her hands. As she looks out on the streetscape she sees children hard at work—washing clothes and carrying baskets alongside adults doing the same. The harsh realities of inequality are becoming clearer to Malala as she grows. Malala then comes to think about the magic pencil in terms of using it to 'draw a better world, a peaceful world.' Malala is pictured in the bottom left-hand corner, fixing the cityscape with her pencil. She explains that she would first erase 'war, poverty and hunger' and draw boys and girls as equals. Years pass, and Malala explains that she stopped wishing for a magic pencil and realised the most important thing she could do is to focus on her schooling and gain an education.

One of the most potent images in the book is a divided, shadowy page, down the middle of the street in which one side is darker and one is lighter. On the left side is a family (a man, a woman, and a young daughter) that look to be hurrying down the street. The woman and her daughter wear the full burka. Deeper in the picture, towards the back are two men holding guns. On the other side of the page is Malala who is in the light, but also looking warily behind her at men holding guns. The picture shows that much of Malala's city is already affected by the darkness (the Taliban's influence). However, Malala does not refer to them as the Taliban but rather as 'powerful and dangerous men.' The content of these pages recognises the importance of connecting to a child readership; to invoke response without fear of transference of trauma. It is most important that the book focus on Malala's experience of growing up and becoming a brave activist and connect on the level of her emotional responses to the events: from fear to bravery and optimism. *Malala's Magic Pencil* offers life-writers an insight into what aspects of life might be shared effectively with child readers and how to achieve this through the combination of well-chosen language and evocative drawings.

In *Malala's Magic Pencil*, Malala ultimately sees life-writing as a potential weapon against the Taliban. Malala is pictured sitting on her bed, writing that 'Someone needed to speak out. Why not me?' On the page next to this, many people of diverse races and cultures and ages are pictured reading Malala's writing, as if the pages have just flown into their hands. This wonderful image neatly explains how Malala's writing—on her pseudonymous blog, Gul Makai—went viral. In just a couple of pages, Malala describes how she spoke out for the girls who couldn't speak for themselves (Anonymous).

In one simply designed page, Malala summarises the traumatic events of 9 October 2012. The left-hand side of the page is black with white writing:

> My voice became so powerful that dangerous men tried to silence me.
>
> But they failed.

The first sentence is represented in the adjacent picture of Malala. The right-hand side of the page is Malala looking out the window (she is most likely in hospital in the United Kingdom given that she is wearing a blue hospital gown and hospital admission bracelet and given that she stands next to central heating bar heater). We cannot see her face (which would have been traumatised by the gun shot); the overt trauma is hidden from a child reader but coded for an adult reader. For the child reader, the words that follow are the most important in the book.

The second part of the quotation, 'But they failed,' is represented in the final pages of the book. Malala explains that her 'voice is louder than ever,' and the picture shows many people holding placards of support and photos of Malala. Malala asks again, 'Do you still believe in magic?' The pictures summarise the events in the book (Malala witnessing the children working, Malala watching TV, Malala writing) and Malala watching some young women entering the school. She explains that she had found magic in her words and her work. The final page depicts Malala speaking at the United Nations.

Thus, the moral of *Malala's Magic Pencil* is that she was not silenced. It is incredibly powerful that Malala omits details of her shooting. The simplest explanation for this omission is that you must not tell four- to eight-year-old readers that a young girl was shot point-blank by religious extremists; this must not and should not be shown. But, more potently, in not representing this event, Malala powerfully erases it, at least temporarily, from her history. In doing so, she focuses on a simple, inspiring message: the power of speaking up and speaking out. She will not allow the trauma to define her life; instead, the triumph is foregrounded. The book focuses on what children can do by way of advocacy. Education is something children of this age will know about, so the book's foregrounding of the power of education is important. Malala shows a new generation of would-be life narrators that life stories are a powerful genre and that there are many potent ways to interpret the facts of life and to show the impact of particular life events. As Grace Lin notes, *Malala's Magic Pencil* reminds us 'as long as there are artists, there will be an important place for the pencil in our lives. It continues to be a forceful tool, revealing its powers to us in the passion of an artist, the struggles and joys of the creative journey, and the inspiration to fight injustice.' The pen really is mightier than the sword, and every pencil has the potential to be magic.

Conclusion

The adapted picture book memoirs of Ahn Do and Malala Yousafzai remind us of the broad potential of life-writing as a genre. Life-writing texts that are widely successful with adults, and particularly those that address timely social issues like trauma and displacement have obvious potential for child readers. Non-fictional picture books are widely used with children in educational contexts because of their accessibility for children at different levels of literacy and for their instrumental value in encouraging children to learn about and reflect on the world they live in. There are important cultural politics and pedagogical ideologies which underlie the publication and circulation of life-writing for and amongst children. I consider Do's and Yousafzai's autobiographies for children as potential case studies for a deeper consideration of the role that autobiographical writing for children might play within life-writing genres more generally. Although it is not within the remit of this chapter to discuss these, they are worth further research. I envisage that this aspect would also have interest for scholars who seek to 'read' child-authored texts within academic contexts. As Kadar argues, 'As much as it is difficult to agree about the age at which a child/youth/young adult should read painful historical narratives, the difficulty is worth encountering. … we want to hope that as adults, our children will have the understanding and willingness to act 'at the right moment'' (55).

Although readers and writers must be mindful of minimising or universalising experiences of trauma in representations for children and of the possibility of being overly simplistic or patronising in these representations, the picture books by Ahn Do and those by Malala Yousafzai show some of the ways these issues and texts can be adapted successfully. Through their creative collaborations with co-authors and illustrators, Do and Yousafzai have used diverse literary techniques to blend visual and verbal narratives to reach a new readership. For instance, the juxtaposition of different visual styles works effectively in both texts to contrast the child's eye with the more knowing, adult perspective. Both texts offer only one or two representations of traumatic experience to stand for the wider experiences of the children and their families, thus offering strategies for how to best represent trauma to child readers and to offer direction on the limits that writers and illustrators might impose in life-writing for children. Malala's achievements also reveal the possible contributions that young authors might make to this growing genre—to tell stories about their own lives in their own voices. Again, collaboration (from adult writers, editors, publishers, and so forth) might prove to be a useful strategy to ensure that young writers are able to make a positive intervention in these new and emerging modes of life-writing.

 ACTIVITY

Questions for practice

- If you were adapting your memoir for a young adult readership, what might be some of the key issues you need to attend to?
- What might be some of the pitfalls in writing for a child or young adult readership?
- Why might reading non-fictional texts be particularly valuable for young readers?

 Recommended Reading

Abrahamson, Richard F., and Betty Carter. 'What we know about nonfiction and young adult readers and what we need to do about it.' *Publishing Research Quarterly*, vol. 8, no. 1, 1992, pp. 41–54.

Beah, Ishmael. *A Long Way Gone*. Farrar, Straus and Giroux, 2007.

Beckton, Denise. 'Bestselling Young Adult fiction: Trends, genres and readership.' *TEXT*, vol. 32, 2015. www.textjournal.com.au. Accessed 7 Dec. 2017.

Brien, Donna Lee. 'What about young adult non-fiction? Profiling the young adult memoir.' *TEXT*, vol. 32, 2015. www.textjournal.com.au/speciss/ issue32/Brien.pdf. Accessed 7 Dec. 2017.

Brown, Daniel James. *The Boys in the Boat: Nine Americans and Their Epic Quest for Gold at the 1936 Berlin Olympics*. Penguin Books, 2015.

Cart, Michael. 'From insider to outsider: the evolution of young adult literature.' *Voices from the Middle,* vol. 9, no. 2, 2001, pp. 95–97.

Carter, Betty. 'Reviewing nonfiction books for children and young adults: Stance, scholarship and structure,' in *Evaluating Children's Books: A Critical Look: Aesthetic, Social, and Political Aspects Of Analyzing and Using Children's Books*, edited by Betsy Hearne and R. Sutton, pp. 59–71. U Illinois P, 1993.

Carter, Betty, and Richard F. Abrahamson. *Nonfiction for Young Adults: From Delight to Wisdom*. Oryx, 1990.

Couser, G. Thomas. *Memoir: An Introduction*. Oxford UP, 2011.

Douglas, Kate. *Contesting Childhood: Autobiography, Trauma and Memory*. New Rutgers, 2010.

Hodge, Robert. *Ugly*. Hatchette, 2013.

Nazario, Sonia. *Enrique's Journey: The Story of a Boy's Dangerous Odyssey to Reunite with his Mother*. Random House, 2007.

Schlosser, Eric. *Fast Food Nation: The Dark Side of the All-American Meal*. Houghton and Miffin, 2001.

Wilson, Charles, and Eric Schlosser. *Chew On This*: *Everything You Don't Want to Know About Fast Food*. Houghton Miffin Co., 2006.

Zailckas, Koren. *Smashed—Growing Up a Drunk Girl*. Ebury Press, 2005.

 Works Cited

Abrahamson, Richard F., and Betty Carter. 'What we know about nonfiction and young adult readers and what we need to do about it.' *Publishing Research Quarterly,* vol. 8, no. 1, 1992, pp. 41–54.

Anonymous. 'Diary of a Pakistani school girl.' *BBC news*, posted 19 Jan. 2009, updated 27 Aug. 2014. news.bbc.co.uk/2/hi/south_asia/7834402.stm. Accessed 9 Dec. 2017.

Beckton, Denise. 'Bestselling Young Adult fiction: Trends, genres and readership.' *TEXT*, vol. 32, 2015, pp.1–18. www.textjournal.com.au. Accessed 9 Dec. 2017.

Brien, Donna Lee. 'What about young adult non-fiction?: Profiling the young adult memoir.' *TEXT*, Special Issue Series, vol. 32, 2015, pp. 1–20. www.textjournal.com.au/speciss/issue32/Brien.pdf. Accessed 9 Dec. 2017.

Bruce.Whatley.com. 1 Nov. 2017. www.brucewhatley.com. Accessed 9 Dec. 2017.

Carter, Betty, and Richard F. Abrahamson. *Nonfiction for Young Adults: From Delight to Wisdom*. Oryx, 1990.

Carter, Imogen. 'Malala's Magic Pencil by Malala Yousafzai review—an enchantingly light touch.' Review of *Malala's Magic Pencil*, by Malala Yousafzai and Kerascoët. *The Observer*, 10 Oct. 2017. www.theguardian.com/books/2017/oct/10/malala's-magic-pencil-by-malala-yousafzei-review-picture-book. Accessed 9 Dec. 2017.

Couser, G. Thomas. *Memoir: An Introduction*. Oxford UP, 2011.

Davis, Rocio G. 'Asian American Autobiography for Children: Critical Paradigms and Creative Practice.' *Lion and the Unicorn: A Critical Journal of Children's Literature,* vol. 30, no. 2, 2006, pp. 185–201.

Do, Ahn. *The Happiest Refugee: My journey from Tragedy to Comedy*. Allen & Unwin, 2010.

Do, Ahn, and Suzanne Do. *The Little Refugee*. Allen & Unwin, 2011.

Douglas, Kate. *Contesting Childhood: Autobiography, Trauma and Memory*. Rutgers, 2010.

———. 'Silence speaks: Shaun Tan's *The Arrival*,' in *Telling Stories: Australian Literary Cultures 1935–2010*, edited by Tanya Dalziell and Paul Genoni, pp. 546–51. Monash UP, 2012.

———. 'Malala Yousafzai, Life Narrative and the Collaborative Archive.' *Life Writing,* vol. 14, no. 3, 2017, pp. 297–311.

Douglas, Kate, and Anna Poletti. *Life Narratives and Youth Culture: Representation, Agency and Participation*. Palgrave Macmillan, 2016.

Douglas, Kate, and Pamela Graham. 'Go back to where you came from: Stunt documentary, conversion narrative, and the limits of testimony on Australian television.' *Biography: An Interdisciplinary Quarterly,* vol. 36, no. 1, 2013, pp. 124–47.

Ellick, Adam B., and Irfan Ashraf. 'Class Dismissed: Malala's Story.' Documentary by Adam B. Ellick and Irfan Ashraf. *The New York Times*, 27 Aug. 2015. Times Documentaries www.nytimes.com/video/world/asia/100000001835296/class-dismissed.html. Accessed 9 Dec. 2017.

He Named Me Malala. Film, directed by Davis Guggenheim, produced by Davis Guggenheim et al., written by Malala Youseafzai. Fox Searchlight Pictures, Imagenation Abu Dhabi, FZ Participant Media, 2015.

Kadar, Marlene. "Literary and Historical Uses of Life Writing for Young Adult Readers: 'She's Only a Gypsy, after All.'" *Canadian Children's Literature/Littérature Canadienne pour la Jeunesse,* vol. 34, no. 1, 2008, pp. 43–59.

Lin, Grace. 'Gorgeous Picture Books That Reveal the Power of the Pencil.' *The New York Times*, 23 Nov. 2017. www.nytimes.com/2017/11/03/books/review/malala-yousafzai-magic-pencil-drawing-writing-children.html. Accessed 9 Dec. 2017.

Makai, Gul (Malala Yousafzai). Original blog entries. *BBC Urdu*, posted 9 Jan. 2009, updated 11 Sept. 2015. www.bbc.com/urduu/pakistan/story/2009/01/090109_diary_swatgirl_part1.shtml. Accessed 9 Dec. 2017.

Martens, Prisca, et al. 'Building Intercultural Understandings Through Global Literature.' *The Reading Teacher,* vol. 68, no. 8, 2017, pp. 609–19.

Petronzio, Matt. 'Malala wrote an inspiring new children's book, and we have a sneak peak.' *Mashable.com*, posted 12 Sept. 2017, updated 23 Nov. 2017. mashable.com/2017/09/11/malala-magic-pencil-picture-book-kids/#iwrEyCaaROq1. Accessed 9 Dec. 2017.

Publishers Weekly. 'Children's Book Review: *Malala's Magic Pencil*, by Malala Yousafzai, illustrated by Kerascoët.' 31 July 2017. www.publishersweekly.com/978-0-316-31957-7www.publishersweekly.com/pw/reviews/index.html. Accessed 9 Dec. 2017.

Sharp, Heather, and Vicki Parkes. 'Representations of national identity in fictionalized history: Children's picture books and World War I.' *New Review of Children's Literature and Librarianship,* vol. 23, no. 2, 2017, pp. 126–47.

Short, Kathy G. 'Critically reading the word and the world: Building intercultural understanding through literature.' *Bookbird: A Journal of International Children's Literature,* vol. 47, no. 2, 2009, pp. 1–10.

Smith, Sidonie, and Julia Watson. *Reading Autobiography*: *A Guide for Interpreting Life Narratives.* 2nd ed. U of Minnesota P, 2010.

Webb, Steve. 'Featured Books for 7+ readers.' Expertly selected books for 7 and 8 year old children—Books. www.lovereading4j=kids.co.uk/genre/7/7-plus-readers.html. Accessed 7 Dec. 2017.

Yousafzai, Malala, and Christina Lamb. *I Am Malala: The Girl Who Stood Up for Education and Was Shot by the Taliban*. Little, Brown, 2013.

Yousafzai, Malala. *Malala's Magic Pencil*, illustrated by Kerascoët. Little, Brown Books for Young Readers, 2017.

Yousafzai, Malala. 'Moving moments from Malala's BBC diary.' Posted 10 Oct. 2014, updated 27 Aug. 2015. www.bbc.com/news/world-asia-29565738b. Accessed 7 Dec. 2017.

Yousafzai, Malala, and Patricia McCormick. *I Am Malala: The Girl Who Stood Up for Education and Was Shot by the Taliban (Young Readers' Edition)*. Little, Brown, 2016.

Notes

1. It is not clear what roles Ahn Do and Suzanne Do took in the authorship of the book.

2. Whatley's 'award-winning titles include *The Ugliest Dog in the World*, *Looking for Crabs*, *Detective Donut and the Wild Goose Chase*, *Diary of a Wombat*, *The Little Refugee*, *Flood*, *Fire*, *And the Band Played Waltzing Matilda* and *Cyclone*' (Bruce.Whatley.com).

3. The book has an instrumental goal beyond sharing his story with young readers: all profits from the book will go to 'Victorian nun Trish Franklin's Loreto Vietnam-Australia Program, based in Ho Chi Minh City, which provides shelter, food and education for disabled and destitute children' (Webb).

4. Neither *The Little Refugee* nor *Malala's Magic Pencil* include page numbers, so I do not cite page numbers in this discussion.

ABOUT THE CONTRIBUTORS

Professor Caroline Mcmillen commenced in the government role of Chief Scientist for South Australia in October 2018 after serving as Vice-Chancellor of the University of Newcastle for seven years, starting in 2011. She is a Fellow of the Australian Academy of Health and Medical Sciences, a Fellow of the Royal Society of New South Wales and a Bragg Member of the Royal Institution, Australia. She holds a BA (Honours) and a PhD from the University of Oxford and completed her medical training, graduating with an MB BChir from the University of Cambridge. She has served in academic leadership positions at Monash University, the University of Adelaide, and the University of South Australia, where she held the role of Deputy Vice-Chancellor of research and innovation prior to her move to Newcastle.

Professor Mcmillen's research focuses on the role of the environment in early development in determining the metabolic and cardiovascular health of offspring in later life. Her research group was funded for two decades by both the ARC and the NHMRC; she was a member of the PMSEIC Working Group on Aboriginal and Torres Strait Islander health focusing on maternal, fetal, and postnatal health; and she has been a chair and member of international and national research policy, review, and assessment panels. She has also served on a range of industry boards, including the National Automotive Industry Innovation Council, Cooperative Research Centre for Advanced Automotive Technology, Cooperative Research Centre for Rail Innovation, the South Australian Premier's Climate Change Council, and the NSW Innovation and Productivity Council, as well as a range of state industry leadership groups and government leadership groups.

Professor Mcmillen has been invited to speak in international and national forums on the critical role of STEMM in driving innovation and on the role of universities as national and regional catalysts of economic and social transition. Throughout her career, she has been committed to building collaborations between universities, government, industry, and communities that deliver a positive impact on the economic, social, and cultural health of Australia. She was honoured at the end of her term as Vice-Chancellor to be presented with the key to the city of Newcastle by the lord mayor of Newcastle.

Emeritus Professor Hugh Craig, FAHA (Fellow of the Academy of the Humanities, Australia), formerly Deputy Head, Faculty of Education and Arts, is Director of the Centre for Literary and Linguistic Computing, University of Newcastle, Australia. A world-leading Shakespearean and renowned expert in early modern English literature and computational stylistics, Emeritus Professor Craig has authored a great many works and has held visiting positions at Magdalen College, Oxford; the Istituto di Linguistica Computazionale, Pisa; the University of Canterbury, New Zealand; the University of Victoria, Canada; and the University of Wuerzburg, Germany, to name just a few. An excerpt from the Academy of Humanities, Australia, website reveals that Emeritus Professor Craig 'is one of the few world leaders in the highly skilled development and application of quantitative, statistical and other computing techniques of literary and linguistic computing to early modern English literary studies.' His work has changed ideas about Shakespeare by showing that Shakespeare collaborated with Christopher Marlowe in three early plays, wrote old-fashioned dialogue compared to his peers, and does not have a prodigiously large vocabulary. Recent publications include *Shakespeare, Computers, and the Mystery of Authorship* (with Arthur F. Kinney, Cambridge UP 2009) and *Style, Computers, and Early Modern Drama: Beyond Authorship* (with Brett Greatley-Hirsch, Cambridge UP, 2017).

Dr Amanda Norman is a Senior Lecturer in inter-professional studies at the University of Winchester, UK. Amanda holds an EdD (Doctorate in education) from the University of Southampton, UK, where her research explored auto/biographical writing in education. This led her to developing innovative ways of researching and teaching identities and life journeys as a vehicle for self-reflection and creative thinking within a pedagogical frame. Her research interests arise from her experience of working in early years and listening to the voices of those caring for infants, and who are less heard in political and social contexts. Prior to this, with a background in education and qualifications in the therapeutic arts and psychology, Amanda was part of the early childhood team at University of Roehampton, teaching a range of professional and learning-related modules. Amanda has published widely in scholarly journals and magazines, using personal stories of practice, and is currently working on a joint-funded project with Western University,

London, Ontario, on perceptions about nature and the outdoors. Her most recent book, *Conception to Infancy*, is aimed at raising awareness of the complexities of care beyond the home. Additionally, she is a core member of an *All Party Parliamentary Group: Fit and Healthy Childhood* (UK) and contributed to a recently published report on Mental Health in Childhood. Amanda is co-convenor for the Early Years Research Centre at University of Winchester and is embarking on research into how obituaries can reveal professional identities and the professions of those identities during specific times in history.

Professor Donna Lee Brien is Professor of creative industries at Central Queensland University, Australia. Donna holds a PhD in creative arts and writing, from the Queensland University of Technology (QUT). She is co-founding convenor of the Australasian Food Studies Network and commissioning editor of special issues for *TEXT: Journal of Writing and Writing Courses*. Donna has authored over twenty books and monographs and over three hundred refereed published journal articles, book chapters, scholarly conference papers, and creative works, many of which deal with forms of life-writing. Donna is the editor of the *Australasian Journal of Popular Culture*, and past president of national peak body, the Australasian Association of Writing Programs. Donna's publications include *John Power 1881–1943* (1991) and the *Girl's Guide* self-help series. Her latest books are *New Directions in 21st Century Gothic*: *The Gothic Compass* (with Lorna Piatti-Farnell, Routledge, 2015); *Forgotten Lives: Recovering Lost Histories through Fact and Fiction* (with Dallas J. Baker and Nike Sulway, Cambridge Scholars, 2017); *Offshoot: Contemporary Life Writing Methodologies and Practice in Australasia* (with Quinn Eades, UWAP, 2018); and *The Routledge Companion to Literature and Food* (with Lorna Piatti-Farnell, Routledge, 2018). Donna is currently working with Margaret McAllister on two books on nurses and their professional identity: *The Shadow Side of Nursing: Exploring Complexities, Understanding Struggles, Revealing Opportunities* (for Routledge, UK) and *Empowerment Strategies for Nurses: Developing Resiliency in Practice* (for Springer, US).

Emeritus Professor David Walker, ASSA, AAH, is Honorary Professorial Fellow at the Asia Institute, University of Melbourne, and Emeritus Professor at Deakin University, Melbourne. He holds visiting professorships at Renmin University of China, Beijing, Foreign Studies University and Inner Mongolia Normal University. He is a Director and board member of The Foundation for Australian Studies in China. David Walker recently became a member of the Order of Australia (OA). He is a Fellow of both the Academy of Social Sciences Australia (ASSA) and the Australian Academy of the Humanities (AAH). He has held visiting professorships at Georgetown University, Washington, DC—here, he held the Monash chair of Australian Studies—and the University of Copenhagen, Denmark. Emeritus Professor David Walker specialises in the historical examination of Australian responses to Asia. He served as a consultant to the Australian Studies programme at the Universitas Indonesia, Jakarta, from 1986 to 1993, and has contributed to the development of the Australian Studies programme in Jiangsu Province, PR China, and at Shiga University, Japan. David has written extensively on the history of Australia's relations with Asia from the mid 19th century to the present, including his prize-winning book *Anxious Nation: Australia and the Rise of Asia, 1850–1939*, and then more recently with Agnieszka Sobocinska, he has edited *Australia's Asia: from Yellow Peril to Asian Century. Anxious Nation: Australia and the Rise of Asia, 1850–1939*, published by University of Queensland Press in 1999, was awarded the Ernest Scott prize for the best history of Australia or New Zealand published 1990–2000. A new departure came with *Not Dark Yet: a Personal History*, an exercise in life-writing. It examines loss of sight, war memory, and family history in South Australia from the mid 19th century. Currently, David is researching a book that he is writing with a Chinese colleague about his family history—starting in the 1890s, when the family moved from the impoverished Shanxi Province to find a better life in Inner Mongolia.

Dr Jo Parnell holds a PhD in English and literature and writing from the University of Newcastle, Australia, where she is a Conjoint Research Fellow to the Faculty of Education and Arts in the School of Humanities and Social Science. She is a reviewer, essayist, memoirist, conference speaker, creative writer, and practitioner and analyst of creative non-fiction. The main focus of Jo's research, literary docu-memoir, is an unusual and little-known form which involves the creative non-fiction writer audiotaping ordinary people for their unusual experience and thoughts and feelings as the resource material for a literary production. As a writer of literary docu-memoir herself, Jo has evolved a new way of writing lives, adapted from the form pioneered by Tony Parker. Jo has won numerous awards, and her work has been published nationally and internationally and in scholarly journals, such as *Humanity 2010* and *2012*, and the online journal the *European Journal of Life Writing*. One of her works, 'Translating and conveying the damaging childhood in Our Kate,' was requested for inclusion as a central chapter in *Catherine Cookson Country: On the Borders of Legitimacy, Fiction and History* (Ashgate, 2012), a world-first text book on Catherine Cookson, edited by Julie Anne Taddeo. Currently, Jo is drafting a sole-authored work, *A Collection of Short Stories, Tales and Essays* (working title), and planning a further edited collection. Jo's most recent publications include this book, *New and Experimental Approaches to Writing Lives*, (Palgrave Macmillan International Higher Education, 2019), and a work for Lexington Books titled *Representations of the Mother-in-Law in literature, film, drama, and television* (2018).

Dr Michael Sala is a Lecturer in English and writing at the University of Newcastle, Australia, where he gained his PhD in creative writing. Michael Sala has published articles and essays in scholarly journals, including *Life Writing*, Francis and Taylor online; *TEXT*; *HEAT*; *Best Australian Stories 2011*; and *The Adelaide Review*. Michael's memoir, *The Last Thread* (Affirm Press, 2012), won the Glenda Adams/UTS Award for New Writing at the NSW Premier's Literary Awards and was the Pacific region winner of the Commonwealth Book Prize. His second book, *The Restorer* (*TEXT*, 2017), was shortlisted in 2017 for the fiction prize in both the Victorian and the NSW Premier's Literary Awards and longlisted for the Miles Franklin Literary Award. Michael is currently working on a third novel, which is due for release by *TEXT* in 2020.

Associate Professor Sonya Huber is a Lecturer at Fairfield University and Director of Fairfield's Low-Residency MFA programme. Sonya holds an MA in journalism and an MFA in creative writing from Ohio State University. Sonya has authored five books, including the collection *Pain Woman Takes Your Keys: and Other Essays from a Nervous System* (U Nebraska P, 2017), which was awarded the Independent Voice gold medal from the Independent Publishers Association and the Silver Medal in the essay category from the Foreword Book Awards. Her other books of creative non-fiction are *Opa Nobody*, an exploration of her family's labour and socialist activism in Germany, which was longlisted for the Saroyan Prize, and *Cover Me: A Health Insurance Memoir* (U Nebraska P, 2010). Other non-fiction books include *The Evolution of Hillary Rodham Clinton* (Squint Books/Eyewear Publishing Ltd., 2016) and a textbook, *The Backwards Research Guide for Writers* (Equinox Publications, 2011). Sonya's essays appear in many outlets and scholarly journals, including *The New York Times*; *The Washington Post*; *The Atlantic*; *Creative Nonfiction; Brevity*; and *Florida Review*.

Dr Vanessa Berry is a Lecturer in creative writing at the University of Sydney, Australia. She holds a PhD in media from Macquarie University. Vanessa is a writer and researcher who works with history, memory, and archives. She is the author of the award-winning essay collection *Mirror Sydney* (Giramondo Publishing Co., 2017) and the memoirs *Ninety9* (Giramondo Publishing Co., 2017) and *Strawberry Hills Forever* (Local Consumption Publications, 2007). Vanessa has exhibited widely and has written a number of books chapters, newspaper articles, and scholarly journal articles, including for the *Sydney Review of Books*; *HEAT*; and *The Lifted Brow*, to name just a few. Working in both literature and visual arts, Vanessa produces and researches interdisciplinary and non-traditional forms of literary work, such as blogging and zine making. Her zines and hand-drawn maps have been exhibited at major Australian institutions, such as the Museum of Contemporary Art Australia and the National Gallery of Australia. She is currently collaborating with the Museum of Applied Arts and Sciences, Australia, on the Time and Memory project, which investigates time, memory, technology, and material cultures.

Dr Emma Newport is a Teaching Fellow at the University of Sussex, UK, having previously been a Research Fellow at King's College London, from where she had earlier gained a PhD in English. Emma is the founder of the series of conferences Women, Money and Markets (1700–1900), from which a new edited collection is forthcoming. Emma's research interests include women's positions in a network of global exchanges of ideas and objects. An article from Emma's research in this field is published under the title 'Porcelain Fictions: Lady Banks's 'Diary Book' and Narratives of Discovery and Display,' in the Special Issue: Material Fictions, *Eighteenth-Century Fiction Journal* (Autumn 2018). As a member of the Centre for Life History and Life Writing Research at the University of Sussex, Emma is currently working on the cytoarchitecture of end-of-life writing and new digital forms of memorialisation. She is also interested in the intersections between the creative and life-writing. Emma is the Director of Sussex Writes, a writing programme which builds creative writing communities between the university, school students, and local citizens. Using life-writing and creative writing, Sussex Writes encourages new and aspiring writers to gain new skills and confidence in their approaches to writing; at the same time, the programme facilitates research into creative writing pedagogies and its impact on well-being and attainment.

Professor Page Richards is a Lecturer in the School of English at the University of Hong Kong, where she offers courses in life-writing, poetry, drama, and creative writing. Page Richards holds a PhD in English and American literature and language from Harvard University. Page has also studied at the Playwrights' Theatre in Boston and has contributed to theatre and film production in Hollywood. She founded the first MFA in creative writing in English in Hong Kong and the region. Page also founded the HKU Black Box Theatre and Creative Studio. She is Director of the HKU Black Box Theatre, the MFA at HKU in creative writing, and the HKU International Poetry Prize. Page has published widely on poetry, biographical lyric, American literature, drama, and performance. Currently, she is completing a book on the biographical lyric and a new book of poems. Her essays and articles have appeared in the *Harvard Review*; the *Journal of Modern Literature*; *The Dalhousie Review*; and '*After Thirty Falls*': *New Essays on John Berryman*, to name a just a few. Page Richards is the author of *Distancing English: A Chapter in the History of the Inexpressible* (OSUP 2009) and the book of poems titled *Lightly Separate* (Finishing Line Press, 2007).

Dr Jessica L. Wilkinson is a Senior Lecturer in creative writing, at RMIT (Royal Melbourne Institute of Technology) University, Melbourne, Australia. She holds a PhD in creative writing and literary studies from the University of Melbourne. Her first book, *marionette: a biography of miss marion davies* (Vagabond, 2012), was shortlisted for the 2014 Kenneth Slessor Prize. Her second poetic biography, *Suite for Percy Grainger* (Vagabond, 2014), is a long poem which won the 2014 Peter Porter Poetry Prize. Jessica received a Marten Bequest Travelling Scholarship to research her third poetic biography, *Music Made Visible: A Biography of George Balanchine* (Vagabond Press, 2018). Jessica has written numerous articles on poetic biography and non-fiction poetry that have been published in international journals and critical volumes, including *Criticism* (US), *Biography* (Hawaii), *Axon* (Australia), *Cultural Studies Review* (Australia), and *Truth and Beauty: Verse Biography in Canada, Australia and New Zealand* (U Victoria P, 2016), to name just a few. She also co-edited *Contemporary Australian Feminist Poetry* (Hunter Publishers, 2016). Jessica Wilkinson is an internationally known poet and the founding editor of *Rabbit: A Journal for Nonfiction Poetry*.

Dr Willa Mcdonald is Senior Lecturer in media at Macquarie University, Australia, where she teaches and researches creative non-fiction writing and narrative journalism. Willa holds a PhD in Australian studies from the University of New South Wales, Australia. A former journalist, she has worked in print, television, and radio, including for the *Sydney Morning Herald*, the *Bulletin*, the *Times on Sunday*, ABC TV, and ABC Radio National. She has also written many speeches for the lord mayor of Sydney and documentaries for radio and television and has initiated and produced various series for television and radio. While working full-time for ABC TV, Willa researched and helped to produce the following award-winning programmes: *The Time of Your Life* (as associate producer, researcher/co-scriptwriter), first broadcast 1991, which won the Logie for Best Documentary and was Silver Medallist in 1991 at the International Film and Television Festival, New York, and *Ladies in Lines*, (as researcher/writer and concept development), winner of a Logie, Penguin (Australian Industry Awards) and a medallist in the 1989 International Film and TV Festival, New York. Willa has published a number of book chapters and numerous articles for newspapers, radio, and television and papers for scholarly journals, including *Australian Dictionary of Biography*; *Literary Journalism Studies*; *Australian Journalism Review*; *TEXT*; and *Crossroads*, to name just a few. Willa's current project is a cultural history of Australian journalism as told through the lives of some of the country's best journalists. Two of her books are *Warrior for Peace: Dorothy Auchterlonie Green* (Australian Scholarly Publishing, 2009) and, with Susie Eisenhuth, *The Writer's Reader: Understanding Journalism and Non-fiction* (U Cambridge P, 2007).

Professor Kate Douglas is Professor College of Humanities and Social Science at Flinders University, South Australia. She holds a PhD in English and writing from the University of Queensland, Australia. Kate's publications include the *Contesting Childhood: Autobiography, Trauma and Memory* (Rutgers, 2010) and a number of co-authored books, such as *Trauma Texts* (Routledge, 2009) with Gillian Whitlock; *Trauma Tales: Auto/biographies of Childhood and Youth* (Routledge, 2014) with Kylie Cardell; *Life Narratives and Youth Culture: Representation, Agency and Participation* (Palgrave Macmillan, 2016) with Anna Poletti; *Teaching Lives: Contemporary Pedagogies of Life Narratives* (Routledge, 2017) with Laurie McNeill; and a forthcoming book, titled *Research Methods for Auto/Biography Studies* (Routledge, 2019), with Ashley Barnwell. Kate is Head of the Steering Committee for International Auto/Biography Asia-Pacific Chapter.

INDEX

Mock, Roberta, 109, 111, 112
Montaigne, Michel de, 9, 193, 194, 202
Moore, Dinty W., 101, 113,
Morgan, Sally, 193, 202
Morton, Timothy, 157, 169
Moses, Rae R., 20–21, 32
   (*with* D. Giana)
'Mourning Walk' (Lavery), 103, 109
   see also Lavery, Carl
Mufid, James Hannush, 67, 80
My Place (Morgan), 193
   see also Morgan, Sally

Nabokov, Vladimir, 4, 82, 89–92, 94, 97
Nagel, Thomas, 156–57, 169
Narayan, Lux, 18, 21, 32
Navarro, Joe, 197, 202
Nazario, Sonia, 204, 216
Neihardt, John G., 72–73, 74, 80
Nelson, Marilyn, 152, 166, 169
netsuke, 2, 39
Night (Weisel), 193
   see also Weisel, Elie
Nobel, Alfred, 1, 25–26, 209
Norment, Christopher, 126, 127, 129, 131
nostalgia, 110, 158
'Nostalgia and Complaint of the Grand-
   parents,' (Justice), 158
   see also Justice, Donald
   see also Longenbach, James
Not Dark Yet: A Personal History
   (Walker), 48

obituary,
   as source of entertainment, 17
   a historical overview of, 16–17
   the meaning and characteristics of,
   15–16
Occupy Wall Street, 107
Olsen, Charles, 172
Oulipo, 5, 106, 108

Padel, Ruth, 6, 8, 152, 169, 171, 174–77,
   179, 181, 184

Parker, Tony,
   purpose in interviewing and writing,
   66
   self-imposed principles and ethics,
   68–69
   social injustice, perception of, 65
   style, 69
   sympathetic objective realism, 67, 68
Parkes, Vicki, 208, 218
   (*with* Heather Sharp)
Patterns of Experience in Autobiography
   (Egan), 134
   see also Egan, Susanna
pedestrian performer the, 103–04
   see also flâneur, the
   see also walker, the,
Perl, Sondra, 64–65, 69, 80
   (*with* Mimi Schwartz)
persona, 3, 9, 23, 27, 67, 68, 75, 78, 194
'The Phantom from Taganrog' (Sanders),
   172
   see also Sanders, Edward
Phillips, Jason B., 23, 32
photographs,
   and ghosts, 49, 50, 76
   haunting effects of, 50, 51, 59,
   symbolism of, 49, 50–51, 76–77,
   108, 110, 158, 213, 249,
   and narrative gaps, 50
Piatti, Barbara, 114, 131
Pickrell, Jacqueline E., 191, 202
   (*with* Elizabeth F. Loftus)
Pilgrim's Progress (Bunyan), 5, 102
   see also Bunyan, John
post-Norman Conquest lyric poetry, 156,
   158–59
Pommepuy, Marie, 210
   (*and Sébastien Cosset*)
   see also Kerascoët
The Prince of Wales's Wedding (Frith), 37
   see also Frith, William
projected, self-written obituary, 1, 25, 28,
Proust, Marcel, 51